# THE WEIGHT IN THE WORD
## Prophethood: Biblical and Quranic

This is a profound and courageous attempt to compare and contrast Islamic ideas of prophecy, as found uniquely in Muhammad, with the prophetic tradition of the Hebrew Bible. It challenges Muslims, Jews, and Christians to understand their own traditions better and to be open to learn from each other. It rests on prolonged reflection about the character of the three Abrahamic religions.
*John Barton, Oriel & Laing Professor of the Interpretation of Holy Scripture, Oriel College, Oxford*

# THE
# WEIGHT IN THE WORD
*Prophethood: Biblical and Quranic*

Kenneth Cragg

BRIGHTON • PORTLAND

Copyright © Kenneth Cragg 1999

The right of Kenneth Cragg to be identified as author of this work has been asserted in accordance with the Copyright, Designs and Patents Act 1988.

2 4 6 8 10 9 7 5 3 1
*First published 1999 in Great Britain by*
SUSSEX ACADEMIC PRESS
Box 2950
Brighton BN2 5SP

*and in the United States of America by*
SUSSEX ACADEMIC PRESS
5804 N.E. Hassalo St.
Portland, Oregon 97213-3644

All rights reserved. Except for the quotation of short passages for the purposes of criticism and review, no part of this publication may be reproduced, stored in a retrieval system, or transmitted, in any form or by any means, electronic, mechanical, photocopying, recording or otherwise, without the prior permission of the publisher.

*British Library Cataloguing in Publication Data*
A CIP catalogue record for this book is available from the British Library.

*Library of Congress Cataloging-in-Publication Data*
Cragg. Kenneth
The weight in the word : prophethood, biblical and quranic / Kenneth Cragg.
p. cm.
Includes bibliographical references and indexes.
ISBN 1–902210–27–1 (alk. paper)
1. Prophets in the Koran.   2. Prophets in the New Testament.   3. Prophets, Pre-Islamic.
I. Title.
BP134.P745C73   1999
297.2'46—dc21           99-20796
CIP

Printed on acid-free paper
Printed by Biddles Ltd, Guildford and King's Lynn

# Contents

|  | Preface | vi |
|---|---|---|
| I | Messengers with Burdens | 1 |
| II | The Casting, The Saying, The Weighting | 14 |
| III | Prophetic Personality | 21 |
| IV | Prophethood and Language | 40 |
| V | Prophet and Situation | 69 |
| VI | Prophethood and Conscience | 88 |
| VII | Prophethood in Suffering | 102 |
| VIII | Prophethood and God | 117 |
| IX | Ongoing Finality | 138 |
|  | Notes | 167 |
|  | Index of Themes | 193 |
|  | Index of Names and Terms | 198 |
|  | Scriptural Citations | 203 |

# *Preface*

Will it be legitimate to link Amos and Muhammad in a single theme? May the four great centuries of Hebrew prophethood (the 8th to the 4th BC) be tied with Arabia in the 7th of the Christian calendar? Muslims, to be sure, have always insisted on a long prophetic sequence anticipating its culmination in the Prophet of the Qur'an. But they have – for the most part – meant the Biblical patriarchs and the Qur'an is totally silent about "the goodly fellowship" that stretched from Hosea, Isaiah, and Jeremiah to Ezekiel and Malachi. These represented the high peak of Hebrew ethicism as a conscience critical of patriarchs and priests alike. They far transcend what "prophecy" had earlier meant as found in seers and soothsayers, or even in the formidable Elijah. Hence the focus here. It is strange that while the Islamic Qur'an is much concerned with the Hebrew patriarchs, it omits the great prophetic figures entirely. This makes some effort to relate Muhammad with them both the more necessary and the more problematic.

Christian habit, too, for its part, has traditionally rejected any such linkage. The Qur'an has been considered pseudo-prophetic, disqualified by allegedly usurping the finality of Jesus "to whom gave all the prophets witness". Since the Qur'an's "witness" to Jesus is equivocal – by Christian criteria – the great veneration Jesus ('Isa) commands among Muslims does not redeem the situation in orthodox Christian eyes. On that score inclusive reflections all the way from Amos to Muhammad would seem either visionary or foolish. Samuel Taylor Coleridge made the point in familiar terms around 1809 in an unfinished poem on "Mahomet":

> . . . th' enthusiast warrior of Mecca
> Who scattered abroad both evil and blessing.
> Huge wasteful empires found'd and hallowed slow persecution,
> Soul withering but crushed the blasphemous rites of the Pagan
> And idolatrous Christians . . . veiling the Gospel of Jesus . . .

## Preface

The poet would have Jesus, not Muhammad, claim community with Isaiah and kindred "friends of God." On many grounds he would be right.

Yet traditional attitudes have to give way to new ventures of scholarship and hope. Despite all that is mutually at odds between things Biblical and Quranic, there are vital, discernible territories that are capable of careful reconnoitre, and not only – as Coleridge conceded – in respect of idolatry. Even with disparities there, the passion for the unity of God stakes an arguable kinship. Less controversially, the personal incidence of Scriptures (if we may so describe the gist of prophethood) involves the several dimensions the chapters here explore, namely personality, language, situation and circumstance, conscience and suffering. Even those whose faith-loyalty may require them to hold all these incomparable in either Scripture must nevertheless allow their comparability for honest scholarship. The urge for community relation might also be pleaded in the same concern. The underlying questions of finality and theology will not be ignored (CHAPTERS 8 and 9) but they can never be rightly addressed if features on which they turn admit of no common study. The confidence that Amos and Muhammad – and all between – can feasibly be brought together can only prove itself in the going. Such is always the way of hope.

The title "The Weight in the Word" is taken from Surah 73.5 of the Qur'an where, on a very early occasion, Muhammad is given to understand himself to be undergoing the onset of "a heavy saying", or "a weighty word". CHAPTERS 1 and 2 explore the import of the text and how its significance at once tallies with the familiar term "burden" among the Biblical prophets, which is a basic descriptive alike for their vocation and their meanings.

Thought on this coincidence of theme leads naturally into the several realms comprising the "burden", the whence and whither of its origin and its destiny. There is the mystery of speech itself. Things find themselves in words only by finding words for themselves. How do they come upon lips? How do lips, in this hallowed context, belong with minds? What, in "inspiration", obtains between source and soul? All clearly enters into personality and persons have biographies. How may history, private and public, domestic and tribal, bear upon "the weighting of the word"?

The issues multiply. The need we may register to pursue them with a jealous solicitude for our respective vantage points of belief need not dispute the common factors we have to heed and elucidate. Indeed, that very activity may serve to search and refine the concerns our doctrines cherish. For, in no sense do we have a merely academic exercise in view.

The several themes the main chapters list entail a certain repetition for which the readers' indulgence is sought. The themes are so intertwined that it was dubious to have to treat them serially. Indeed the chapters could readily have exchanged places in a different sequence. Should the strange incidence of words precede the election of persons? Yet only in deliverances was identity discovered, whether inwardly to the prophet or publicly to society.

Hence the inevitable overlap of the chapters. Perhaps the fact of it may serve, rather than encumber, the justice we need to do to a strenuous but rewarding study. The theme of "burden" should expect no easy exoneration, for only in the onus does significance reside. Even tolerance is about what we can carry and sustain.

Commenting on Surah 73.5, the celebrated Qur'an exegete Al-Baidawi stresses from its context "the vigils of the night", as serving to "quieten the heart" and brace the spirit for the daylight task. He realizes that the "burden" stems from the very will to escape it. Human nature – even in prophets – shrinks from hard demands. Al-Baidawi detects the "weight" also in how the word bears down heavily in warning to unbelieving wastrels. For the Prophet there are physical symptoms, he avers – a nervous distress that may take the form of "feeble knees", or swooning. Furthermore, the "weight", Qur'an-wise, is also in the obligation to allow no tongue to slip, to give divine words perfect reproduction.

Biblically, one might say, the onus is more inherently personal, in the very springs of utterance and the essential loneliness of being, like Athanasius, *contra mundum*. There is a far gulf between the terms in which Jeremiah, for example, was "burdened" and those that obtained for Muhammad in Mecca.

One common feature, however, is how, in almost every case, the sense of "burden" leads to the recruiting of "disciples." Something of what Aaron was to Moses, Baruch may have been to Jeremiah. Muhammad had his "Companions", while 'Isa in the Qur'an had his *Ansar*, "disciples who are his helpers unto God". Though the status and the task belong to the "chosen vessel" alone, these "associates" are guardians to whom we owe the "sealing", the preservation, of the words. Hence our deliberate focus here only on Biblical prophets known as "the writing ones" – if only thanks to their amanuenses.

To be sure, much that remains open to study surrounds the written legacies of prophethood throughout the Semitic range. Of the crucial role of auditors and scribes there can be no doubt. Must it not be, as far as in us lies, the same kind of intimacy with the source we too must covet? In part, this means an effort of will. Oddly the Arabic word *thaqil* in Surah 73.5 can describe unwanted company. Ostracism, enmity and isolation were the common experience of prophethood. For it focused into crisis evils which, otherwise, would have remained un-accused. The messenger incurs the antipathy the message arouses. Our study-task now is to reach a just measure of what being "charged with what is weighty" meant in time and place, there and then. Its four dimensions were – situations in history, meanings via language, personality in travail, and travail as a suffering proxy for truth as God's. The final category, then, is the place of the whole in the economy of God, of how the prophetic role stands in vicarious relation to the purposes of the Lord who sends.

There is no probing the mystery of "God-weighted word" without realizing how, in some sense, what is divine moves through the human and what is human underwrites what is divine. If we can rightly reckon with this ultimate fact, we may be nearer to the perceptions we need to bring to the Qur'an than if we stayed woodenly with familiar inhibitions and stances that left them to silence, whether the silence be secular or dismissive. "A theology of prophethood" must be our final goal, thinking into what the Islamic *Shahadah* simply comprises in a sort of "comma" between: "There is no deity save Allah, Muhammad is Allah's apostle." How should we comprehend that conjoining?

An Islamic sincerity will not disallow the question, "God and the Messenger" being – in the Qur'an – repeatedly its dual unity of creed and command. For Christian theology, via Messiah crucified, the theology of prophethood is found in knowing "the weight in the word" by the wounds in the soul.

Such, as we will discover, is the point of deepest encounter in the effort to align prophethood in the Bible and in Islam in one denominator. So problematic for many, in both mosque and church, will that alignment be that the task of a first chapter, before coming to our fivefold exposition, will be a careful justification of it. It will be clear that in studying "prophets" we do not have in view mere "futurologists", or "foretellers" of things to come. That, though a popular notion, is only sometimes the relevance of the figures "prophethood" presents and, then, only sequential to far more significant meanings that belong with the living present and, indeed, with time's eternal bearings.

I extend my thanks to the V&A Picture Libary for permission to reproduce the "The Lonely Tower" etching by Samuel Palmer as part of the jacket design.

*Kenneth Cragg*
*Oxford, February 1999*

By the high noon and by the deep silence of the night your Lord has not forsaken you.
Surah 93.1

I have set thee for a tower among My people.
Jeremiah 6: 27

I will set me up upon a tower and will watch to see what He will say to me.
Habakkuk 2: 1

And thou, O tower of the flock.
Micah 4: 8

Up unto the watch-tower get
And see all things despoyled by fallacies.
John Donne

His soul had wedded wisdom, and her dower
Is love and justice, clothed in which he sate
Apart from men, as in a lonely tower.
Percy Shelley

Or let my lamp at midnight hour
Be seen in some high lonely tower.
John Milton

(Samuel Palmer's) "lonely light" –
An image of mysterious wisdom, won by toil.
William Yeats

All I have is a voice
To undo the folded lie,
The romantic lie in the brain
Of the sensual man in the street
And the lie of authority
Whose buildings grope the sky.
W. H. Auden

# I

## Messengers with Burdens

### 1

Prophets – "Secretaries of the Holy Spirit", the poet, John Donne called them. How far are we justified in bringing Biblical and Quranic prophethood together under the one category? Centuries of Christian thinking have been minded to withhold any Biblical-style recognition from Muhammad and the Qur'an. Islam, for its part, has insisted on a veritable continuity among all divinely sent "messengers", from the first to its own as the last, in one dependable sequence "confirming what (human) right hands possess", the sacred deliverances mediated to earthly spokesmen and "bearers of the word".

The issue of a discernible continuity cannot be separated from the enigma of finality. It has always been assumed that after Malachi Biblical prophethood either passed into apocalyptic or was overtaken by the sort of zealotry with which the Maccabees understood their destiny. Had Hebraic prophecy spent itself, or had its highest vision in the Isaiahs, in Hosea and Jeremiah, achieved what would for ever suffice all ensuing time? So much one might conclude from the closure of the Hebrew Canon. Could that Canon, then, or its mentors in Judaism, anticipate or approve what emerged, with confident sanction, seven centuries later and in unhallowed Arabia?

A negative answer seems hardly in doubt, seeing that first a Jewish ambivalence, and soon a Jewish demur and hostility, entered circumstantially into the very fabric and text of Muhammad's Qur'an. An experience of rejection at the hands of Jewry in the aftermath of the Hijrah from Mecca to Medina was embedded in the Book itself. Thus it came to spell disavowal of Jewish self-perception in very vigorous terms, even while also claiming a confirmation of, and by, all previous prophets. Surely, then, much doubt must attach to the idea of any ready "harmony" of all the prophets Biblical and Quranic.

Moreover, Christian faith perceives prophethood as having passed over into "Sonship" and "the Word made flesh". Fulfilling the "prophetic" we reach Jesus as the Christ, the sense of truth, nor merely by persons, but in personality. Prophethood culminates there in something to which it had always pointed and where it is seen to be consummated. "The voice of one crying" becomes "the image (i.e. the iconic drama) of the invisible God", "the Father" cognizant in "the Son" in whom comes our human cognizance of "the Father". This dimension of divine revelation – to be explored duly in later context – has acute question to bring to the claim of a subsequent return to vocal prophethood as ever compatible with such Christian conviction concerning Jesus.

The fact that the Qur'an counters this growth of the prophetic into the filial, by a virtual recall to "recital" alone, sets it at odds with things Hebraic as well as Christian.[1] For Biblical prophethood is inherently biographical. The point was finely made concerning Jeremiah when the scholar A. B. Davidson wrote:

> The Book of Jeremiah does not so much teach religious truth as present a religious personality. Prophecy had already taught its truths, its last effort was to reveal itself in a life.[2]

Citing this conclusion, John Skinner adds his thoughts concerning Jeremiah, after noting his kinship with Hosea:

> He breaks through the limitations of the strictly prophetic consciousness, and moves out into the larger filial communion with God.

Jeremiah "knows God in being likeminded with Him".[3] So that what, from his persona, we are given to know is not verbal only, or informative, but deeply incarnational and vicarious. He is "secret-ary" with God in the most ultimate shape of character through experience. This would seem a far cry for Biblical studies from the traditional Muslim, oracular, understanding of the role and function of the Qur'an, aside from the issue of chronology as test of what is "final".

Yet all that is at stake here need not disallow hope or be held insuperable for a Christian mind-set. There are aspects of the Qur'an – and indeed of the mystique of Muhammad in Islamic devotion – which engage personality in deeply experiential terms. So much is evident from the "weight in the word" theme which we are undertaking as index to the Qur'an's meaning. Its quality throughout is highly situational. It is assumed that the text must be read in the context of the life. For its own insistent reasons, Islam will never see the "prophetic" as ever passing into the "filial". "Son" language is adamantly divorced from "servant" by Islamic lights.[4] Yet there can be grounds whereby alert Muslims may come to appreciate how what is, for them, exclusively verbal utterance in prophethood still entails the servant-agency which the Gospel sees brought essentially into significant life. For their part, Christians, as heirs to that life-significance which is Christology, may be ready to relate – for Muslims' sake – to a verbal preaching, disallowing that Christian perception, yet returning to antecedent concepts of divine spokesmanship. The lapse of intervening centuries need not veto that readiness.

There will, remain, nevertheless, the difficult hurdle for Christian minds of the Quranic disavowal of the status and the suffering of Jesus in venturing a positive reception of Muhammad's prophethood. What is at stake here can be more fruitfully handled, as later intended, in the context of where prophethood itself takes us all when fully weighed in the perspectives which attend its path. If the Christian starts with an *ab initio* refusal to accommodate the prophethood of Muhammad within that descriptive, what will be forfeit is not only intelligent discourse with the Muslim but also any relevant entry, by either party, into the criteria they have to bring. Only in positive terms can even negative conclusions – if we reach them – prove themselves necessary.

Accordingly, there is wisdom in the pragmatic realism which acknowledges that the Qur'an is here in human history and affords the house of Islam its scriptured focus, heritage and frame of reference. Inevitable tensions for Biblical loyalties are entailed by such acknowledgement. They are not faced if we renounce their claim on Christian patience and perception. The long interlude between Malachi and Muhammad poses endless questions as to why and how prophets should have been in such sustained eclipse and how and why a sort of Biblical resumption should have allegedly arrived in terms so sharply contrasted or – indeed – why prophethood should *ever* finalize itself anywhere, given the unfailing obduracy of a wayward and incorrigible world. Could the Qur'an ever credibly claim either legitimate succession or ultimate conclusion, in a sequence so long urgent and so far burdened? The question presses harder still if we comprehend, as Christians, a point in history where prophethood had registered both its inherent incompleteness and its ultimate completion in "the Christ of God".[5]

There will be strains then for Jews and Christians alike, but no false compromise, in being receptively related to Muhammad and the Qur'an.

## II

Indeed, only so do we fully incur the liability in which evident disparities place us. Whether tentative, or assured, inclusion of Muhammad in the broad prophetic tradition requires the recognition of sharp issues and contrasts. Some of these will have ample place in the areas of "casting", "saying" and "weighting", proposed for CHAPTER II – the studies set by the words of Surah 73.5. In present context, the first duty is to note the sharp difference in the *mise-en-scène* of Mecca and the Hijaz in respect of Muhammad and that of the major prophets of the Hebrew tradition in the 8th to the 6th centuries. The former is a setting of paganism unrelieved except by the incipient monotheism of the *Hunafa'*, or "Abrahamic Semites" in quest of a single worship, whom we find in the prophetic formation of Muhammad. The latter is that of Hebraic theism and political order, well-schooled in Yahweh and covenant but caught in successive crises of actual or threatened invasion, and chronically susceptible to spiritual declension from its given standing under God.

The territory of the Qur'an and of Muhammad's destiny is not in fee to the rise, fall or rivalry of great world powers between the Nile and the Tigris. It is remotely aware of the mutual attrition of Persians and Byzantines beyond its northern reaches and has dim memories of Jewish arms in Najran to the south. But its politics are those of a city-shrine in pagan *Haram* sanctity with a growing commerce, liable to kindle or abet tribal feuding and economic unrest. All this is a far cry from the turbulence of Jerusalem and the frustrations of Josiah's reformation, as they burdened the likes of Jeremiah.

There is a resultant contrast in the concept and the context of prophethood. Biblically there is a long retrospect to covenant and Exodus, to a Sinai made focal in the Deuteronomic reforms. Quranically a pagan establishment has to be confronted in all the "ignorance" of an obstinate Quraishi mind-set. It might be said that the burden of Hebraic prophethood is about what ought to be and is not, while Muhammad's undertakes what is not and ought to be. The former has the Torah in being and "the prophets" are sequential to "the law": the latter is a prophethood whence Shari'ah must emerge as its sequential fruit. The Biblical prophets address, accuse and admonish a "kingdom of priests" already self-aware as "elect" and long sancto-politicized since David. The Qur'an belongs with a pagan tribalism only precariously on the way to a monotheist politics of statehood which it will attain, without benefit of ethnic "election", by dint of the very text its prophethood affords. That text will proceed in tandem with the very process that waits on its sequences and stems from its incidence in the time and the terms the duality constitutes.

The contrasted *sitz-im-leben*, in either case, arouses the sharp disparity evident in the shape and the temper of the two Scriptures – the cycle from Amos to Malachi and that from Mount Hira' to Medina and Tabuk.[6] The scenario for Muhammad means that the Qur'an's vision of all previous prophets tells itself in terms identical with those of his own encounter in Mecca, namely obduracy around plural worship, denunciation of dire wickedness and warning of dire requital. It is as if all his predecessors had confronted his own Hijazi situation and, therefore, toiled with the same essential burden, as the Qur'an's own minor ones, Salih, Hud and Shu'aib, did among the peoples of Mada'in Salih or the Banu Thamud. Not for them the scenario of an Amos indicting the social iniquities of Samaria or the powerful ironies of Jeremiah's famous Temple sermon.

It is perhaps in this context that we must seek a reason to explain the absence from Quranic retrospect of all the greatest figures in Hebraic prophecy. Was it that successful patriarchs like Noah, Abraham, Moses and David, aligned more readily with Muhammad's setting and the logic he read in it towards vigorous political action and the criterion of "manifest success"? Or was it that the kind of irony known to Hosea and Jeremiah would have had no purchase on minds in Mecca, stemming as it did from the depths of a personal travail arguing something akin to accompany it in the heart of Yahweh himself?[7] Only rarely does the Qur'an allow the reader insight into the personal experience of its incidence within Muhammad's soul nor would the ardour of the "Confessions" of Jeremiah be ever congenial to its genius.[8] Reflecting this way must be the clue to what otherwise remains puzzling, namely the absence from the Qur'an of the personalities in whom Biblical prophethood came to its surest glory.

Perhaps we should conclude that Muhammad's *in situ* was a more elemental mission. There was no Torah yet in being and no Shari'ah grounded in a power-community. These the Scripture would inaugurate through its own incidence via the Prophet. By that circumstance something inherently political was entailed in Muhammad's setting. The paganism his message denied was expressed in Quraishi hegemony and prestige. These, in their pagan quality, could not be challenged in solely verbal terms. So much the pre-Hijrah preaching learned. His very message in its there-and-then carried a logic arguing the necessary dethroning of the structure that opposed it.

Biblical prophethood faced a situation in which covenantal divine order, politically in being, came under the fluctuating threat of external powers. Their menace had to be interpreted as potential, if not actual, divine discipline of social disorder and retribution of its moral guilt. In this setting, the Hebrew prophets were not political in any Quranic sense as seeking prophet-power with a view to state-making. They were political only as subverting guilty power-forms. They stood in courts, to be sure, coming to them from "the court-counsels of the Lord", but only to arraign the compromises and alert the conscience of the powers that were. In contrast to the Islamic logic that made for the Hijrah, theirs was a mandate inherently moral and spiritual. If, as with Amos, they seemed subversive, or as with Jeremiah, even treacherous, that was no more than the honesty of their divine words.

It is vital to register this fundamental contrast in the whence and whither of the Biblical and the Quranic prophethoods. Nowhere is it more dramatically measured than in the Exile and the Hijrah as the pivots of each, as events constitutive of the outer and the inner worlds they negotiated. The Hebrew prophets anticipated and interpreted and survived the exile experience. It was the fulcrum of their whole vocation. It evoked their deepest personal emotions as well as dominating their engagement with history. On either account it has no parallel in the setting of Muhammad in the Qur'an. Rather, his experience both counselled and accomplished a theology of attainment and triumph out of an origin awaiting the status it did not yet politically enjoy. The Hijrah from Mecca on the part of the Prophet and his first disciples was, indeed, an exile costly to their emotions but voluntary. It related past and future in terms entirely other than those of Jeremiah in the desolation of Jerusalem or of Ezekiel sitting with the exiles by the river Chebar. The emigrés in Medina were not grieving by "willows on which they hung their harps", nor pondering how to "sing the Lord's song" in a strange land. They were still within "inviolate territory", if not in Hebraic terms,[9] and, turning from a Jerusalem Qiblah to a Meccan for their prayer, were oriented towards a physical return which they, not some remote Cyrus, would engineer.

The contrasts give the whole clue to the dissimilarities of Biblical and Quranic prophets. Muhammad was set to become "head of state", in the formula: "Obey Allah and obey the Prophet."[10] It was never so with the sequence from Amos to Malachi. These prophets were never "kings", only their mentors, emissaries from God within an establishment already launched via Moses and David and requiring to be addressed in its given identity as Yahweh's realm of covenant.

## III

Another significant consequence of this contrasted milieu must be the shape of futurism in the two prophetic traditions. We have insisted from the outset that any popular notion of prophethood as merely "forecasting", has no place either in reality or in this study. Nevertheless, since reading of past and present have a future logic, the future is inseparable from the moral relevance and inner dynamism of the prophetic task. Things Hebraic were bound to look beyond exile to redemption or restoration. Hence an implicit Messianism with its dimension of hope. A sort of "Messianism", not awaited under God in possibly distant terms, but immediately or presently predicated as action in the wake of Hijrah, characterizes the ethos of the Qur'an. A voluntary emigration to Medina lay within a situation clearly tending to a strategy of armed recovery by which a purposeful and resourceful body of believers would attain an auto-restoration. So much their history would suggest. So much in fact the post-Hijrah Qur'an indicated and achieved. It had its own decisive and physical implementation that had its future in its own hands.

Here is another aspect of what differentiates the Biblical from the Quranic. It may help to explain the absence from the Qur'an of any Biblical-style Messiah and perhaps thereby, also, its presentation of Jesus as lacking Messianic import in his exclusively didactic, preaching, role. To be sure, the formula: *'Isa Ibn Maryam al-Masih* is regularly used for the Jesus of the Qur'an. The matronymic and the Messiah title, however, do not have the "restorer" or the "redeemer" connotation. They merely indicate an "anointing" to the role of "messenger".[11] Jesus is firmly incorporated into that which, for Islam, is the only shape of divine agency in the world, namely "bearers of words".

For, unlike the Biblical word-bearers, Muhammad did not have to decipher the ways of God in the seeming bankruptcy of covenant that the Jewish exile represented, nor to investigate the measure of human wrongness which that exile reproached and from which its burden derived. He had only to bring the scriptural concomitant of his people's Hijrah and their campaign to retrieve what they had voluntarily foregone. The enigma of their persecution and suffering in Mecca had not spelled a cumulative divine requital of their misdoings to be divinely resolved in God's own time. Its vindication lay potentially in their own resolve and the concert of their politics.

It is in these terms that perspectives of far history did not come into the frame of the Qur'an, nor measures of human perversity like those registered by Amos, Zephaniah and Zechariah. "The angel of the Lord" in rebuke was not there standing beside the representatives of Jewish crown and temple. Rebuke was set on a pagan Quraish whom Muhammad would have within his own final reckoning of city-siege and conquest.

There are, in this way between the two prophethoods, divergent conceptions of human evil and wrong. Jewry and their prophets, to be sure, had ample "woes" to utter against the heathen nations, witness the diatribes of Ezekiel upon Tyre or earlier of Amos upon sundry nations in enmity to Israel. But the sharpest anathemas and verdicts of Biblical prophethood were against their own domestic guilty – priests and people and false seers. This interior accusation is not blunted or elided by concentration on the sins of foes. Islam, in its genesis and its *mise-en-scène*, had ample occasion for reproach of external iniquities, the sins and heedlessness of pagan tribes, rather than deep self-scrutiny of heart. Where reproach comes it is in the context of reluctance for the risks of war or of *fitnahs*, seditions, inside the Muslim enterprise under way against the obdurate Quraish. Zealous causes are always liable to find alibis for what might inculpate them and to silence self-queries where "conscience might make cowards of all", and what we need is heroes.[12] Was it not the distinctive notion of covenant and election which gave to things Hebraic their capacity for deep self-interrogation, even when it also argued a lively self-assurance and an obsessive self-admiration? Was it not precisely inside that paradox that the whole reality of Hebraic prophethood belonged? Election was its supreme impetus, actual apostasy its ultimate burden. The patterns of Islam in the Qur'an exempted it from both sides of this paradox. Evil lay in its own foes, vindication in its own efforts. Allah was "with" them in the circumstances of their own devices. When decadent Jewish kings and people thought that way, as they often did, the great prophets had for them nothing but reproach.

We must postpone here all the implications of this analysis for any theology of divine agency in prophethood. In present context, the fact that future vindication is not Messianic in the Qur'an but vested in the Prophet himself, and comprised inside the Scriptures as "manifest victory", gives a distinctive quality to its theme of patience – that vital requisite of the prophets, evermore exemplified in the saga of Job, the Quranic Ayyub.

*Sabr*, and its cognates, are a frequent theme in the Islamic Book. The term is somewhat akin to the New Testament *hupomone*, as "staying power" in adversity, "endurance" against odds. While "endurance" matters, there is a different virtue in positive "long-suffering", which overcomes evil, not by how well it resists but how far it surmounts and retrieves. We shall be brought back to this theme via the meaning later of "the weight in the word". Here the "Confessions" of Jeremiah will prove the ultimate measure. It may be that Islam, too well and too soon, assumes vindication and success and so fails a full register of what prophethood must undertake in the non-coercive persuasion of the world.

It is clear that there is much anguish in the *Sirah*, or life-career, of Muhammad. We will meet it under "weighting" anon. Yet it is of a different order from the Biblical experience measured in Hosea and his intimates, and supremely in Jesus. Presently, we are only concerned to have the mutual bearings of the Biblical and the Quranic in honest focus. What happens to "patience" is an aspect that holds a clue to much else, just as it tallies with all we have to explore. It is surely in such frank appraisal of the differentials that we can rightly comprehend both traditions under the single category of prophethood.

# IV

It follows that our confidence in doing so may find warrant in discerning the part played by the Hebraic in the forming of the Quranic, in respect, that is, of Muhammad's experience. The subject is large and contentious. Much of it will better come in CHAPTER III. Here we make the case for the interplay of the two prophethoods by tracing the shape of the continuity between them.

The familiar Quranic phrase "The people of the Book" may well hold the key, with its bond between a Scripture and an identity. That "messengers" belong with "books" and that communities having both possess what distinguishes them and gives them cohesion, seems clear enough. Deferring local factors to the later chapter, Muhammad's mission, read in the light of the Islam's credal accent on "books" and their human bringers via revelation, could be seen as turning on his consciousness that his own people thus far lacked both "book" and "apostle". They were subtly excluded from Judaic identity and were, in the vital sense of the word, *ummiyyun*, "illiterate" by the absence of "an Arab/ic Scripture".[13]

Here was a double objective to be satisfied, namely a drawing of feuding, tribal Arabs into unity by means of their being scripturized in their own native tongue.[14] By Judaic precedent the two could well be one attainment. Why should not native people find fulfilment in a native Scripture? The theme is there squarely in the Qur'an's stress on its being "an Arabic Qur'an" "in a clear Arabic speech", via *al-rasul al-nabi al-ummi* whom Muhammad – clearly in the sequel – proved to be.

If this perception, which needs an elaboration we defer, reads the association rightly, then the impulse of the Biblical tradition, discernible in local Jewry, is one factor in the making of Islam. The large disparities between "Book" and "Book", i.e. between the Biblical "Canon" of the prophets and the text of the Qur'an, need not disqualify this measure of inter-association. The Qur'an has the right to its own originality but, on its own showing, bears the clear traces of the debts in its historical incidence. The Islamic doctrine of its "uncreatedness" and thus its "independence" of human factors is not impugned, in its intention to safeguard the divine source-origin, by the recognition of the earth-located setting in which any enterprise of scripturizing humans must proceed.[15]

The Qur'an, in its own contents, looks back to Biblical patriarchs and "sent Ones", whose mediations of meaning it claims to corroborate and finalize. Muslim orthodoxy, then, can have no quarrel with the inter-association of Bible and Qur'an *The Weight in the Word* assumes. To be sure, the Qur'an claims continuity on its own terms as a sort of corrective even of its debts. Those will always be in dispute but, without the linkage we are exploring, there would be nothing to have at issue.

There is one interesting feature the Biblical and the Quranic have in common. The Preface made the point that the primitive forms of prophetism, the professional "seers", were excluded from the status of Amos and all his peers in "the goodly fellowship" of those who were prophets indeed. His urgent disclaimer: "I was no prophet, nor a prophet's son" (Amos 7: 14) underscored his status as truly sent by Yahweh. Many of his Biblical successors made the same protest or suffered the competition of the professionals, the temple-associates, the soothsayers and the routine poesysers. From these historically the great ethical spokesmen may have had their nurture. For – as under "casting" and "saying" in subsequent chapters we must note – the impulses to vision and to utterance are mysterious and lie deep in the psyche.[16]

What is here significant is that the Qur'an makes a similar dissociation of *waḥy*, as Muhammad experienced it, from the skills or vagaries of professional poets. He was at pains to disavow the charge of the Quraish that he was merely of their number. Important as the "matchless" language of the Qur'an was as evidence of its heavenly origin, it was in no way attributable to a poetic art. Poets might be challenged to match it but this was not, in any sense, an exercise to bring it into their orbit but, instead, to demonstrate its claimed unearthly character.

An unbelieving reckoning may discern some perplexity here but Muhammad's urgent disavowal of professional prophetism is clearly comparable, in its own locale, with that of Amos in his mission to Samaria. As a bare phenomenon the *afflatus* by which prophetic utterance proceeds may seem the same: the authentic is known only in the content and the sequel. It transcends what it shares as that by which, undifferentiated, it might be misconstrued; namely verbal power, poetic genius, or professional adeptness. Hence the urgency of lively repudiation of such sources, the more squarely to assert truly religious quality. Despite their large contrasts, Amos and Muhammad may be seen akin in this respect. Both were despised as pretending to a familiar role; both repudiated a charge that would have belied their genuine errand; both had to repudiate what they were not in order to affirm who they truly were. That measure of common experience between them may justify the risk we run in associating things Quranic with things Biblical.

The incidence here, and elsewhere, of a broadly comparable issue as to the credentials of prophets does not allow us to neglect the large categories in which the two Scriptures are at odds with each other in their radically different perspectives on history. The Qur'an has within its own sequence the Hijrah and the institutionalizing by which "God's religion" is finalized. Hence its impatience in its enmities (identified as these are in its immediate campaigns) and the rigorous nature of its verdicts on the future states of Paradise and "the Fire". Hence, too, the absence of that Messianic expectation by which Hebrew prophecy interpreted the vicissitudes of a turbulent history – the expectation which the Christian Church found fulfilled in the suffering Christ through whom it held the exclusive realm of Jewish hope thrown open to all and sundry on the sole ground of faith. Islam, for its part, brought a universality about, but in terms of its own ambition to have actualized "God's religion" via given *Din* and *Dawlah*, the final faith in the care of the Caliphate.

In multiple ways the prophethoods diverge and tangle in their perspectives on history, their mandates from heaven. Yet does not that very conclusion require that we also align them as closely as we honestly may? Biblical loyalties are not forfeit in perceptive readiness for clues and parallels in the Qur'an.

# V

What of a readiness – and its potential benefits – in the other direction? Islam has long insisted on the confirmatory role its Scripture has in relation to all previous prophets. It has, however, qualified that approval by assuming that all pre-Quranic texts and text-bringers should be, and were, identical in their themes and meanings. Thus it "confirmed" them on condition they were confirmable on its own terms. In this way, Islamic scholarship has long denied itself a real reckoning with the subtle complexity of prophethood. It has claimed to exemplify in ultimate terms what it assesses only in its own Islamic dimensions.

That the prophets "had all the same message" might be verified in respect of the unity of Allah, the reality of creation, the entrusted creaturehood of humanity, and the divine will enshrined in a concept of law. These, however, were attended by sharp disparities of perception, such as Judaic exceptionality (Abraham but only via Moses and Sinai), human amenability or perversity, readings of time and its vagaries. Could Jeremiah be "among the prophets" by any Quranic criteria, given the tragic burden of his pleas to God and the unavailing nature of his long ministry? Could Hosea by a Quranic prophet with a pathos about Yahweh drawn from a deep domestic anguish?

The questions multiply and may go far to explain why – otherwise inexplicably – these supreme Hebraic prophets are absent from the Qur'an's roll of honour from Enoch to Elisha. They may also explain why the Jesus of the Qur'an is restricted to "prophet", i.e. verbal status and the meaning of Christology is ignored or dispelled. For it was the essence of the ultimate prophets of the Bible, as we have seen, to point forward to that crucial "truth through personality" and personal travail that Christology enshrines.

It is thus that a hopeful bringing together of prophethoods, Biblical and Quranic, may serve to invite Muslims into appropriate study of how their familiar terms of reference as to what prophethood means and entails might come to compass the whole range of prophetic experience, however uncongenial its content to the ethos of the Qur'an. Such study is long overdue. For, by their ready thesis of approximation to the Qur'an, Muslim scholars have proved reluctant to test the very confidence with which they hold it and forfeited an appreciation of all that awaits them in the "burden" – whether of Amos or Jeremiah, or of Micah with his "spears into ploughshares".

The point might be illuminated by reference to the Biblical Book of Psalms. For so many of its contents derive not from David, but from unknown prophets whose travail they express.[17] There are superb passages of nature celebration in the Qur'an but little akin to the inner soul-searching of prophet-born Psalms. That these "cries from the heart" might constitute divine revelation contradicts the Islamic norm that revelation only "comes down" in *Tanzil*, and happens only when God addresses men, not – inconceivably not – when men, even out of the burden of their prophetic task, are addressing God. Yet such responding to the pain of truth and the mystery of word-taking may be the very crux of divine disclosure. So it proved with Jeremiah and so it was that psalms could take due place in divine Scripture.[18]

It may be that, on Quranic prescripts, this perception of what fits to be Scripture is impossible of recognition. Yet, some effort after recognition there must surely be if the common task of "weight in the word" is shared by both religions. The Qur'an's ambition to be confirmatory of all prophethood that preceded it must cast its net more widely and suspend its prior judgement in the arbitrary pre-requisite of Qur'an-conformity.

If it can do so, the rewards can be great. Doing so will involve the realization that those themes, earlier listed, that are discernibly already mutual, entail sharp contradictions in their outworking. How does divine unity square with human perversity – in condign judgement, or in suffering grace? How does our given creaturehood square with supposed theocracy? How actually feasible in the human world is absolute divine law? How do "messengers" receive, relate and realize their "message"? How far can being on behalf of God in spoken agency translate into the human psyche and, conversely, how far is the divine implicated in the message-bearing consequences for the prophet as a self, endowed with mind, heart and will?

Clearly it is impossible to hold to some continuity of all prophethood, some supposed identity in all means to "holy words" and sacred "books" from God, without conceding this measure of interrogation of them all. The hope of the chapters that follow is to pursue this wealth of puzzlement and diversity belonging to the prophethoods we are bringing together under the Qur'an's own rubric of "casting", "saying" and "weighting" – these being at once biographies, personalities, destinies and Scriptures.

## II

# The Casting, The Saying, The Weighting

### I

Given that prophethoods, Biblical and Quranic, admit of a discerning comparative study, it will be well to take the verb, noun and adjective of Surah 73.5 for an overview of what is entailed in the venture. "We will cast upon you a heavy saying." The experience of a prophet has these three dimensions. Each will need exploration in subsequent chapters. The immediate aim is to measure the "burden" theme as comprising vocation, expression and tribulation. A summons is explicit in all three – the claim of a calling, the bidding to heed and the demand of a meaning. Everything from Amos to Malachi could be comprehended in the terms of this one Quranic verse, seeing that the Hebraic "burden" holds the same three in one – the mission undertaken, the message told and the cost in the sequel paid.

The Arabic verb in Surah 73.5, *nulqi* is frequent in several contexts and cases in the Qur'an, of fear cast in the hearts of the obdurate, of mistakes Satan casts into recital, of Moses casting down his rod, or of the earth casting out all her contents at the climax of judgement. Elsewhere the word is used of a beast giving birth, "casting from the womb to the ground", or meaning "to throw", or to "lade" camel or donkey. A nounal form has the sense of "encounter". The word can even be used for the delivery of a lecture.

Many of these senses come together, as it were, in the pregnancy of prophets, their enloading and unloading, their quality as receptacles and carriers of meaning, and so undergoers of liability.

What the Arabic will not allow may be suggested by the term "cast" in other languages. Two intriguing nuances of the English word are obvious at once and they serve our context well, namely the "casting" of a

# The Casting, The Saying, The Weighting

producer in the theatre and the "casting" of iron in the furnace. Both are apt clues to the mystery of prophetic vocation.

By what criteria does the country boy from Anathoth, gentle in nurture, sensitive in soul and a very private self, become a supreme exemplar of prophetic heroism? Casting in drama is a rare art, fitting character possessed to character portrayed, detecting who is best potential for the roles in repertoire. It is not inapt to sense here a measure of the incidence of the choice of God's persons in the drama of the several books and the incidence of inspiration. It is vital that our Quranic study undertake the setting of Muhammad's becoming the Prophet of Islam, the factors which helped to initiate and sustain vocation, rooted as these were in the social context and the personal realm.

Unlike Tradition, the Qur'an itself – as we must study in CHAPTER III – yields few clues to these. Biblically, it is notable how frequent and how central are call-narratives like those in Isaiah 6 and Jeremiah 1 and the sense they carry of a born destiny. By what impulse does the "herdman" from Tekoa betake himself to the northern Kingdom in the 8th century, armed, for all his apparent rusticity, with alert antenna for the world-scene and a rich power of rhetoric and vivid imagery? It will be both fascinating and reverent to examine divine "casting" for prophetic roles and right to do so in full cognizance of sacred mystery.

As for the other "casting" the story of Joseph – if we may return to patriarchs – tells how "the iron entered into his soul".[1] Prophets, including Muhammad, had to be "steeled" for their task, tempered by its adversities and toughened in the process. Jeremiah certainly knew this meaning. "I have made thee this day . . . an iron pillar and brazen walls against the whole land" (1: 18) by whom "the sin of Judah is written with a pen of iron" (17: 1). Ezekiel is bidden to be "iron-plated" in his confronting the city of Jerusalem (4: 3). The Qur'an's "Surah of Iron" (57) is so named for its mention of "iron" (v.25) but does not carry an "iron in the soul" significance. It celebrates martial feats that required the toughness for lack of which others were reproached.

Whatever light these bearings of the English word may hold, the casting is essentially the entrusting of what will take its toll and demand courage. Prophethood is no realm for cowards. Its crux is a sense of destiny, if need be from birth, spelling its own logic in exacting terms of exaltation and despair. It contrives a marriage with meanings "for better or for worse". It signifies a load which will take all that a man has. How personality is recruited, moulded, sustained and prophetic part imparted belong with personal time and local place.

## The Casting, The Saying, The Weighting

## II

The vital noun in Surah 73.5 is *qawl*, lit. "a saying", with the verb *qul* among the most frequent in the Qur'an. "Say: He is God, the One" (Surah 112.1) is an early key to the thrust of the Qur'an and the command echoes through the whole. The saying is sublimely simple, cogent, brief and commanding yet these very qualities hide deep issues. The concept of divine speech placed on human lips and heard by human ears involves the entire realm of language, the whence and whither of its warrant to mean. Theology, both Christian and Muslim, has long been involved in lively appraisal of what "divine word" can signify, how "Thus says the Lord" can be understood. Late modern philosophers, if they have not discredited the theme altogether, have sharply complicated it by notions of "language/games" and "reader control". The threat to any scriptured confidence which these embody may serve, in some measure, to give both Biblical and Quranic scholarship common cause. But they will, by the same token, reveal the very different perceptions of revelation, of "word from" to "word through", on which the two Scriptures are based.

This theme is, of course, bound up with that of the "casting" which we have understood as the "election" and the "making" of the prophet as agent of the divine text through the impact of biography and locale. But such "casting" to and for "a saying" can only transpire through the mysterious fusion of "word-bearer" and the "word-borne". When *The Wisdom of Solomon* speaks of wisdom "in all ages entering into holy souls . . . making them friends of God and prophets" (7: 27) the beauty of the concept leaves to silence the hard questions of how the "friendship" contrives with their souls the shape of the language they will utter, and of how that language holds and gives what had possessed the soul. Or, as the Quranic situation would seem to require, is there somehow a direct verbal in-voicing of the very words so that the soul is not consciously engaged?

This alternative, if such it be, is specially relevant in respect of the Qur'an. For, as exegetes have often observed, to none but Muhammad was Allah ever speaking in Qur'an-terms. He was the sole and sufficient recipient, so that the completion of the Book coincided precisely with his death. Biblical prophethood in its panoramic quality through the crucial centuries admits of very diversified experiences of inspiration, its means and contents. The "Go, prophesy . . ". of Amos (7: 15) has a different feel from the "Say . . ." to Muhammad. Judging from the journey Amos took and the metaphors he savoured, all from his habitat, one could well imagine him shaping his utterance as he went, gathering impulse in language from the thrust of his errand. The "saying", when it happens, is no less "cast" on him but the pattern is altogether different from Muhammad's recital of what is known to him – as Islamic faith holds – from recorded text. Ezekiel, again, is a highly contrasted figure for whom sometimes the command to "say" takes shape in "exhibition" by contrived imagery even embracing prolonged, but presumably significant, silence. Such purposive ostentation has no place in the Qur'an where "saying" is consistently oral. Yet its sustained oral nature has vital situational bearings and occasions. These enter crucially into both immediate and exegetical reception of the sense.

These and kindred problems of "the word and the casting", of "the saying and the voicing", the thing in its origin and in its mediation to and from its chosen bearer, are the duties that following chapters must take up. They aim to bring two prophetic traditions together, if only – in the event – to register them as disparate. "The Word of the Lord came by Haggai ..."; "Say: 'People, I am an apostle of God to you all, of God who is sovereign over the heavens and the earth'"; "Say: 'I am not a new phenomenon among apostles'"; "Hear this word which the Lord has spoken"[2] – how should we read claim and content in their incidence in such examples of religious "saying"? What is their provenance in the intimate experience out of which they speak? The "saying" is never exempt from that "I am" of Muhammad nor from identification with the Micahs or the Zechariahs from whose lips it falls. Yet the enigma of how and why they should be who they are and what they speak is the core mystery for ever attaching to the status and the authority alike of Bible and Qur'an. The phrase "Cast upon you ..." captures that juncture, the human means as the condition of divine meaning.

# III

This "casting" of "saying" is on every count a "weighting". There is no mistaking the Arabic adjective *thaqil* in this regard. "Grave", "profound", "onerous", "grievous", "momentous", "formidable" are all apt synonyms. Surahs 7.57 and 13.12 use the word for heavy, louring clouds, while 76.27 *yawman thaqilan* means "the dire day" of judgement. The verb akin is used of the "weight" of good deeds in the scales of that day, while 7.187 warns of how that judgement is "heavy in the heavens and the earth". Elsewhere the word has the clear sense of "burden" as when Surah 52.40, like 68.46, remonstrates that Muhammad in his preaching is asking no "fee" from his hearers by which they might be "burdened". They were familiar enough with the burdens of insolvency stemming from the usury against which his words were set.

Elsewhere in the Qur'an, notably in 94.3 ("the burden weighing down your back") Muhammad's message-bringing is known to him as a "heaviness" both of import and cost. *Thaqil* is sometimes currently used of people whose company is unwelcome or hard to take. There may be in that usage a remote hint of the essence of prophetic burden, both Biblical and Quranic, namely the unwantedness it has for those who say: "Let us hear no more of the Name of the Lord." Hostility to messengers is a dominant and permanent theme in all prophetic story. Muhammad is one with Hebraic antecedents in the certainty and pain of this experience of calumny, ridicule and harsh rejection. It is the central feature that theology has to interpret. Many of "the sent" have had cause to say to themselves, in a Shakespearean image: "Thou art no Atlas for so great a weight." Yet "Atlas" in the realm of truth in the human scene is the right analogy, where the constraints of meaning "hang weights upon the tongue".[3] Or, changing the imagery, the saga of prophethood might borrow the famous words of William Bradford.:

> All things stand upon them with a weather-beaten face and the whole country, full of woods and thickets, represented a wild and savage hue. What could now sustain them but the Spirit of God and His grace?[4]

The inhospitality of the suqs and shrines of Mecca to Muhammad fits the situation well. The "thickets" of conspiracy were daunting to Jeremiah and intimidation was the lot of all his peers.

This obvious sense of "weight" and "burden" is not the only – or indeed for Muslim exegetes the first – reading but it is the core of all the others, whether things dire in warning to heedless miscreants, or threats against the godless, or radical issues of life and death, or crises present or impending in history. For all these return back to the travail of the speaker risking the enmities they arouse, the recriminations they excite, the threat they represent to a stubborn *status quo*. Ahab's questioning gibe to Elijah: "Art thou he that troubleth Israel?" (1 Kings 18: 17) echoes through all such confrontations.

Nor is this ultimate burden allayed, still less measured, by a distinctive interpretation given by some Muslim exegetes in reference to the "weight" language "on the back" or in the "saying", namely that the onset of *wahy*, in *tanzil* or "inspiration", caused Muhammad to fall to the ground or experience a physical limpness he could not sustain. This reading and this phenomenon need study in a later context. Whatever psychic or mystical import they have must surely be no more than a feature in, or a parable of, the central burden of articulate and existential prophethood – the burden which belongs inherently to being vicariously on behalf of God in the human world. The weight accompanies the vocation in a full engagement with place and time.

These psychic manifestations have often been cited as appropriate evidence and proof of the supernatural origin and working of inspiration. Be that as it may, the clue to real "burden" must surely lie beyond the range of these symptoms in its incidence. Conscious spiritual "weight" must surely mean that personality, however conditioned, is where the crux is found. It is hard to conclude, for example, that Ezekiel was a normal man, with his vagaries, his impulses and his at time neurotic demeanour. Whatever the psychic price of the divine agency authentic prophets fulfill, whatever the idiosyncrasies they display in its discharge, the spiritual import and its "heavy going" in the world must always be, and remain, the meaning of the burden, as – precisely – the burden of that meaning.

"Vicarious" is a word broadly uncongenial to the Muslim mind, given the Qur'an's steady emphasis on no "burden-bearing" of guilt or liability other than one's own.[5] Yet is it clear that what prophets undergo as a consequence of their (unsought) sentness, they undergo for God's sake. To forebear to preach would flout vocation, but it would escape the burden the preaching entails. Thus fidelity is anxiety, word-taking is pain-taking. Both are in God's Name and for God's sake. Religion may not be as the philosopher A. N. Whitehead saw it "the last refuge of human savagery";[6] it is, nevertheless, certainly a prime theatre of human perversity. Prophethood experiences in concentrated force the hard going in this world of goodness and truth, of the ideal as for ever the vulnerable, of the latent human antipathy to the divine when the divine impinges through messengers on the complacence or the cussedness of society or on the vested interest of hierarchies, institutions and cultures. Sin and wrong are never quiescent when challenged and always restive under reproach.

It is for this reason that prophethood, aside from the political crises in which, in the Hebraic mode, it so often moved, has always been compelled to question its own adequacy. It has an instinct to feel that there must be something beyond itself for the sake of the "desire" to which it points but seems of itself unable to reach. The New Testament implications of "Yea, I say unto you and more than a prophet", to be sure, have no meaning for Muslims. Muslims hold that prophethood is all, the ultimate of what there needs to be, Allah being Allah and the world being as the world is.

Yet, in the significance of the Hijrah, there *is* more than prophethood, more than the *balagh*, or "message" to which Muhammad, pre-Hijrah, was repeatedly and strictly confined.[7] He experienced acutely what all prophets came to know, namely the unpersuadedness of obdurate humans, their capacity to belie and resist the hortatory, the directional, the prescriptive. The central Quranic concept of *kufr*, as wilful unbelief, is eloquent enough of this situation. The proof of its chronic quality lies in the necessity for the Hijrah itself as a perceived need, in the sequence of Islam, to pass from failing persuasion to urgent *jihad*, from ardent verbalism to martial ardour. The whole logic of the second division of both the Qur'an and the Prophet's *Sirah* springs from the impasse of the first. It was an impasse of the undeniable word and its ever deniable claim, such as all great prophets knew as the explicit travail of their calling.

Hebrew prophets, for the most part, knew exile, not Hijrah. They moved in the courts of political power but did not usurp them. Their experience, comparable in this sense to Muhammad's in Mecca, coped with adversity and the distresses of their words, by invoking Messianic hope, not as the self-help of some Hijrah, but as fit to be anticipated from "the Lord of the vineyard" they believed their Israel/Judah to be. A "redeemer" safeguarding the divine future would need to be "more than prophethood". So much their experience round the proven insufficiency of words led them to anticipate. It was logical, too, that when such futurism both consoled and fulfilled them, they read its shape in the same prerogatives of suffering they had themselves known in registering their own travail. Hence "the suffering servant" imagery in their reading of the ultimate shape of hope. It was for this reason, and by this legacy, that – at length – Christianity understood that the human world was, and is, a crucifying place. The cross of Jesus as the Christ was the very shape of "the God of the prophets" being there in the realism to which all His messengers had pointed. It is sobering to realize that the very same pregnant incompleteness of prophethood that, for the Qur'an, led to the Hijrah to Medina, brought Hebraic thinking into that Messianic expectation which the New Testament identified in the ministry and the suffering of Jesus. For that ministry underwent, in its movement into crucifying rejection, precisely the same eventuality of resented teaching and unwanted presence that prophethood at large had habitually known. The disciples, when questioned, were perceptive enough to recognize in "the prophet of Nazareth" the lineage of Jeremiah. The words "more than a prophet" which Jesus applied to John the Baptist (Matthew 11: 9) had even richer meaning in the Sonship of Jesus. It was in line with what would always be needed in the divine economy as the ultimate measure of all prophethood, divinely sent and divinely wrought. This brief chapter has in summary what needs to be scrutinized and underwritten in the chapters that follow.

# III

## Prophetic Personality

### I

An old Muslim tradition says that "God has sent no prophet who was not a shepherd of sheep".[1] "All we like sheep have gone astray", once on the lips of an Isaian community of hearers, could give the tradition metaphorical point. Otherwise, in literal terms, it could only be true of Abraham, Moses and David. As far as prophetic biography knows, Hosea, Jeremiah, Ezekiel with others in Judea, and Muhammad in the Hijaz, would not qualify, though by conjecture Amos might.[2]

Apart also from any figurative sense, associating prophets with shepherds hardly does well by the intractable human world. As CHAPTERS V and VII will underline, the task of "messengers" to people, Israelites or Meccans, is far removed from "green meadows and sweet pastures and still waters". They are not monitors of docility but parties to a divine encounter with a turbulent world. The "lostness" of sheep – and their recovery by shepherds – are only distant analogy for what is wrong with humans and what its retrieval exacts. "The voice of one crying" will not be making gentle music from a shepherd's pipe.[3]

However, the tradition – with these reservations – can serve us here. De-romanticized, it implies that where prophets originate bears strongly on what they become. Their antecedents are significant for their destiny. Whether shepherds, priests, citizens, state-counsellors, merchants or thinkers, the dimensions in their origins will colour their language, shape their perceptions and situate their vocation. The spiritual and circumstantial making of prophetic personality is the business of this chapter, exploring more curiously the "casting" in the "weighting" remitted from CHAPTER II. All that follows concerning style, life-scene, conscience and travail will be the register of personhood as gathered into proxy-hood for God in the sending that mysteriously He wills, the errands He requires.

The work of shepherds, one may assume, is uniquely self-preoccupying. The task finds them often wrapped in their own thoughts. For sheep know where the grass is and amble slowly over it. The vigilance of shepherds is not always at critical stretch. There is ready occasion for interior awareness free from the besetting intrusions that happen in the market and the work-place.

In this feature they can be seen to point to the great distinctive quality in prophethood. Not, to be sure, any reprieve there from the crowded scene, the stressful claims – but a role that takes selfhood into isolation, a business that means a high self-consciousness. "Him that crieth", in Isaiah 40: 3, leaves all other detail about "him" as though it were irrelevant. The "crying" is all and the "crier" is only in the "crying". All that matters about him is "a voice", so complete is the fusion of word and personality. The Hebrew text in Isaiah 40: 3 leaves open the possibility that "the voice" is that of Yahweh himself. When the evangelist cites the passage it is from the Septuagint that he identifies a human speaker, John. Then there is immediate characterization about one "clothed in camel hair" and nourished with "locusts and wild honey". Personality is vividly introduced but the "voice" is dominant.

Prophets, then, are so taken up into vocation that their significance is in the word they carry. That task commands their whole identity, takes it into a total equation. Prophetic language is the heart of prophetic personality. So intertwined are these that, arguably, CHAPTER IV ahead ought to have preceded this CHAPTER III. Is not the onset of "utterance" what makes prophethood and ought, therefore, to be prior? Meanings only tell themselves by finding words to tell them. Language then is primary. Yet words only find themselves on lips and have their "tellings" from persons.

Much, too, that derives from personality determines the tenor and the drift of words. Prophets only find themselves such in words: words only come on prophetic leave and lip. They are one and the same reality.

## II

This mutual finding happens in the Biblical prophets in ways significantly different from how it obtains in the Qur'an. With the exception of the unknown "Isaiah(s)" of the chapters 40 to 66 so ascribed, Biblical prophets are all personally named.[4] Identities are there with the formula: "The word of the Lord came to . . .". The Qur'an does not use such formula. One, un-named, is bidden: "Recite in the Name of your Lord . . .". In fact the personal named, Muhammad, occurs only three times in the Book, a fourth having to do with his having no surviving son. *Al-Rasul*, in "messenger status", is sufficient designation. The personal pronoun addressing him is used with great frequency.[5] Whereas a choric quality in the Bible extends from Amos to Malachi, Muhammad is Allah's sole addressee in the Qur'an.

This difference between the two Scriptures derives from a deeper contrast still. The Biblical "word-coming" enlists the personal idiosyncrasies it commissions. We recognize them in their deliverances in ways that make their naming – and dating – significant. The Qur'an's imperative "Say . . ." means that what follows "recites" the pre-existent, heavenly text.[6] Vocabulary, style, verbal usage, of course, tally with what is locally current. It matters that Muhammad is a "native" Arab messenger. But locality and personality do not enter in the way they do as *mise-en-scène* when Isaiah finds his vocation "in the year King Uzziah died", or Jeremiah posts himself at the Temple to disillusion its "vain oblations".

Despite this distinctive perception of the role of the person in the text, Muslim tradition and philosophy have engaged in far-reaching reflection on Muhammad's status, endowing his passive role in the Book itself with large cosmic and ontological dimensions, to be noted later. In tension, as they are, with the immediate pattern of how he received the Qur'an, they justify an effort to study Muhammad's experience in something like the terms involved for Biblical messengers. The command: "Say . . ." is both a verbal imperative suggesting what is wholly from without and a summons to a mysterious participation in soul. There are numerous Quranic hints of a deeply personal experience, despite the peremptory form. Muslim Qur'an study has long been at issue with itself on this score. Part analogy with things Biblical may assist its problems.[7]

Biblical scholarship, in line with the Bible's own evidences, normally has no hesitation about probing the inner psyche of prophetic experience. It would be idle to come to Amos, Hosea, Ezekiel and the rest without a lively cognizance of biography and its bearings. They are, to be sure, aware of a commission to "say . . ." but not in the absence of the immediacies, the outward scene, the inward cares of sense and soul. What these yield has its place in what they utter.

It is subtly different in the case of the Qur'an. While the landscape of the Hijaz and the markets of Mecca, even the shipping of the Red Sea, supply rich imagery in the text the Prophet is allowed no Jeremiah-style soliloquies and is rarely depicted in a personal capacity outside the controversies the message itself arouses or the directives concerning his official status and access to him. No biographical prelude is given with the inaugural "Recite in the Name of your Lord" in 96.1, for the subsequent hearer or reader to locate its incidence in Muhammad's self-awareness. Likewise the great vision in Surah 53. 4–11, and a second (vv. 13–18) "near the garden of abode" are told without prelude, as so overwhelming in their incidence as to make "background" superfluous. In this way they are powerfully in line with the Qur'an's status. The "Night Journey" from Mecca to Jerusalem in 17.1 has the same dramatic brevity, for all its profound significance. In these ways, it is almost as if the Qur'an is majestically dispensing with any circumstantial credentials that, like minor characters on a stage, might serve to interpret or illuminate the action. The text itself carries all the weight it needs.

While the Qur'an is thus silent about how Muhammad came to these absolute moments of being Scriptured in its terms, there are a few latent clues which later Tradition copiously develops in detail beloved of the faithful. There are, in the Qur'an, no birth narratives concerning him, nothing parallel to the long accounts of 'Isa's birth in Surahs 3 and 19. The two allusions in Surahs 73.1 and 74.1 both address Muhammad as "Thou . . ." and surely take us as close as we come to "seeing" his calling.

He is one "wrapped in a mantle", one "enfolded". "Mantles", of course, befit prophets, mark and designate them. But they also suggest personality "engrossed" in awareness of reality and commission from it. It may even be – as some Sufi exegesis holds – that the "mantle", thrown over the upper body, helped towards *fana'*, the escape from empirical selfhood into "the only real". Is there not a usage that speaks of being "wrapt" in thought?

The context in 73.6 tells Muhammad that "impressions by night are more intense and emphatic". Day brings busy-ness. Here we are certainly given a sight of Muhammad at the incidence of the early Qur'an, though from the reference to opponents who must be answered with "patient courtesy" it must seem that preaching had been in hand for some time.[8]

The call "O Thou . . ." in 74.1 is followed by five precepts which confirm the central experience as that of "enwording a vision", or giving utterance to meaning made known.[9] They are:

> Your Lord magnify, your garments purify, and shun defilement. Give not with a view to self-increase and turn patiently to your Lord.

If we take these precepts not only as directives for Muslim practice communally but – the imperatives being singular – as conditioning Qur'an reception itself, then we are close to the spirituality possessing it. They indicate a total personal surrender to a calling that demands purity of heart and will, and unselfish intention and a sustained devotion.

These are all descriptive of what tradition knows as *tahannuth*, or "meditation", in which Muhammad had withdrawn to a cave on Mount Hira' outside Mecca in the months or years that preceded his Qur'an-experience.[10] It may well be to these antecedents that Surahs 73 and 74 refer, though it is significant that no explicit narrative about them finds its way into the text. They are veiled in the "mantle" allusion. It is the command to "Recite" which is all important, lest personal detail about its incidence should detract from the overwhelming reality that is "the word" alone. It is not that Muhammad's personality is over-ridden, still less excluded – else how could inspiration ensue? It is that the initiative – albeit necessarily engaging agency – must be entirely with Allah. Biblical prophethood is no less totally mandated from Yahweh but are we not right to find the human instrumentality more deliberately, even assertively, involved?

Yet though excluded from the Quranic text – in the terms by which the Qur'an understands itself – deliberation on the Prophet's part was by no means excluded from the personal situation into which the text was given. His recourse to the cave and reflection seems to have been inspired by the influence of "Abrahamic monotheists", or *hunafa'* (sing. *hanif*) to whom the Qur'an refers.[11] "Neither Jews nor Christians", but somehow linking their Arabism with a conscious repudiation of its pagan expressions in Mecca, they went behind Sinai, and all that Moses and things Mosaic symbolized for Jewry, and invoked Abraham as their progenitor, relating them via Ishmael to Allah and so defining an identity the Jewish "covenant" could not disadvantage.

That inspiration may have been seconded in Muhammad's antecedent experience by revulsion of conscience against the patterns of Meccan society, its tribal conflicts, its economic inequalities of wealth and poverty, its infanticide and soul-wasting feuds. Nor did the *Hanif* factor preclude the impact of Judeo-Christian elements from which it distinguished itself. For these were variously available to Muhammad in his merchant-travels whether north to Jerusalem or south to Najran, and among the scattered tribes around the Hijaz and beyond.

A phrase in Surah 42.51 alludes to only three forms in which Allah addresses humankind. Two obvious instances are the incidence of *wahy* by which prophets speak His word and the recital they make audible to hearers. Between is the second – "From behind a veil" – a theme which has entered far into mystical debate thanks also to its Biblical association with Moses and various epiphanies. The "veil" symbolizes both distance and discernment, a sort of less than immediate awareness. The otherness of the Revealer is safeguarded inside the reality of a revealing.

Could it be that the phrase, at least for our perception, captures what belonged with Muhammad in his Mount Hira' withdrawal into *tahannuth*, as a "preparation" standing proximate to the incidence of *wahy* and so to the activity of preaching the word? The Qur'an, however, leaves to Tradition and later piety the telling of it. The text suffices to be "recital in the Name", with nothing biographical where only the command is relevant. No birth story is needed to undergird authority or justify credence by listeners. Biography will have incidental place later only in respect of how it impinges on the sequences of the Book's "descent", and so illuminates the bearings which its meanings carry. Muhammad's need of patience belongs with the intervals of its coming to him, with their temptations to haste, anxiety or despair – "the burden that was breaking down your back" (Surah 94.2). We are allowed to know that the Prophet was an orphan but his father and mother are unnamed in the text.[12] His intensely personal role is strangely depersonalized so that his significance is entirely taken up into the weight of the word.

## III

A reader who moves from the Qur'an to the Book of Hosea – superb in his quality among the Biblical prophets – will find a fertile contrast casting light in both directions. In Hosea personality is clue as well as instrument. Something in biography is the very fabric of the book; not – to be sure – as merely when deliverances happen, but supremely why they did.

This, in measures differing from those unique to Hosea, is the case with all the Biblical messengers. Often we are given an ancestry. Hosea is the son of Beeri, Joel of Pethuel, and Zephaniah of four named forebears. Such was Hebrew custom concerned for the "chosen-ness" of "seed". Such is barest accreditation, like the tribal origins of Micah, a Morasthite and Nahum, an Elkoshite. It matters who the sent-ones are. But, beyond such lineage and the frequent datings that go with it, is the inherent substance of *dramatis personae*, of private people enshrining public roles in the full recruitment of their individual identity. In their making as prophets is what prophethood is making of them. Experience enters into the shape of utterance. Words are only delivered to them as experience speaks through them. They are ushered into meanings prior to being charged with language. There is room and occasion for their individual idiosyncrasies in the sequence.

Here the "occasionalism" – to use a Quranic term[13] – has a different feel from that of the Muslim Scripture. The events that are clues to commentary are birth-pangs to the messenger. The sundry Biblical situations in major prophethoods will concern us in CHAPTER V. The point now is that, more than being where the text arrives in a sequence, it is where the text comes about as a burden. The distinction belongs squarely with the ethos of the two Scriptures.

Either way, whether as text set on to lips or as burden fleshed into life, the person as instrument is the vital agent. There is proof of this in the theme – common to both Bible and Qur'an – of prophets being "native" in their mission. "A prophet from among their brethren", Deuteronomy 18: 17 has it, in pledge to Moses: and in those terms "likeness to Moses" was the criterion of authentic prophethood. It was "Let *my* people go" that had been his challenge to Pharaoh. Muhammad's being *ummi* (of his own as yet unscriptured people) was throughout crucial to his status.[14] Was it, perhaps, that alien "prophets" were nothing better than mere soothsayers?

Being "native sons", these mouthpieces, whether for Yahweh or Allah, were thoroughly conversant with their communities. They were "native" in a more ultimate sense than that of tribe or race alone. There are even parallels in literatures at large of the "homespun-ness" of a people's writers. There is unmistakable fusion, for example, of Russian soil and soul in the writing of Gogol and Dostoevsky as of New England in the poetry of Robert Frost. The eloquence of the prophets is no less steeped in the vat of their society like the dyer's hand.

With one like Hosea, however, this native-ness assumes a deeply ethical fervour. A prophet to the Northern Kingdom, his Hebrew identity "enpeoples" him (if we may invent the word) in terms of "covenant" and divine "election". That sense of things makes acutely pressing the problem of miscarriage, of an "elect" people disowning in moral terms the very destiny they cherish in congratulatory terms. "Native" in every fibre of his emotions to this situation, he is impelled to summon his people to face this contradiction between who they are *qua* covenant and how they are *qua* society and politics. Hosea summons his nation to what, in him, are the deeply personal criteria of what that nationhood should be. It is in this sublime sense that he is "native . . ." and out of "nativeness" becomes the prophet. His prophethood, we have to say, is the intensity of personal moral religion made to press upon the national society seen in its very peoplehood as covenanted to righteousness. Thus Hosea represents the tension between personal integrity and corporate destiny which is the heart of prophethood. Writing on Jeremiah but taking in Hosea, John Skinner makes the point precisely:

It is his own personal knowledge of God which he reads into the relation between Israel and Yahweh, and is the standard by which he judges the actual religion of his people.[15]

No one could be "native" in more authentic terms.

It is through this personal dimension in prophethood as made such only out of being participant in peoplehood that the later concept of "the remnant" arose. For, as we must see in CHAPTER VII, the vocation led into sharp loneliness and deep isolation. Prophets came to feel that, in their register of divine claim, they were more and more solitaries inside an apostate people. The point emerges compellingly later in Jeremiah. It then came to seem that the entire future lay with a faithful minority, a prophet's immediate hearers, fated to undertake, on behalf of a nation of "recusants",[16] the destiny they had foresworn. Being "native" in those terms was the most pregnant meaning of all and underlay the Messianic hope itself.

With Hosea, to resume the theme of "casting into a role", this "native" shape of prophetic personhood sprang from private domestic travail. His analogies, to be discussed in CHAPTER IV, are drawn from an experience of marital betrayal – if we take the "Go, marry an adulteress" in 3: 1 as typical Hebrew prolepsis whereby, in marrying genuinely, he proved – in the upshot – to have been unwittingly heading into a betrayal. For all vows and troths, precisely in binding a future, enclose and entail what that future, for good or ill, will prove to be.[17] Unless Gomer had been initially a true bride, it is hard to see how Hosea was ever betrayed – this, apart from the incongruity of reading 3: 1 as any literal order.

Thus Hosea's deep register of a people's disloyalty to Yahweh took cognizance from, and found eloquence in, what had supervened in his own heart and home. He drew both the thrust of his mission and the force of his conviction from the fusion of two tragedies. It was the situation that engendered the imagery by which he told his mission. There could be no more tender example of *dramatis personae propheticae*.

There is no call narrative as such, no tracing Hosea back to his mother's womb. "The beginning of the word of the Lord" to Beeri's son lay latent in his own nuptials (1: 2). Could there be a richer inaugural of personal prophethood than at "a time to marry", when Qoheleth might have added: "A time to understand" (Ecclesiastes 3: 1f.)

## IV

Of Biblical call narratives that of Isaiah in 6: 1f. is the most celebrated. It captures vividly the personal register of the social community we have noted in Hosea. It also locates prophetic vocation in the bosom of cultic worship. For the two are historically merged, seeing that it is as "a priestly people" that the "royalty" of Judah is so compromised. Cultic hymns and ritual norms are embedded in all prophetic traditions.[18]

The young Isaiah is bereft of his youthful enthusiasms by the untimely death of his icon-mentor King Uzziah. It is within the year of his dying that the Temple vision breaks upon Isaiah and turns him into Yahweh's messenger. He "sees the Lord" enthroned in splendour with the seraphim waiting on the throne with their six-winged obeisance and their salute in the thrice "Holy" cry destined to reverberate as the Trisagion through the long centuries from Isaiah's Jerusalem to the ends of the earth. The young prophet is overawed by the quivering of the doors, the ringing shouts of praise and the spreading clouds of incense. The vision brings together all the elements of sovereignty, wonder, mystery and power.

Yet at their very core is the emotion of shame and unworth in the human order. For the first time in Isaiah's awareness, if not in the bosom of Israel, we encounter the supreme reality, namely that "the holy" is "righteous" and the ethical is holy. For unremittingly to proclaim the truth of this unison will become the very *raison d'être* of prophethood. How could the two be other than inseparable? instinct might enquire. All too readily, history tells how they are sundered when the holy preens itself in the pride of ritual, the privilege of covenant, to neglect the demands of honesty and compassion in the social order. Then the insouciance of priests calls out the candour of prophets and oblations, empty of integrity, must stand arraigned.

The very meaning of Isaiah's vision is that he knows with a conviction that prostrates him the guilt, the sinfulness, he shares with his people. He and they are alike unclean in lip and life. This is what it means that he, with his very eyes, "has seen the King, the Lord of hosts." The relentless indictment of the nation with which Chapter 1 begins holds the meaning of this Chapter 6. Maybe the reversal of the order is significant, giving textual precedence to the reproach before the experience which gave it birth.

As the drama in the Temple unfolds it holds the holy and the ethical in their mutual reality the other way round. Just as the thrice "Holy" cry convicted Isaiah-with-his-people of their moral shame, so now it is from the "coals of the altar's fire" that his lips are cleansed. A seraphim moves from the role of worship to the task of human hallowing, whereby "iniquity is taken away and sin purged". When duly transacted the things of holiness bear effectively on the business of living in the human scene.

But, for Isaiah, it is lips that are touched with the fire from the shrine. With prophethood the lips symbolize the whole meaning of existence as "voice for the Lord". The experience is no indulgence in sentiment. At once the summons comes: "who will go for Us?" The Lord, throned in seraphic tended majesty, is in need of the human emissary. Utterly abasing as the vision was, the recruit must come by his own volition. There is no press-gang in the work of prophecy. The very sovereignty that overwhelms the spirit of a man is nevertheless appealing to his freedom. Isaiah's response is immediate and entire. "Lord, here am I, send me." The paradox is complete of a soul that "can do no other" and yet is only commissioned as a volunteer.

The message he is to take is forthwith known to be a heavy burden. Isaiah is allowed no illusion of a ready audience or a contrite people ready to hear and answer. On the contrary, the mission from which there is no escape will be one from which there is no respite. The prophet will be "without honour among his own people". Has he not already recognized how adrift they are from godliness and truth? Indeed, the first consequence of his message will be to harden their obduracy. By the same Hebraic prolepsis we saw in Hosea's call, the preaching of Isaiah will first evoke a popular self-vindication that will render hearers deaf and their hearts closed. Truth has to know that, in the context of guilt and wrong, its case is not promptly proven by words nor its ends reached by persuasion. Truth has to be ready to be maligned and rejected, even crucified, as the cost and condition of its own honesty. It is not made thereby less true, but only more self-expending in its steady perseverance.

Faced with this daunting prospect, who would not ask with Isaiah: "How long, O Lord, how long?" The divine answer is not consoling. Wrong is not undone without the price of its own perverse wilfulness in striving to escape the truth of itself and the outworking of its own retribution in the wasting of the land and the desolation of its soul. "A holy seed" has to be patiently awaited.

Isaiah's Temple vision and Muhammad's in the mouth of the cave on Hira' are two worlds it would be precarious to relate together. The culture settings are too distant from each other. Yet something of the same elements belong. Other than an idolatrous Mecca, there is no ritual establishment within which a prophet's summons might arise. But there is a revulsion from social perversity and a sense of inevitable encounter with bastions of popular unworthiness which promise a long, hard road for an accusing word. Both in their different errands will find the same destiny awaiting their words, the same fate of preaching to entertain disdain and discover the limits of its own persuasiveness. In the wake of that experience there comes the incidence of suffering. Wary, as we must be, of the risk in linking otherwise disparate missions, it would be folly to mistake what is akin.

# V

When we pass Biblically from Isaiah to Jeremiah the place of personality in prophethood deepens even further. The Isaiahs of the Bible have no lineage (save father Amoz in 1: 1): he of chapter 40 is anonymous and the more eloquent in being so. They lack all birth-narratives.[19] So, indeed, story-wise, does Jeremiah, but his inaugural vision gives him to know that he was ordained from his mother's womb.

> The word of the Lord came to me saying: "Before . . . you came forth from the womb I sanctified you and ordained you as a prophet to the nations."
> (1: 5)

He was not to think of himself as ever having some existence or meaning other than prophethood, no pursuits or directions from which he might be temporarily diverted or to which a preaching role might be added. His life, *ab initio*, was unilaterally this task of messenger.

His response in 1: 6 does not dispute the point but pleads the very child-imagery to excuse him from the task. His tensions respond in their own coin. In the climax of subsequent distress he has occasion, like Job, to return to that all controlling womb:

> A curse on the day I was born, the day my mother bore me that it be for ever unblessed . . . since death did not take me before birth and my mother did not become my very grave – her womb great with me for ever. (20: 14, 17, 18)

That bitter cry was at the height of his long travail with the unavailing word among an unrelenting people. His inner turmoil even went behind due procreation in his parents' weddedness and likened the summons that made him a prophet to the "seduction" – even the "raping" – of an innocent girl.[20] Yahweh had "taken advantage of his simplicity", inveigling him into a biography he could neither escape nor endure. Never were prophetic words a more intolerable burden than in this man from Anathoth. In him supremely in time of the old covenant, prophethood told itself in a life. His perception of having been called from birth is that he has undergone a life-long take-over of his existence, the burden of which makes him cry: "Woe is me, my mother, that you have borne me, a man of strife and dissension for the whole land" (15: 10).

There is a measure here of what, in the Qur'an situation, is *takdhib* – whereby a prophet's truth is held to be "lies and deceit", fit to be maligned and vilified so that the truth-bearer – in the words of Surah 18.6 – is "killing his own soul with grief because of them". We take up the ultimate implications of this proxy-suffering on behalf of God's commission in CHAPTER VII. Here the threat to Jeremiah's life in rejection of his words (the very same issue which prompted Muhammad to the emigration) creates a situation in which personality undergoes prophetic status. The burden shifts dramatically from word to audience into dialogue with Yahweh. The mouthpiece becomes a puzzle to himself as individually enshrining in his own psyche the fate of the unwanted word. It is no longer simply a word he has to speak: it becomes, in some sort, an initiation into Yahweh's own "rejectedness" at the hands of a people who are both Jeremiah's and Yahweh's.

Thus a strange dialogue ensues between them in which the prophet seeks light on his inner tragedy from its source in God's sending of him. It is almost as if Jeremiah, as a single self, replaces the entire people as the crux of the divine/human association. For it is the people who have rejected the word he brings. We may discern in this development the seed-plot of "the new covenant" concept to which Jeremiah himself was led (31: 31f.) – no longer formally with "chosen masses" but with the private heart, with personal integrity. His actual experience at the hands of his people gives a heightened meaning to the old prophetic sense of having "stood in the court of the Lord to know his mind". Jeremiah is now party to Yahweh in a more profound order of things made so by the very trauma of his tragic reception as the messenger.

His life has come to know and to symbolize what is awry in the wrong of his people. He knows and reads them in his own wounded soul and it is increasingly out of that measure that he accuses them. He registers in his own prophet-soul the ultimate dimensions of what they are doing to Yahweh. In being sent as a spokesman he emerges as a sacrifice for whom the "lamb" imagery (11: 19) is right in no ritual sense but in the soul-reality of his personal life. Hence those intense "Confessions" in which he pleads with Yahweh for the clue by which to know his own meaning and sustain his inner crisis.[21] In disdaining him, his people have registered their abandonment of Yahweh, so that the messenger has come to incarnate in personal burden the perversity of a world in the wrong. The implications of this radical measure of prophet-personhood will reach far into the story of the New Testament.

## VI

There is only one Jeremiah in the canon of the prophets. The idiom captured in his Confessions is unique. However, among his near contemporaries, notably Zephaniah and Habakkuk, there were men whose personality was drawn into individual patterns of divine/human dialogue. Immortalized in the concept *Dies Irae*, "the day of the Lord", Zephaniah's whole text was based on a serial interchange of seven speeches between Yahweh and his messenger, almost like the parts in a Greek drama, though the pronouns shift from the first to the third persons. "The Day" which had been a theme of powerful irony in Amos[22] and figures as "final judgement" in the Qur'an, is announced by Yahweh as total retribution on all false worships. Zephaniah cautions against protest or disregard. Yahweh renews in vehement terms his reproach of Israel, vowing to "search Jerusalem with candles" as he warns the sceptics. Responsively the prophet stresses the imminence and desolation of "the day". After further emphasis from Yahweh, Zephaniah visualizes a "remnant" of penitent folk who might salvage legitimate hope and the Lord turns to focus his anger on Moabites and Ethiopians, Assyria and Nineveh, with the prophet confirming and drawing Yahweh, chorus-like, to pledges of a redeeming "remnant". The whole sequence, finely structured, ends with the Lord pledging, in the first person, the rescue of cripples and the reversal of shame and captivity. The literary form draws the persona of the prophet into a partnership in which the message contrives to become a colloquy.

Things dialogical in Habakkuk occupy 1: 1–2.4, prior to a series of pronounced "Woes" (2: 5–20). These give way to a personal psalmody celebrating a kind of intimate theophany. In the "Woes" he is a traditional "announcer" of what Yahweh bids him utter. In discourse and psalm he enters as a soul into the Lord's converse. The "burden" he "sees" becomes (1: 1) the perplexity he offers so that what he has in answer is what he gives as message. Or the message consists in the substance of his own seeking. He is Job-like in his urgency concerning unrequited evil, open defiance of right, and the cruel tyranny of the heathen. His vivid imagery celebrates the utter purity of Yahweh's righteousness. For it is precisely this which poses the mystery of historical events and the violence of great powers.

The response is reassuring only to faith – the "faith by which the just will be vindicated". "Though it tarry wait for it." Habakkuk's witness is the education of his own perplexity. Out of the interrogatives that occupy his inner self, his public vocation is born. It is, then, highly fitting that his book ends in musical lyricism. For he has not been sent on an errand: he has been initiated into a conviction – one destined, via Paul of Tarsus, to open the key to the Christian experience of faith.[23] In 3: 1–16 we have strains of historical retrospect and poetic irony set to characterize, if not indeed to echo, so many of the (so-called) "Psalms of David". This interfusion of psalm and prophethood yields us the full measure of how ministry enters into personal life and personal measures into public teaching.[24] Whether Habakkuk's psalmody with its dedication to "the chief of musicians" belongs in some way with Temple offices is widely debated. But without the Temple, its compromises and its rituals, the personal antecedents of many vocations to prophethood would have lacked the stirrings of soul that gave them origin.

Of all prophets with priestly impulses Ezekiel must be the most intriguing. The mystery of the divine *Shechinah*, the "Presence" hovering over the sanctuary then forsaking it and heading into exile with its banished heirs, is his most telling concept. His deliverances are full of curious devices, stratagems of interpretation and arresting visual parables. One is sometimes dubious of his very sanity, so extra-ordinary, or incredible are his skills with *mise-en-scène*. Individualism with him is at its most emphatic and bizarre. Whether with the exiles by the river Chebar, or returning (whether physically or in vision) to the holy city, or organizing the meticulous details of a restored Temple, he – or the authors concealed in his canon – is both the mentor and the medium of his spoken mission.

Even his haircut and his behaviour with its cropping are contrived to signify (5: 1f.). He builds a model of Jerusalem to foreshadow siege (4: 1–7) and makes ostentatious lamentation (21: 6f). He accepts a command to "eat" the cautioning roll, making "taste" a sign of content (3: 1f). What is being "said" gains in force and impact by what is being "done". Throughout the personal ingenuity – if as such we may see it – is firmly inside the remit of Yahweh but this "son of man" (as Ezekiel is termed) is very much "the priest, the son of Buzi". More than "visual aid" his antics, reverently so termed, are a way to transact, as do pledge or curse, the things they intimate. Through them runs a sense of divine compulsion, while it incorporates all that makes the prophet-figure the man he is.

## Prophetic Personality

The actual situation of Ezekiel will concern the next chapter. One final point here around his personal part has to do with what is arguably a resemblance to Muhammad. His "eating of the roll", with no detail about what was read there, indicates that what he tells is verbally dictated to him in the very form in which he must give it voice. After call, he is struck with dumbness (3: 17) and can only await the next disclosure patiently. This dumbness may imply that he is a mouthpiece only when he is made verbal by the given text. One recent scholar writes in terms that unconsciously echo the language Jalal al-Din Rumi used about Muhammad:

> The prophet (Ezekiel) is simply the conduit through which the unaltered divine word comes and it is impossible to accuse him of speaking falsely.[25]

That gives Ezekiel, in that roll-context, a kind of Quranic quality. Yet, nevertheless, and in both cases, there is no mistaking *who* is being recruited in what is presented as a divine take-over. It is noteworthy, in Ezekiel's case, how authorial power of metaphor and irony enters into his descriptives of Tyre (chapters 26 to 28).

When Thomas Carlyle, celebrating heroism in history, looked for its incidence in prophethood, he turned to the personality of Muhammad. The terms of his tribute were less than satisfactory to Muslim minds. But he had identified a tenacity, a staying-power, a quality of endurance worthy to be variously attributed to all the Biblical figures here under review. As subsequent chapters must explore, all had to brave themselves for calumny, steel themselves for loneliness and match the crises in events with their quality of soul. They found themselves, in turn, moulded and discipled to the things they said by the pains and passions in the telling. There was always this interplay between selfhood and the task, between the going and the being sent. All that this meant, both for biography and insight, belongs with chapters to follow around situation, suffering, conscience and finality.

It remains here to note how posthumous theories around their personhood, guesses as to the sources of their wisdom, the secrets of their stature, developed from their legend. Several Biblical figures were made to lend their names to pseudo texts and apocryphal writings sheltering under their prestige. Some were granted "ascension" into heaven or were hypostasized in realms celestial. Surprisingly this process was most marked in the case of Muhammad, perhaps because his human role in the Qur'an was so far made superfluous by classic conceptions of "inspiration". The *dramatis personae* in prophethood would be incomplete without study of what happened to their silent legacy, to which such large audience was lent.

## VII

The aura around prophetic personalities and the fascination their peoples felt concerning the mystery of their "inspiration" inevitably led to mystic scenarios about the whence, the how and why of their origins and their repute. Contemporaries denied and vilified them in finding their message offensive or menacing but, for later generations, the tenacity which outfaced and survived such hostility only added to the legend it bequeathed. If it could be said of one so remote and unsung as Abel that "he being dead yet speaks" (Hebrews 11: 4), how could towering figures like Isaiah, Jeremiah or Muhammad fail of large posthumous repute and veneration?

The beginning of what we may call "prophetology" can be attributed to the emergence, whether from Persia or Egypt, of the idea of a personified "Wisdom" and its association with the major prophets. It is explicit in The Wisdom of Solomon where "Wisdom in all ages enters into holy souls, making them friends of God and prophets" (7: 27). This awesome feminine figure "companions" God in the very business of creation and is eternally partner in celestial counsel – those courts where prophets are found as auditors. Her presence mediates between the divine mind and the human spirit, igniting what is "the candle of the Lord" (Proverbs 20: 27). The imagery of wind and fire, so apt to "the way of Wisdom", readily fitted the phenomenon of the likes of Amos or Joel or Haggai with their impulse to speak, their power of language, their urgency of warning or comfort.

The Hebrew word *hokmah* is akin to the *al-Hikmah* which the Qur'an uses of itself, as a title; while *Al-Hakim* from the same root is a frequent Name of Allah, usually coupled with *Al-'Aziz*, "the strong".[26] In the developing "Wisdom" tradition of the fourth and third centuries BC Greek influence helped to enlarge the scope of ideas to bring together the principle of ordered reason discernible in the material universe and the moral insightfulness belonging with the mission of the prophets.

In this way it became necessary to link the fundamental perception of "person and word" in prophethood as being wholly revelatory, with something, at the same time, rational and cognitive. Whereas the basic religious comprehension of what made prophets had excluded any such rational element, it became necessary, under the impact of "Wisdom" concepts, to think supreme intelligence as their endowment. The paradox was one to contain rather than to resolve. The Wisdom literature, embracing, for example, the Book of Proverbs, Sirach and the Wisdom of

Solomon gathered aphorisms drawn from contemplation of the human scene with a sanity that invoked experience and reasoned observation. It seemed, for all its godly tone, a far cry from "Thus says the Lord" in the old prophetic passion. To listen to Amos was not to be invited into reflective philosophy on the human condition. Isaiah was no purveyor of disingenuous advice to novices in the management of living, nor of saws to bring nodding assent from old men.

It was not that Wisdom writing repudiated divine sources: it reverently invoked them. It did not, however, see them as mediated to a burning passion that preached "the fearful day of the Lord". The fear of the Lord" to be sure was "the initiation into – or beginning – of wisdom", but in the sense that "the fool" would be warned of the snares in sexual indulgence or the folly of excess, by having God soberly in awe. "The weight in the word" of the wise was its gathered store of guidance from life's spectacle, the lessons elders had for gullible youth. It was as if the dire religious burdens of exile, the trauma of the flux of marauding empires had brooded too long on anguish and turned, under Persian or Greek influences, to a smoother melancholy or found refuge in counsels of the inner mind, away from the thunders of prophethood.

The puzzle of the abeyance we have noted in those thunders will concern a final chapter later. It has to do with a variety of factors within the Jewish culture of Maccabean, Greek and Roman times. The Yahweh of the passionate prophets was unfailingly the God of creation and of Sinai. The Wisdom literature was more than faithful to these two dimensions of faith, with "Wisdom" in some way co-presiding with the Lord in the shaping of the worlds and belonging inherently in the moral ordering through Moses and everything from Sinai and Temple. These it had securely in its own splendid custody, but in terms different from the urgent fervour of the prophets. They, as we saw, were long and sharply at issue with "covenant" and "holy peoplehood".

The contrasts being so marked between prophethood and sages like Sirach and pseudo-Solomon, speculation towards "rationalizing" the genius of the prophets could be indulged calmly enough without undue anxiety in Jewish circles. The great prophetic writings survived the succeeding centuries to be had as we know them, while "Wisdom writing" made its own way. The suffering which, in CHAPTER VII, we find so central to the story of prophethood held its relevance in the shape of Messianic hope, to become the vital clue to the New Testament. Suffering in Wisdom writing had to do with day-to-day pessimism and mortal transience, as in Ecclesiastes, or the injustice of events, as in Job, or the deceptiveness of fame and riches, as in Proverbs. These were not the primary burden of

Amos or Hosea or Ezekiel, who were occupied with social guilt and betrayed covenant, with calamitous history. They knew tragedies that made them preach, not broodings that had them philosophize.

This evident duality in the Biblical literature from Amos to the close of the Apocrypha moderated the Jewish impulse to rationalize "revelation" and reconcile prophetic Yahwism with a philosophy that might explain its genius.

The situation was otherwise for Islam, in whose ensuing centuries there developed a remarkable prophetology seeking to understand Muhammad's role in the reception of the Qur'an in terms of a philosophy of genius. Perhaps one reason for this lay in the solitariness of his *persona* in the economy of the Qur'an. As the climax and "seal" of a long continuity, he was the sole recipient of the text in which the sequence was finalized. His predecessors had only narrative place in its pages. "The weight in the word" belonged only from his personal receiving of its *tanzil*, or "sending down".

This meant an exclusive significance in his whole *persona*, his origins, his birth, his antecedents prior to *tanzil*, his conduct and biography inside it. His unique status gave rise not only to *Hadith*, or Tradition, as a source of law and ethics, but also to fertile theories of mental "illumination" and of intellectual genius. These theories were not deterred by their obvious contradiction to the classic thesis of an "unlettered" prophet who had spoken the Qur'an only by audible receiving, in its actual undeviating Arabic, without the intervention of his personal will or being, except as entailed in such entire passivity.

Apart from the appeal of curiosity and of esoteric lore, there are two factors within the Qur'an that can be linked with the development of doctrines about Muhammad's *persona*. The one is the *Tasliyah* theme from Surah 33.56; the other the mystique, so cherished by Shi'ah Muslims, around *Ahl al-Bait*, "The people of the house" in Surah 33.33 and the hereditary principle. That "God and His angels call down blessing on the Prophet" is well explained by orthodox thought as simply the "satisfaction" of Allah in Muhammad's discharge of his task – a "satisfaction" which, in due exultation, Muslims must also celebrate in the given formula. But as the Qur'an's direct injunction to them, concerning Muhammad and no other, it was well capable of implying, or being held to imply, some theosophic significance by which he is exalted. This perception finds ground also in the Night Journey (17.1) to Jerusalem and that *sharh al-sadr* (94.1) which coincided with his exaltation heavenward.[27] This "purifying of the heart" signalled a revelatory experience which was more than a receiving of words. It readily lent itself – for those so minded – to a theorizing about Muhammad's mediating status between Allah and humankind. It exceptionalized his *persona* beyond that of a bare mouthpiecing of a message to that of a divinely endowed vessel of truth. It was a clue which imaginative piety was all too ready to explore and enlarge, despite the Qur'an's own firm insistence on Muhammad's "mere" humanity.

The theme of a mystique of hereditary status in his tribal lineage and the "immaculate" associations of *Ahl al-Bait* inspired a mythology (in the strict sense) around his family and call.[28] This became the more assertive by its involvement in the politics of caliphal succession after 632 but, long after the Shi'ah schism had become permanent, the "immaculate House" belief generated commemorative traditions of piety and fervour concerning the "mystery" of Muhammad – acts of devotion in which popular Islam among Sunnis also shared, despite the reproaches of purists who disowned such "superstition".

Narratives of Muhammad's lineage, portents of his birth, legends of his weaning, foretellings of his destiny found their sure way into Muslim folk religion – though not into the fabric of the Qur'an itself.[29] More significant, however, for our study of "prophet-as-person" was what philosophers in the middle centuries did with this aura of "truth-possession" as intellectual "genius" or "illuminationist wisdom". Platonic language could be recruited concerning "the philosopher-king". Muhammad might be almost "divinized" as Allah's "deputy".[30]

These aberrations – as Wahhabi-style orthodoxy must count them – are instinctive, intellectual tribute to the entire "event" of Muhammad and to the abiding mystery of the Arabic Qur'an. That Muslims have struggled both to formulate and to denounce these exaltations of the human Muhammad is a paradox which takes us to the ultimate dimension of prophethood, namely that "the weight in the word" must somehow include a theology of the Word. This must await CHAPTER VIII. Meanwhile we must take stock of language, situation, conscience and suffering.

# IV

# Prophethood and Language

## I

That meaning finds itself in words only by finding words for itself is an aphorism with which few will quarrel. But how are the twin findings to be traced and how understood? Everywhere in language there is this puzzle concerning the mutual play between content and form. The issue is most crucial of all in what purports to be the language of word-mediation, *wahy* – as Islam terms it – by which there is a text for "one crying" and the "one crying" is caring with a text. What is the event which transpires between the "casting" and the "saying" as CHAPTER II drew the terms from Surah 73.5?

The event is clearly both in the psyche and in the speech. It belongs with soul and mind and voice. An impulse in the person proves the making of a prophet. From where beyond him does it contrive to happen through him? No authentic prophet is self-made but none is self-absent. There is a necessary fusion of what is inherently human and what is humanly inhering, so that words said carry meanings given. Language in prophethood becomes somehow the place of a rendezvous, the coming together of the two-in-one called "revelation" and "inspiration", as the making of Scriptures. The point of their incidence is "the voice of one crying" whose language is the text. It is this phenomenon in its Biblical and Quranic incidence we have now to explore.

That those two realms are widely disparate has been conceded in CHAPTER I. There are obvious aspects that disqualify setting them side by side incautiously. The ethos of the Qur'an cannot readily align with the temper of Micah or Habakkuk and their peers. Yet we are assuming that the common themes of personality, conscience and claim to finality – though not situation – are possible of fruitful comparison. Of these, language proves the most exacting. Biblical and Quranic Scriptures proceed on deeply contrasted premises concerning how divine and human engagement in their language, its role and formation, must be understood. Were we to think to apply to Amos, Isaiah, Jeremiah, Paul or the four Evangelists, the implications defining *wahy* in the Qur'an, we would find the notion quite impossible. The contents respectively contain what they hold to be given, in very different concepts of how language houses them and of how those contents have negotiated their arrival through the human mouthpiece.

# II

Before embarking on a careful study of these contrasts sharply obtaining in what is still a common territory of language as Scripture, it will be useful to enquire about the genius in literature at large and in the poets most of all. "From where did it come and in this shape?" is the almost universal query attending on all creative writing. Poets are often a mystery to themselves. There is endless surmise around the apparent paradox of effortlessness and effort, of genius and labour. Writing flows while composition frustrates. It is stupid to ask "How many miles in an hour?" seeing that space and time are different realms. Yet truly the question fits because ventures or crises relate them. Comparably one may well ask about genius and its medium, about words wrestling with cares and coming to a perfect match. Great art is a coinciding drawn from personality only in being received from beyond.

The mystery of men being possessed of perceptions, and of the words sublimely suited to them, so that the two blended as one, fascinated the Greeks. Plato's *Dialogues* muse on personal consciousness being somehow over-ridden, or even imperiously eliminated, if authentic inspiration was a-coming in the soul.[1] It was as if a rational normalcy was incompatible with an onset of divine wisdom. If things divine and human could not share the same dwelling, there must be some eviction of the regular tenant of the mind. To poetic pens inspired ideas flow unbidden. By a sort of paradox, response happens in irresponsibility. Mere artistry is overpowered by an afflatus, "a wind listing where it blows" so that there is no "invention" in the recipient.

Mystery, no doubt, persists but this notion of near "frenzy" seems – at least among Scriptured prophets – altogether incompatible with the situation-quality we see to be central to all prophethood. It would return them to the level of those ecstatic seers and soothsayers whom the great prophets we are studying left far behind. The insistent intelligibility – sought and urgently offered – of the ministry of these requires that we give due weight to their total personal engagement in it, however elusive the mystery of their vocation and the gift it brought them.

The Qur'an, for its part, is insistent in its denial of Muhammad's being "a poet", while the "matchless" eloquence of the Book is its valid credential.[2] That is the Islamic form of the Biblical juncture of qualities of language-utterance carrying the imprint of spiritual truth. In either case, the inspiration that evidences itself in form and eloquence does so only because, and on behalf, of the import of truth. To identify only a virtuosity of style would be to disavow the divine word as ever truly revelatory. Yet to look for the latter and find it only a dull and lifeless prose would be to misread it altogether.

It is intriguing in this way to find a similar tension around prophet and poet, between the scriptural and the lyrical, obtaining both for the Hebrew Bible and the Qur'an, in their respective idiom. Poetry and song are prone to be admired for their own sake or be suspect as no more than an exercise in gratification, conveyed or indulged – self-centred in a way quite unworthy of a genuine prophet of the Lord. Ezekiel, in this way, was charged with mere musical skills but only by people unconverted by his message (33: 32–33). Yet the impact of holy words may not renounce what literary force and artful power of expression may bring to their mission.

Thus it was perceived to be, in Muslim doctrine, from the "excellence" of the Qur'an's Arabic discourse and poesy. For many of the early Surahs are eminently poetical in their rhymic music, their lyrical strophes. The Biblical prophets are superb users of words and shapers of language, with vivid metaphors and heavy ironies. To hold "the Bible as literature" can be an unhappy secular reductionism, but it is also a sure dimension of its revelatory claims. Appreciation can deny God's word and yet also be apprentice to heeding it.

Either way, words are themselves an event when they come in the way of prophethood. As in poems they offer an induction, or at least an invitation, into experience. They subject the hearer or the reader to the subject they enshrine, even while hearer and reader think themselves handling an objective text. To possess and to exercise that power is a prerogative of Scripture precisely as being a thing of words. For words, given due range and eloquence, have exactly that vocation. It is a vocation the prophethoods we are studying profoundly exemplify.

It is thanks to this perception that texts may find a reading beyond the knowledge or intention at their first onset – a point we have noted. Thanks to the literary aspect by which the content is offered as an experience, it may pass beyond historical criticism, and its first range, and thus come to possess, and be possessed in, terms wider than it first conveyed. Such is the nature of literature. Since it proceeds verbally, prophethood has the same potential, kindling inwardly with the prophet and kindling outwardly from him in the souls of his audience. We have come upon yet another clue to "the weight in the word". For "the word" is set to bear it,[3] as the heeder is to feel it.

## III

However, classical Sunni Muslim view of the role of words in the mediation of revelation, as the Qur'an embodies it, moves on lines very different from these. To see "the Qur'an as literature", while in one sense warranted, in theological terms would be quite improper. The orthodox concept of how language constitutes truth in the way the Qur'an does is a doctrine of a text divinely constituted as "the speech of God" in its literal sequences. These were serially ministered to Muhammad's lips as the conveyed text of "the Book in heaven", so that this, when faithfully recited by him, is – in human ears and hands – "the Book on earth".

Musings around this comprehension of the Qur'an's divine nature – which concerns us throughout – wrestle with the problems it sets. Its being fully warranted, however, for the faithful is not in doubt. Many aspects of the Islamic Scripture underwrite it. For "slips of the reciting tongue", to which Satanic wiles are directed, would suffice to disqualify the recital. Recital, verse by verse, in *tajwid*, or due "beautifying", is the basic recognition of the Qur'an, its inherent right, just as calligraphy is the crown of art. Both attest this strictly literal quality of what reveals and enshrines the divine will.

This sense of a verbatim Scripture answers to the sense of Allah's care that His revelation stands "error-proof", free by this means, from what, otherwise, would be susceptible of human error. Revelation is so crucial an enterprise from God that it is not left (as we find Biblical meanings left) to the competence of minds using their own range of words, their own idiom and persona in an "inspiration" which leaves them also veritable "authors".[4] Instead, it ensures – as critical to revelatory status and guarantee – the very words that thus infallibly carry these. The human factor in Quranic prophethood, on this classic view, is limited to a recipience that is believed to have no essential role either in the comprehension or the expression of the content in the words. These are, and could only be, faithfully echoed from their given audition in the Prophet's experience. That experience, on this premise, had no other role.

This passive reception of the given text attests the absolute authority, there being no admixture of human risks, no occasion of human spoiling such as could potentially occur in a shape of recipience allowing a measure of human authoring. By its doctrine of itself the Qur'an secures its immunity not only from "slips of the tongue", but also from what a more participatory prophetic human share might put in hazard.

It is in this context of an abeyance of normal, natural human powers in divine Scriptuarizing of a people that the traditional view of the "illiteracy" of Muhammad belongs. Surah 7.155 and 157 describe him as *al-Rasul al-Nabi al-Ummi*, "the Apostle, the Prophet, the unlettered". It is on that third word that the whole discussion turns. Were Muhammad to have been altogether unable to read or write, then the case for the Qur'an's being a miraculous deliverance to him in which he was no more than a conduit would be incontrovertibly confirmed. This would be still more the case, given the marvellous eloquence achieved in it as only present from beyond him. That case is made from within the Book itself in the frequent challenge to its detractors to "bring a Surah like it".[5]

Is there not, however, a case for reading *al-ummi*, not as personally illiterate, but rather as sharing the as yet unscriptured status of the Arab people? The translation "native" captures this but obscures in what sense the "native-ness" signified. For good or ill, "prophets and peoples" went together.[6] The Qur'an notes the importance of the fact that they normally came from among, and were commissioned to, their own kin. That Muhammad had "got his words from a stranger" was one of the dismissive gibes of the Quraish. That he was "from their own midst and their own kin" was a vital fact in his credentials. His being a "native", then, indicates that, prior to the Qur'an's coming, he belonged with a people as yet "unscriptured". His being a successful merchant with the trading caravans would also call in question "illiteracy", while coinciding with the implications of divine *wahy* by reminding us that Muhammad was neither bookish nor an academic student.

Understood as "thus far without Scriptures", *al-ummi* fits exactly several other characteristics of the Qur'an. When the word occurs in the plural there it almost invariably denotes "non-Jews". For the Jews, as "the people of the Book", were manifestly Scriptured as their most obvious item of identity. Furthermore, was it not that very fact which engendered the aspiration that Arabs too might become enscriptured and have a heavenly Book of their own? Since that hope could only transpire by means of an Arab prophet ("books" being always reciprocal to "messengers") – as pondered in CHAPTER III – we may have in *ummi* a clue to the actual antecedents of Muhammad's call. If so, we will be doing the fullest justice to the word.

Thus to conclude is strongly in line with the intriguing emphasis in the Qur'an on the necessity of its being Arabic. Scriptures at large, to be sure, are in the speech of those among whom they originate and for whom they are first intended. Even so they may exist in different languages like the Sanskrit and Pali of the Buddhists' *Dhammapada*. Hebrew is the language of the Biblical Scriptures (less Daniel) but that Bible's being Hebrew is not a doctrine of necessity guaranteeing its being itself so that, for example, it could not readily – in the Septuagint – consent to be Greek. The Christian New Testament as a document took Greek form in which to scriptuarize a Christ-event of word and suffering in a Palestinian, Aramaic milieu arriving to a trilingual Cross.

Islam is thus distinctive in holding Arabic quality as essentially, not merely circumstantially, determining its Scripture as authentic and God-given. "We have sent it down an Arabic Qur'an (Surahs 12.2, 20.113, 41.3, 42.7 and 43.3). Both the fact of its being Arabic, and the excellence of the Arabic it is, are what attests it as the Islamic Scripture. The force of that dogma explains the long assumption that it was, and must, remain "untranslateable" and such – not in the literary sense that any classic is diminished when no longer in the original tongue – but in the categorical sense that to "de-Arabicize" is to "de-Quranize".[7]

This uniquely Muslim doctrine of how sacred language does not simply suit sacred text but exclusifies the one sanctity in the other, makes for a remarkable concept of how language belongs with meaning. It also entails several problems, given that this Scripture in inviolable Arabic form is also – and emphatically – "a mercy to the worlds". All religious "universals" have to submit to "minute particulars". One cannot have eternity in time without giving it a place and date. But, by the same token, the would-be universal must find and enlist particulars from which it can translate itself into all cultures with their languages and do so inherently undiminished and unimpaired. It is surely a strange thesis both to employ a language and disallow its belonging with language at large, in the will to be the restrictive organ of its themes and witness. A tongue may indeed be held "holy", but not so that its grammar, its vocabulary, its syntax engross that "holy" to themselves or do more than give expression to what, on its own showing, exists for currencies other than its own. As a human, and an inter-human, phenomenon, language surely cannot admit to a privatizing of what it does by any singular member in the art common to them all, namely giving shape and voice to meaning. Least of all can such monopoly be conceivable in things religious. Moreover, a faith that places its credentials firmly inside the eloquence of one speech thereby makes them inaccessible to all non-speakers. For then only impaired meaning can reach these.

In practice, despite the ongoing thesis, Islam does not do this. The very thesis about "untranslateability" based on those several Surahs is overridden by the verses themselves inasmuch as the reason for Arabicity is explained by the urge to be intelligible to Arabs. If comprehension is the intention of the Arabic form among Arabs, translation *must* follow outside the Arab-language world. It becomes obligatory. This, of course, is what has happened in the world-wide outreach of Islam.

Happening, it still leaves intact the assurance once, and still, brought to Arabs by what Scriptured them in their own tongue. That limited but legitimate role of "an Arabic" as the Qur'an's milieu and voice remains authentic in its context. Translation in the service of world-wideness does not invalidate it but must surely imply that a single language cannot enjoy exclusive status in the incidence of "the weight in the word". However, in all cases, the original language of Scriptures will characteristically influence the yield of their mandatory translations in the duty of belonging to mankind. For meaning in translation is always susceptible to what the original can bear and what the receiving speech can tell.

## IV

This issue, so central in the Qur'an, about the bearing of language on the how and the what of revelation into Scripture, goes deeper than we have thus far explored. It does so in two directions. The one relates Godward into the "uncreated", the other manward into what, despite all the foregoing, the human realm must afford if ever a sacred literature is to exist in the textual fabric necessary to its purpose.

Muslim thinkers, taking the former first, were long preoccupied with how the language of the historic Qur'an could conform to the "language" of the heavenly original, inscribed eternally on "a preserved tablet" (85.22). In what did the heavenly one consist, given that all extant or lost languages had an earthbound vintage of place and time? Words as doing the work of the world are in the flux of the world. Their very "weight" belongs with a human gravity. Moreover, the sequences of the Scripture partake, as we must see in CHAPTER V, of incidents and accidents of mortal circumstance. Must these, then, be supposed eternally prefixed when, in fact, they precariously transpired?

Such, in crude lay-folk terms, was the issue of the Qur'an's being at once, somehow "uncreated" and yet "created", entire in heaven and cumulative on earth, as eternal as its author-Allah himself yet *in media res* with Muhammad among the Quraish. There is no necessary place here for the minutiae of this long debate, except how it bears on the prophetic role of language.[8] Its presence with respect to the viability of the Qur'an is only the Islamic form of a perennial problem implicit in the very concept of divine revelation. It will be present in whatever terms any faith believes it has eternal truth in mediation to it.

What is at issue for Muslims is whether their urge to be certified, as to such eternally given truth, by a Book of this order, is more apt for divine ends and human means than a Book more historically contingent – as the Bible is – on human partnership. Insofar as facts of belief are facts for the faithful, the looked-for certitude will be had, but the confession of it will still be responsible to justify the shape in which it believes it given.

There is a sense in which choosing how to formulate this ultimate question about revelation is the key to any answer to be had. How the Ayatollah Khomeini does so is as good a handling of the answer and its question as any. He writes that "the Qur'an is not verbal in substance". *Tanzil*, its "causing to come down" upon the Prophet, is a passing through many layers of meaning until "finally it assumed a verbal form".[9] The "heavenly language", then, is only humanly thought of in language terms. Insubstantial, as verbal, it is certainly not Arabic, unless there be, imaginatively, a celestial "Arabic". Its becoming on earth "an Arabic Qur'an" happens within – and only within "the mystery of its mediation". What our curiosity wants to know about it eludes us in the mystery with which, beyond our own conceiving, we have to do.

As, inevitably for all faiths in this context, the answer we get returns the question we put. It suffices that "the faithful messenger" bore it down "upon the Prophet's heart" (26.193) "on the night of power" (97.1). What that meant heart-wise for Muhammad faith cannot penetrate in empirical terms. "Prophets are like men who have seen a dream they cannot describe."[10] Human language, in this case Arabic, yields itself as the chosen vehicle of that mediation and "the mother of the Book" is with Allah (43.4). Without words nothing is given or received, since words are its human shape. When they are received, and what they carry and, by carrying, impart in cognizance – first for the Prophet and then for his auditors – proves humanly accessible to comprehension and obedience. That purpose is believed fulfilled, via language, as the means devised to that end. If this formulation of what *wahy* constitutes seems to be circular that circularity – the Book into language and language for the Book – is in the nature of the event of *Tanzil* as faith confesses it. Bound up in the whole is a destiny of Arabic to be "the chosen language", for which no further warrant is needed. In the ultimate sense "the weight in the word" – as the Qur'an sees it – is just that destiny. Language as a human possession becomes, in Arabic, a divine instrument. It suffices for faith that *Tanzil* is the name of the transaction. Islam stands in and by this distinctive theology of language. It is one no other faith shares in the same absolute terms.[11]

If that is how we must leave the Godward direction, we are left, inside it, with the manward dimension seeing that it is "upon the heart" that *Tanzil* comes. "Upon the tongue" – though the phrase is never used (nor "lips") – would seem more akin to the theme of a total passivity in reception on the Prophet's part. Yet, clearly, on the evidence of the Qur'an on every hand, it is imperative to realize that a receptive dumbness is no part of prophetic experience as Muhammad undergoes it and, in its sequences, the Qur'an documents. There is participation on personal terms in every part. CHAPTER V following has to undertake a study of all things situational in the Qur'an's incidence over some twenty-three years of *waḥy*.

Taking the language theme here prior to "situation" was a question of exposition. Either way round we would need to anticipate what would have to follow. We do so now in relation to the historic "eventings" in the Qur'an's sequence, in order to occupy ourselves, pre-supposing them, with how the language factor on which *Tanzil* proceeds partakes of Muhammad's own "literacy" as necessarily the reception of *waḥy* required him to deploy it. If this seems in tension with orthodox concepts, tension it must remain. For it is implicit in there being a Qur'an at all. It will bring us part way towards the much more forthright quality of the human partnership with revelation in the Biblical order of things.

# V

CHAPTER III has already taken us into personhood as central to prophethood, via study of call-narratives and human idiosyncrasies inseparable from all human agency. The task now is to see how style in the Qur'an fulfils *waḥy* in powerful qualities that are all its own. If, as Muslim doctrine sees it, language *per se* is the elected instrument of divine revelation (rather in the way that Jewry saw itself the ethnic election of God) and, among languages Arabic has this privilege, it happens via what must seem an impressive human artistry. Leaving doctrine to contain, rather than explain, this fact, it is an artistry even the outsider can appreciate.

That there was a culture of poesy of love and war in the pre-Islamic scene is familiar enough. Arabic, such cultural habits apart, lends itself readily to rime, alliteration, consonantal assonance and rhythmic diction. These are already present in its pattern of derivatives from the triliteral verb-root. They abound via regular and broken plurals, in the vowel recurrences and word frequencies in which the language structure excels. The Qur'an is richly heir to these assets and employs them powerfully. There are passages that, if they enthuse the insider, almost defy the translator. Take a notable example in Surah 91.1–6, with its invocation of sun, moon, night, sky and earth in a chorus of celebration.

> By the sun and the midday glory and the month that follows after; by the day telling its splendour and the night that envelops it; by the heaven and its rearing; by the earth and its shaping: by the soul and its shaping . . .

The *wa* ("and") that invokes also conjoins. The clauses have the rime of the pronoun attached in a poetry eliciting nature's witness in a solemnity that stands in awe of it.

The theme is perennial and makes a clear *confessio* in the Qur'an's theology. It has a genuine kinship with the majesty of an Isaiah in the same context of landscape and wonder. Surah 77. 1–11, with its elusive title *Al Mursalat* (lit. "sent-forth-ones"), is even more resistant to being taken out of its Arabic where alone it can be fully sensed.

> By the chartered winds in their familiar courses,
> And tempests in their stormy pride,
> By the dispersing, fructifying rain-clouds,
> By all that deciphers and discerns
> And brings home a reminder as plea and as warning –
> All that you are promised will assuredly happen.

The English clauses and participles do only scant justice to the eloquence of the original. It is little wonder that Islam has always insisted on the Qur'an as a book to hear and recite, never a tome only to peruse or study. Its literary power belongs squarely with its religious intent. The two are wedded in its sheer human quality. If it takes poetry to arrest and summon in these terms it is because the meaning is urgent.[12]

In purely linguistic terms this quality would be described as rhetoric – the art of convincing and convicting by the skill of a way with words. And rhetoric is well aware of unpersuadedness and is set to overcome it. In that sense it takes its cues from the situation it has to convince. Like a good navigator on troubled seas it learns to make assets of its hindrances. The speaking art of the Qur'an is no exception. Hence the strong array of questionings posed to necessitate the answers they require.

A crucial example is Surah 7.172 where Allah demands to know: "Am I not your Lord?" challenging humanity at large to acknowledge in a cosmic oath the sovereignty implicit in human responsibility over creation. The reply can only be a resounding affirmative, given the dramatic impact of the question, phrased as if the reality could ever be in doubt. This universal confession of human liability under God transcends and precedes what Sinai has only in strictly ethnic terms. In final judgement humanity will have no chance to plead: "We were unaware."

Similarly arresting is the question (Surahs 4.82 and 47.24) to the yet unpersuaded pagans: "Do they not reflect on the Qur'an?" with sequence in the first case that its divine origin is attested by its evident freedom from contradiction, and, in the second case, with the further query: ". . . or do their hearts have locks upon them?" Making rusty locks turn is the business of urgent rhetoric.

In similar vein are the numerous invocations of nature as evoking gratitude and alert perception of divine wisdom, mercy and power. No Arabic rhetorician could ignore the force of the word *La'ala*, the "maybe" or "perhaps" that both teases and tests the hearer. It occurs more than a hundred times in the stride of the Qur'an with a retinue of following verbs. "Perhaps you may register gratitude", "perhaps you may come to your senses", "perhaps you will recollect". In its own idiom this usage might be compared with the parable method of Jesus' teaching where appeal is made to what might be comprised in common consent by reason of its sheer day-to-day evidences.

For all its "implacable" character – a descriptive often used by Muslims –[13] the Qur'an's style clearly anticipates its hearers' intelligence and comprehension beyond the bigotry or apathy in which their pagan tradition holds them captive. Islam has its own religious reasons for not ascribing this quality to personal authorship or conscious rhetoricizing. Yet, even so, it effectively characterizes the way the style works – cajoling, arousing, querying and summoning the listener and the reciter with allusions, imagery, irony and word-play, calculated by their force and familiar idiom, to evoke assent to their logic.

The theme of the futility of idol-credence is an obvious example. It may not be pressed so satirically as by Isaiah and the psalmist[14] but it is no less vigorous. "God has created both you and what you manufacture", Surah 37.96 tells the idol-worshippers.[15] The very material of idol-shaping is within the creation of the Creator. The folly of reliance on created things "to the exclusion of Allah" Himself – another refrain in the Qur'an –

underlines the habit of moving through things visible to their source and ground in God. Hence, for example, the repeated refrain of Surah 55.10–32: "which of the blessings of your Lord will you discount and deny?" coming some eight times to crown inclusive references to aspects of "the good earth" – fruits, palms, dates, grain, fragrant herbs, the dawns and the sunsets, humans from clay made, seas salt and pure – bounded by shores, coral and pearl. The argument for reverent gratitude is made between the integrity of social ethics ("weigh with a just balance") and the "everywhere encompassing face of your Lord in majesty and glory all His own".

The poetical power of this passage in the original belongs with the insistent querying refrain but also in the dual pronoun: "your (2) Lord" preceding the verb *kadhdhaba*, often translated "you and you" (*yukadhdhabani*) is also in the dual. Why not a straight plural since the dual is two individuals? Some exegesis thinks of two collectives, namely humans and jinns. But can these be conjoined in the same quality of sentient recognition of created things, these being only (as the Qur'an insists) in the technological competence of humans?[16]

The poetry is clearly serving the rhetorical as the rhetorical is serving the religious. Perhaps then the force of the dual, confined properly to humans, belongs with the range of the verb "deny". Hence the rendering used here: "discount and deny". We begin by trivializing, slighting evidences that should evoke wonder and we end by dis-connecting from God the giver in a total "there is only us" posture. Is there not always this potential momentum in attitudes from negligence to scepticism? At least, so reading a superb passage, we will not be misreading the whole thrust of Quranic rhetoric in this field.

In the following Surah (56.57–74) comes another striking instance of the religious poetry of the Qur'an, again in urgent interrogation, though hardly "implacable" since it concedes that the answers remain open, turning – as they must – on human cognizance, on readiness *not* to "discount and deny".

> It is We who have created you. How is it that you do not recognise that truth? Have you considered what you do in intercourse? Is it you who do the creating, or We? . . . In what fashion you were created is familiar enough to Us. How is it that you do not ruminate on all this?
>
> Have you considered the soil you till? Is it you who bring the crop or are We the real agent of growth? . . . Have you considered the water you drink? Was it you who made it fall from the rain-clouds or are We the rain-maker? Had We so willed, bitter water had We sent. How is it that you have no gratitude?

> Have you considered the fire you kindle? Was it you who made the tree to grow or are We the source of its being? We devised it to be a point of recollection and to provide solace for those who pass through desert ways. Praise, then, each of you the Name of your great Lord.[17]

Again the same rational appeal concerning earth, air, water and fire, the four elemental things and the procreative power in male and female keeping the eternal creation alive. Human intercourse as the crux of the world's perpetuation is a vital theme of the Qur'an.[18]

It might be claimed that the teleology here is naïve – a universe designed for humans, a geo-centric pretentiousness fit to be discounted in an age when any intelligent mind-set knows it has to be atheist. Away with the misty crudities of metaphysics and theology. But the "crudity" would be all the other way – and the un-Quranic arrogance of a secularity that knows not how to kneel. The verb *ra'aytum*, translated "consider", has also the literal sense of "see" as with the naked eye. Whether sperm, or the soil's chemistry, or how oceans are $H_2O$ etc. (and oases also), or combustion spontaneous or contrived, in what they are and behaving as they do – and as humans organize – belong both with the science that "sees" and the awareness that ponders and wonders.

The teleology is not naïve. It is of the Biblical sort that obtains beyond Darwin, beyond Lamarck, beyond Sherrington, beyond Hawking. In conceding perplexity it admits liability. In accepting to be geocentric, it does not ignore immensity: instead it reveres the more the responsibly anthropic situation it encounters as one which no vastness can dissolve but only "marvellize". "Have you considered?" is the question and "consideration" (itself derived from *sidereus* "of the stars") brings into awareness the *'ilm*, or "science", that explores, and the *Ma'rifah*, or "knowledge", that understands.

It is fair, then, to appraise the style of the Qur'an as an eloquence that addresses the rational mind, as a poetry that appreciates the hallowing of human emotions. It is also sharply realist in its measure of human capacity for *zulm, kufr, fasad, takdhib* and *zann* – "wrong, unbelief, corruption, denial of truth, false suspicion" – and in the sense of doom that hangs over its historical retrospect on destroyed communities and over its prospect of "eternal retribution". In these realms the vividness of its imagery and the force of its vocabulary give condign thrust to its eschatology. Whatever the reaction to the theology involved, the linguistic power of its expression is everywhere perceptible even in translation. The original is all the more compelling on the ear. This moral realism about a sin-prone human scene is aptly caught in a turn of rhetoric in Surah 17.95:

> Say: Had there been angels going about in the earth in tranquility, We would have sent an angel from heaven as a messenger.

The irony is gentle and telling. Humans are no angels, set in "a middle state" between earth and heaven, between the cruder creation and the angels. The verse is in line with the kinship between the sent and the intended in the sending. Humans need a human prophethood, native to its own natives. So much we have seen. For we are not, by nature, in that "tranquillity" that is the mark of angels.[19] The ultimate question, which takes the course of thought – in part – beyond the study of style, is how this realism about human waywardness, authentic as it is, rides with exclusive divine reliance on the sending of messengers. For these bring an appeal – in words, eloquence, warning, counsel and prescript – which is already pre-empted by the very situation it addresses. The first *Iqra'* of Surah 96, at the Qur'an's outset, was countered by *kalla* "Nay, nay!" of pagan obduracy.

It is from this paradox of a divine–human "call-from-to" implicit in a solely hortatory and didactic perception of what *wahy* affords that the verbal passion, even vehemence, of the Qur'an stems. It is powerfully forthright in its diagnosis of human wrong, its warnings against *dalal*, or "erring", its measures of human self-delusion and perversity, its stark prognosis of eternal "forwarding" of life's deposits to the last assize. It is for this reason that no study of Quranic style can isolate itself from Quranic themes, no sense of its poetry can displace the patterns of its theology. The two are fully mutual. By the same token there is no eluding the surpassing range and beauty of its diction, the vitality of its rhetorical recruitment of imagination. Its analogies belong sympathetically with its Arabian locale. It harnesses its landscape to affirm its meanings. It recruits to its revelatory ends the wealth of Arabic syntax and lyricism.

There is one passage, of great import to the commentators, where it passes a verdict on its own quality. Surah 3.7 explains.

> There are revelations in it (the Book) which are quite categorical and explicit. These are the book in its essential meaning and nature. Other verses employ metaphor and analogy. Those who in heart incline to deviant ideas have a habit of following these metaphorical parts with a will for discord and tendentious exegeses. God alone it is who knows the interpretation of it.[20]

The sharp distinction here made between *muhkamat* and *mutashabihat*, "absolutely given" and "figurative", is clearly intended to prevent the vagaries to which the latter are – by their very nature – susceptible. Yet, with its caveat, the Qur'an has no hesitation about anthropomorphic analogy – "the face of God", "seated on the Throne", "the ever vigilant Lord", "the abiding countenance of Allah", "the Mother of the Book", and numerous other "similitudes". *Wahy* itself would be otherwise inconceivable.

Yet the passage gives no clue to how the distinction between "category" and "imagery" is to be known to obtain. Is there not a sense – from the whole nature of language – that they interfuse and inter-depend? What analogy expresses is not, thereby, uncategorical in its truth, nor can the would-be absolute dispense with what the metaphorical contributes to its perception. Thus style and substance are one. The Qur'an achieves a sure marriage of poetry with prophecy with a plain warning that they may not be divorced.

# VI

The theme of "prophethood and language" has obviously much more to do with poetry than with prose. Much, however, has been made, in modern times, of the narrative art of the Qur'an – a topic long inhibited by the classic doctrine of *wahy* as divine mediation of words in a way that left no room for any artistry understood as personal to the Prophet. "Story" in the Qur'an is naturally bounded by its ruling situational concern, namely the eradication of plural worships through the supreme assertion of the unity of Allah against "all that idolaters associate". This crowning mission controls the interest in history. Thus "revelatory historicizing" – if the phrase holds there – makes the Qur'an narratives very different from the Biblical. It may also explain the absence from Quranic poetry of the hymnic, or liturgical, element so notable in the Biblical prophets.[21] For they prophesied within and against an established monotheism with its Temple so central to what had to be rebuked and purged, whereas Muslim worship was only a potential through the early stages of *Tanzil*.

Further, narrative in the Qur'an broadly reinforces the theme of divine *Tawhid*, by reciting the stories of departed tribes and their prophets, like Salih, Hud and Shuʻaib. The tales of *Dhu al-kifl*, "owner of the pledge", and *Dhu al-Qarnain*, Alexander, do not materially add to the impact of the Qur'an. David figures only marginally as the "source" of the *Zabur* or Psalms. The longer, oft repeated stories of Abraham, Moses and allusions to other patriarchs of the Biblical scene, belong squarely with the

Meccan thrust of the Qur'an. Abraham, for example, emerges as the great iconoclast, breaking his peoples' images.

Surah 12, devoted to the tense story of Yusuf and his brothers, the Biblical Joseph, is the salient example of the Qur'an's narrative art. Various claims have been made as to its technical superiority over the Genesis version, with its fuller insight into the ménage of Zulaika, wife of Potiphar, and its moving insights into the psyche of father Ya'qub through the trauma of his suspense and the part a vision of his father had in steadying the soul of Yusuf in his crisis.

Controversy has inevitably surrounded the areas where the Qur'an represents the central New Testament events of Jesus' nativity, his society of *ansar*, or "disciples", their role around a "memorial table",[22] and the Qur'an's strictures on the matter of his crucifixion. These, however, do not belong with the place of language in the quiver of the prophets, except so far as hard questions turn on issues of vocabulary, of hidden pronouns and the rest. These, with all their urgency, arise elsewhere.

When, in a notable tradition, Muhammad described himself as more "vexed" than any other prophet,[23] it must have been his circumstance in Mecca he had in mind. It is a study to which CHAPTER V must come. Meanwhile, the word "vexed" might give way to the word "resilient" as a fair descriptive of how language in the Qur'an returns resourcefully to its themes and deploys its wide Arabic range in the urging of its mission's claims. The language of the Hebrew Bible has a "resilience" of its own different vintage and provenance.

# VII

To enquire about the role of language in the Biblical world, in those books of what Christians called "the Old Testament", from Amos to Malachi, is to enter another world, for all the case made in CHAPTER I for common prophethoods, Biblical and Quranic. Hebrew, to be sure, prevails but there is no stress on a mandatory language with validity turning on preservation from "slips of the tongue" or proven by divine mediation in syllabic sequence. The whole panorama of this prophethood coming to be Scripture is wide and prolonged. The single personality in the Qur'an and the precise span of some three and twenty years gives way to a crowded canvas of four centuries and a "goodly fellowship" of "voices crying" in a welter of political and social flux. The entire logic and poetry of prophethood are changed.

Monotheism is already in place. We do not have to dispute with unscriptured paganism. Rather a sharply ethnicized Yahwism is found at odds with its moral liabilities and prone to disloyalty and irresolution under the menace of powerful foes. These situations concern the chapter following. The arts and strategies of language which they demand release individual powers of rhetoric, satire, cajolery and dramatic symbolism freer than those the classic theory of the Qur'an allows to Muhammad.

His range of metaphor and luminous word-play within the prescripts of *wahy* was eloquent enough.[24] The Biblical theme of "Inspiration" – no less "from heaven" in its character – leaves the personal idiosyncrasy of an Amos or an Ezekiel in full play as the very agent of the word that still announces itself with "Thus says the Lord". Hearers, and beyond them readers, are still made to feel the warrant of a language which is more than an individual's conscious skills. Yet these are imaginatively present in the very fabric of their utterance. There is still, in the public domain, what we may call a psychic "establishment", as in Muhammad's Meccan situation. But it is no longer one defensive of pagan status, basking in the prestige of pilgrimage and bent on holding to its trade advantage. Biblically it is a psyche of people-privilege buttressed by faith in covenant and the illusion of a land inviolate.

Accordingly, the language of critical counter-persuasion – as the moral conscience of the prophets and their political realism devise it – carries their sentiments with a thrust born of their inner intensity of vocation. To study them now is to experience the conviction that, somehow, theme and word have forged a single passion. It is not as if there was a laboured search for imagery or a tedious experiment with vocabulary unconvincingly artificial. Instead, it is as though meaning and passion had spontaneously found each other, either fired by the other – a quality justifying the sense of a "God-breathed" inspiration.[25]

It is this way that metaphor comes so strongly into its own in the Biblical prophetic tradition. With the possible exception of Ezekiel, whose deliverances, as we have noted, have features implying something like divine "dictation", the personal resourcefulness of the prophets in their language is evident everywhere. Metaphors come eloquently from their individual locale, their mental habits, their observant eye. They are made to marry with meaning often in extended form, so that the metonymy involved[26] gives congenial thrust to the original intention and sharpens the impact. Language is not then merely a carrier of meaning but a participant in its shape and content. Examples abound. "Famine" and a plethora of words might seem an incongruous pair but Amos uses this very oddness to bring home that desperate hunger awaits the satiated heedless, replete with their ill-gotten diet of luxury.

> The time is coming, says the Lord God, when I will send famine on the land, not hunger for bread or thirst for water, but for hearing the word of the Lord. People will stagger from sea to sea, they will range from north to east, in search of the word of the Lord, but they will not find it. On that day fair maidens and young men will faint for thirst. (Amos 8: 11–13)

His words inter-weave panic among the well-fed; a heedlessness to calls for penitence ends in an urgency to know where any news of respite is to be had: the drama in the paradox is pressed to its climax.

When, in a different oracle, Amos turns to restoration on condition of repentance, security and plenty are told in the familiar imagery of an "implanted people".

> I will restore the fortunes of my people Israel: they will rebuild their devastated cities and live in them, plant vineyards and drink the wine, cultivate gardens and eat the fruit. Once more I shall plant them on their own soil . . . (seeing that) . . . the ploughman will follow hard on the reaper, and he who treads the grapes after him who sows the seed. The mountains will run with fresh wine and every hill will flow with it. (Amos 9: 13–15)

Language conjures up the idyllic picture which conveys its own cargo of hope.

Amos' language is often charged with historical memory. He is fascinated by "the waters of the Nile", that river of Israel's destiny. His words are redolent with the places of ancient story, with "Gath of the Philistines" and "the sacred way to Beersheba". But he is under no illusion about the uniqueness of the Exodus (9: 7) nor about the extravagant fame of David's music. This he is ready to associate with the vain pleasantries of "ease in Zion" – the very city of David's prowess.

> You thrust aside all thought of the evil day and hasten the reign of violence. You loll on beds inlaid with ivory and lounge on your couches: you feed on lambs from the flock and stall-fed calves: you improvise on the lute and, like David, invent musical instruments, drink wine by the bowlful and anoint yourselves with the richest oils, but at the ruin of Joseph you feel no grief. (Amos 6: 3–6)

The poetry captures the intense reproach in the message, crowding clause on clause in a cumulative arraignment.

But, for all the vivid quality of his "palace" scenes, it was from his native Tekoa that he drew his finest rhetoric, anticipating the Qur'an's practice of questionings that must elicit the negative answer to underwrite the positive point.

> Do two people journey together unless they have first agreed?
> Does a lion roar in the thicket if he has no prey?
> Does a young lion growl in his den unless he has caught something?
> Does a bird fall into a snare on the ground if no bait was set for it?
> Does a trap spring from the ground and take nothing?
> If a trumpet sounds in the city, are not the people alarmed? (Amos 3: 3–6)

Has Amos seen a strange but logical "coincidence" between the ominous rise of Assyria and an Israel rightly in the path of its retributive significance, both by "the hand of the Lord?" So it must be read. But the poetry which breathes this meaning for public heeding is all his own, the product of the very terrain in which he sensed its truth. Language has become the consummate instrument of prophethood.

# VIII

We can hazard the guess that the entire Book of Hosea is extended metaphor drawn from his private experience as the only writing prophet for the northern Kingdom.[27] Scholars are at issue about the "marriage" on which Hosean metaphor turns, thanks in part to the uncertainty between chapters I and III and the identity of the spouses. Gomer may have been some Temple prostitute before, or after, her marriage to Hosea, or the whole episode may be bare allegory. But, given things "proleptic" in the Biblical tradition – by which where they ultimately "arrive" can be thought implicit and latent in them from the start – it seems the most sane conclusion to believe that Hosea, trustingly, married a pure, sincere woman and the marriage proved to have within it his bitter experience of betrayal.[28] At all events, that sense of things tallies entirely with the instinct of his prophetic vision to read in it a clue, an epitome, of all that belonged historically between Yahweh and Israel. That perception became in turn both the theme and the impulse of his prophethood.

It follows that his language fuses the two in its pathos and its tender hope. Hosea might be taken as the supreme example of "words found for meaning known" only because "meaning known had birth in words". Language and revelation inter-act. One might borrow – changing the idiom – the sentiment of one of Homer's poets who declared:

> I am self-taught: a god inspired me with all manner of songs.[29]

Only that Hosea would believe: "Yahweh breathed in me self-taught the language of His travail for my people."

The text of Hosea may well exercise the critical scholars but there is no escaping the burden of his extended metaphor. The very "election" of his nation has to be doubted in the pain of its moral forfeiture. He names his children – the first occasion of a device others emulate – "Unmercied" and "Not My people", alike devastating verdicts to arrest his reckless hearers. His own heart-anxiety inspires him to think comparably of the emotions of Yahweh. A tender retrospect as far back as the Exodus yearns and accuses:

> I led them with bonds of love, that I lifted them like a child to My cheek, that I bent down to feed them. (11: 4)

Tension informs the inner debate between requital and compassion. "By a prophet Israel was tended" says Hosea (12: 13) unwittingly telling his own role in retrospect to Moses, while reality has so far clouded the prospect of Sinai.

The tenderness of Hosea is as radical as Amos in denunciation of the moral compromises of Israel. The love that clings to the beloved may not trivialize the guilt that makes its pain. The necessity for disciplining tribulation rides with the potential of current history to inflict it. The prophet is led to the supreme principle, nowhere else more plainly uttered:

> For I desired mercy and not sacrifice, acknowledgement of God more than burnt offering. (6: 6)

Ritual is futile in the absence of honesty of heart and the integrity of society. Thanks to his inner yearning of soul, Hosea is alive to natural imagery that is at once searing in its condemnation and gentle in its wistfulness. "Morning cloud" and "early dew", "a silly dove without heart", "smoke from a chimney" – are analogies of nature's poetry.

This feature of Hosea extends in a remarkable way to his habit of drawing language arguably sympathetic to the Baal or fertility worship he denounces. He has nothing but reproach for "altars on high hills" and the veneration of the means of "husbandry" with all their sexual connotation yet he is ready to adapt the natural order to his spiritual message. While "their (guilty) altars were like heaps of stone beside a ploughed field", he summons them to repentant faithfulness in the imagery of the farm.

> Jacob shall break his clods. Sow to yourselves in righteousness, reap in

mercy, break up your fallow ground. It is time to seek the Lord till He come and rain justice upon you. (10: 11–12)

This divine–human fertility is still more strikingly celebrated in 2: 21–23 by a benison of nature reversing the "not My people" verdict of condemnation.

> I will betroth you to Me in faithfulness . . . I shall answer the heavens and they shall answer the earth, and the earth will answer the grain, the new wine and fresh oil, and they will answer Jezreel. And Israel will be a new sowing in the land . . .

"God sows" is the meaning of Jezreel, name of Hosea's firstborn taken from the fated city where Jehu made a bloody end of Omri's heirs (2 Kings 10: 11) in a grim harvest of retribution. By the same paradox, Hosea could take "the valley of Achor for a door of hope" (2: 15). His poetic soul was deeply steeped in his people's story.

The inter-text of nature and history, shaped in Hosea's case in personal life-experience, is vividly renewed throughout the four long centuries that belong with the Book of "Isaiah" in its present canonical shape. From "the year when King Uzziah died" (6: 1) to the hailing of Cyrus as "Messiah" (45: 1) the diversity of numerous oracles poses issues that have concerned scholars contentiously. There is, however, one unifying quality which perhaps explains why "Proto", "Deutero" and "Trito" Isaiahs – as the terms go – have been joined in one book. If we allow the possibility of a "community" of disciples of the original Isaiah over several generations, there is a discernibly kindred eloquence, a community of rhetoric, on either side of the great divide between chapters 39 and 40.

It consists, in part, in the fusion of nature-imagery and historical destiny. The Exodus is lyrically celebrated in analogy taken from creation myths of the divided dragon through whose cleaved entrails, like rearing waters, the deliverance – alike from chaos and from Egypt – transpired (cf. 27.1 and 51: 9). "The slain dragon of the sea" inaugurates "the vineyard of red wine". The early Isaiah's loved image of "the vineyard" captures the implanting of Yahweh's "people" as "the pleasant plant" covenantly "enlandized" into Canaan. The song of the vineyard in Isaiah 5: 1–7, turning lyrically into lament and dirge, reverberates in the New Testament and affords numerous allusions throughout the prophetic literature. The unison of nation story and land-benison is one with the poetry of Hosea.

Further, it yields a central poetic symbol of things Messianic, with "every man under his vine and under his fig tree, none making them afraid", when, much later, Zechariah (3: 10) makes it the idyll of divinely pledged security. The dark side of this recurrent language of "the dressed vine" is that the bitter cycle of dispossession in exile can only repossess – as it only originally possessed under Joshua – by the sort of despoilation immediate occupiers will always know at risk, if only from their own experience. Hence the bliss of having "sons of aliens for your vine-dressers".

It is evident that common themes descend through communities of mind whether Joel, Micah, Habakkuk or Haggai and shape their music and their idiom. The last named sees "vine and fig and olive" as mentors of prosperity to come (2: 19).

Imagination might link this prophetic strain with the note in Isaiah 8: 16–20 concerning the "laying up of the scroll for disciples" to come. Whatever may be its political significance, it has to do with "signs of One who dwells in Zion", and the first of these is the union of land and people. At all events there is a brotherhood of Isaian imagery reaching across the sequence that bears his name and through all "the goodly fellowship".

The original Isaiah was a master of Hebrew poesy and style. He conjures up a vivid image for every theme. His opening charge against his people (1: 4–6) is worthy of the Book of Job at its most gruesome in characterizing putrid wounds with "no soothing touch of oil". The intensity with which he turns his vineyard song into bitter woes is as telling as his several oracles (5: 26–30, 10: 28–32 and 13: 19–22) against heathen powers. Or take the lyricism of the celebration of Babylon's overthrow in 14: 4–23, with its sharp irony and the "cedars of Lebanon" exulting "since you are laid low no feller [hewer] has come against us".

Some studies have associated Isaiah's lyric power with liturgical passages from Temple worship. The role of the Temple, as we saw, was crucial to his vocation. Isaiah 12 is a worthy example. If not itself liturgical, it could readily become so. There are throughout what might be called liturgical dialogues with Yahweh, "entering through the gates". After chapter 39, in the new epoch, we find anticipations of deliverance sung in paeans of praise set in the old liturgical tradition of Judah's recitals of history. "Sing to the Lord . . ." (42: 10–16) is redolent with "the sea and the wilderness" and the Lord "making darkness light" in the ongoing path of destiny. Then the familiar rhetorical questions: "Who is blind . . .". The opening of "Deutero" Isaiah in 40: 1–11 had initiated the same theme and turned it into song, rejoicing in the paradox of a plain way through the rough wilderness and the image of "the shepherd gentle with the young".

## Prophethood and Language

It is not, with Isaiah throughout, that a self-conscious artistry is aptly making language tell: it is rather that the very thrust of his theology breathes its own ardour and gives it voice in surpassing verbal power. He is not embellishing his theme by some literary indulgence arguably contrived for mere effect. He finds his passion and his imagery fused into one, recruiting metaphor in the fullest authenticity. Take the famous "roll call" of the stars (40: 25) when the myriad hosts of heaven answer to their call like men on the parade ground: "Present!" The instance takes its place in the crescendo of eloquence where questions set their own ineluctable answers in a climax of sublime theology.

Through all the "Isaiahs", named and un-named, runs the familiar Hebrew quality of lively parallelism, where companion phrases clinch the meaning by blending their separate kinships of imagery. Often there will be a hidden play on words.

> Why are your clothes all red?
> Like the garments of one treading grapes in the winepress. (63: 2–3)
>
> I have trodden the press alone . . .
>
> You . . . spread a table for the god of fate
> And fill bowls of spiced wine in honour of Destiny. (65: 11–12)
>
> I shall destine you for the sword . . .

or, in gentler vein:

> The glory of Lebanon is given to it,
> The splendour too of Carmel and Sharon . . . (35: 2)
>
> A branch shall grow from the stock of Jesse
> And a shoot shall spring from his roots. (11: 1)
>
> Will the clay ask the potter what he is making,
> Or his handiwork say to him: "You have no skill"? (45: 10)
>
> Your children would have been like the sand in number,
> Your descendants countless as its grains. (48: 19)

Or, in double sequence at the very outset in impassioned distress around the sinful follies of a "chosen people":

> An ox knows his owner, a donkey its master's stall,
> But Israel lacks all knowledge,
> My people has no discernment. (1: 3)

Such parallelism and the instinct to appeal to animal nature against the wilfulness of volitional humans are familiar enough in the Psalter and belong too with Isaian colleagues like Joel, Micah and Zephaniah, all in the tradition of Hosea.

In the Isaiah of chapters 40–55 there is a characteristic accent on "holiness" as the corollary of the Judaic land-people reading of the theology of nature – a theology that readily invokes analogies, via land, from things to people, from the sensuous to the spiritual. The theme of divine exaltedness, so crucial in these chapters, means that appeals to external nature constitute, as it were, a court of justice, a frame of reference, the logic of which is a people-holiness. What Hosea 12: 2 and Micah 6: 2 called "the Lord's controversy" rings through Isaiah. The logic of historical retrospect as well as of nature's fecundity, of being "covenanted" in the land, is urged to invoke a holy tenancy, a contrite economy, a reverent agriculture. Isaiah 3: 13 "takes Israel to court", when the Lord . . . argues His case, standing up to judge His people (He) opens the indictment against the elders and the officers of His people. The verdict of "Woe . . ." to the faithless then has all the force of a judicial condemnation.

The theme of "holy liability" reverberates through all the Isaian Canon. Can we surmise that invoking "natural evidences" to sustain the case for "godliness" and against iniquity points towards the "wisdom" concept which developed in the wake of the return from exile, via the influence of Persian lore? If so, its roots were deep in the ardent theological ethics that belong with the literary style, the arresting metaphors of the Isaian texts. For these deploy in sustained energy and power the entire range of Biblical Hebrew and its rhetorical passion. The Isaiah name, meaning "Yahweh is salvation", fulfils itself in the saving graces of speech and pen that drew so eloquently on the streets and markets of his native Jerusalem and on the contours of his haunts and rural sights and sounds.

The supreme feature of the style of later namesakes (though nameless) within the Canon was the world-wide vista mirrored in its perspectives of Messianic future. Yahweh is heard in summons to all the nations to "look and be saved." "The isles wait for His law." In these passages also theme and poetry fulfil each other. Yet, for all the fervour of this universal vision, the "separate identity" of Jewry is never merged into some new ecumene. Israel will still "suck the breast of nations" and "the sons of aliens be evermore her vinedressers". Perceptions long after all Isaianic writings were needed in the New Testament to make good the inclusive, undifferentiating vision of de-ethnicized covenant. Yet those writings celebrated from afar and sang what they could not historically embrace – a circumstance which remains their final glory.[30]

## IX

If we read that virtue of prophetic language in anticipatory terms, doing so takes us to where the excellence of all the Isaiah texts is noblest, namely in the "servant songs" of chapters 42, 49, 51 and 53. Leaving to later study their inner significance in and beyond their where and when in the text, there is here no verdict but emotions of awe around their literary quality. Setting them to recitative arias brought a tearful Handel to his knees.[31] The pathos of their mysterious provenance is deepened by the elusive ironies, the terse phrasings, the cumulative force of the metaphors.

> He will not quench the smoking flax
> Nor break the bruised reed . . .
>
> . . . my tongue a sharp sword
> He hid me under the shelter of His hand.
> He made me into a polished arrow,
> In His quiver He concealed me . . .
>
> No insult can wound me . . .
> I have set my face like a flint.
> One who will clear my name is at my side.
>
> His form, disfigured, lost all human likeness . . .
> He had no beauty, no majesty to capture our eyes . . . Despised and rejected of men,
> A man of sorrows and acquainted with grief . . .
> Who gave a thought to his fate?

In the climax of the 52: 13–53: 12 passage, the language pleads the enigma of an event where language itself found birth in the very throes of conceiving the event in its whole enigma. However we interpret the theme in its origins, the telling knows itself in its own perplexity. So much is clear from 53: 1, where "our report" – the term is close to the later Christian "tradition" – has the double sense of "what has come to our ears" *and* "What we are echoing into yours". The text acknowledges its own incredulity and expects hearers to reciprocate it. It is at once a confession of amazement and an anticipation of it, which together breathe a strange tension into the unfolding drama.

Yet to have this quality in no way makes the language a bare artifice. It stems from the very intensity of thought. It compels every hearer, every reader, to muster into that "we" at its heart. It fascinates by fusing loathing and pity, making repulsion and admiration a paradox of truth.

The allusion to the "eye-avoidance" of lepers – ("we averted our faces from him") – kindles guilt at horror. By the sheer capacity of the language what results is a scrutiny of all "seeing" and "esteeming", as radical perplexity about all familiar evaluations and the society that takes hollow refuge in them. "The servant" here – unlike the earlier passages – says nothing, speaking only by silence and suffering. The only persuasion of the observer is the reality itself – a situation which is the supreme achievement of language. "Who gave a thought to his fate?" contradicts its own irony in the reality of the long sequel.

The beginning of the sequel – and, it may well be, its anticipation – take us to the prophethood of Jeremiah, whose situation and legacy are explored elsewhere.[32] Beyond the vexing problems left us by the Canonists of the Book that bears his name, the reader feels in a different world, stylistically, from the Isaian heights. Yet, in its most tense moments, as in the "Temple Sermon" (7: 1–12) the long prose narratives of the Book give way to surpassing eloquence, with all the qualities of irony, bitter rhetoric and word-play in Hosea's tradition.

Most passionately of all is this so with the several poetic cries, known as "Jeremiah's Confessions", in which he strives with the unwanted burden of a fruitless ministry and its bitter cost in lonely ostracism and slanderous threats. Here the imagery of "the swelling of Jordan" (12: 5), "Yahweh seeming to him as a liar" (15: 18), "a pit dug for his soul" (18: 20), and – most graphic of all – how "Yahweh took gross advantage of his servant's simplicity" (20: 7)[33] that the Lord might seem "a rapist", is the utmost daring of language-intent.

Throughout Jeremiah's heroic prophethood, often tediously dismissed as "weepinghood",[34] his passionate speaking employs the entire range of things ironic, allusive and defiant. "Jeremiad" – in the popular sense – is no name for his oracles and moral calls to heeding by the heedless. "The almond tree" and "the seething pot" (1: 11–13) yield pointed punning to the country boy, while even "in the field ploughmen cover their heads" as if mourners in a grief-ritual (14: 4). Jeremiah uses all the devices of dialogue with hearers, remonstrance with the guilty, expostulation with Yahweh and the long rhetoric of interrogation. Phrases like "a den of robbers" or "cursed be he who . . ." that become, like something Shakespearean, the common speech of centuries, fall from his lips.

With him, too, there is a mode of "word-weight" that becomes more marked with Ezekiel, namely the adopting of symbolic ploys that carry unmistakeable significance. Mysteriously, by command, he wears a dry loin-cloth and later hides it in the bank of Euphrates, to retrieve it by and by all rotted (13: 1–7).[35] More grimly, and by heavy tragedy, his unmarried state is ordained on him to represent privation and barrenness (16: 1). His visit to the metaphorical "potter's house" (18: 1–6), with his open letter to the exiles (29) and his purchase of "the house of Hanameel (32), are well-known examples of truths made visual. Was it his bitter tribulation in the dank and muddy pit (38) that inspired the psalmist "drawn up out of the miry clay"? (40: 1). It certainly set a precedent Jeremiah well understood (18: 20).

But the deepest truth about the language of Jeremiah is the measure of prophetic "incarnation" explicit in his whole long saga, his heart-travail and his personality in tension for, and with, Yahweh as literature-in-life, as "truth through personality". His was "the voice of one crying" in dimensions which, being all his own, were to be essential measure of Messianic realism ultimately acknowledged in Jesus of Nazareth "and him crucified".

## X

The world we have been traversing from Amos to Jeremiah presents itself as a far cry from the Meccan/Medinan world we earlier reviewed. Situations, as we must trace them in CHAPTER V, were so far contrasted. But in Ezekiel – the last of our concerns with literary style – is in one particular close, it would seem, to the Qur'an in *how* "word" is "weighted" to him. Unlike Hebraic predecessors, he seems to speak only as words are put on to his lips.

> Unlike other Israelite prophets, Ezekiel seems to be devoid of free will while carrying out his prophetic tasks . . . The overall effect is to portray Ezekiel as an automaton, an individual who has no personality.[36]

It follows, as with the Qur'an, that "the word" is "divine" by virtue of this (re-assuring?) absence of personal impulse or emotion. Ezekiel cannot be accused of speaking falsely seeing that he is not speaking "from himself". The abeyance of conscious art, or personal arousal, makes him – as Jalal al-Din said of Muhammad – a "conduit".[37] The injunction about "eating the roll" (2: 3–7) may be thought to support this view.

This reading of prophetic language with Ezekiel raises the question: Where, then, is the "burden"? Perhaps we have to surmize, whether in Mecca or by the Chebar, there was a "dictation" simply "taken in", while a measure of spontaneity was also present. If so – leaving now the Quranic point – Ezekiel certainly emerges from his Book as a very idiosyncratic

## PROPHETHOOD AND LANGUAGE

figure. The "word" certainly appears as a vivid event in his mind. He can find the "roll sweet to his taste", and he can demur four times over the command to "eat" it. The word becomes part of him in his destiny to partake of it.

Thus we find a number of near incredible symbolisms which make him a bizarre messenger. Even speechlessness, for a time, is him speaking (3: 22–27, 24: 25–27, 33: 21f.). He bakes strange bread (4: 9–17) just as he is to build a toy city and besiege it (4: 1–3) or "lie" symbolically on left side and right (4: 4–8) or join two sticks together and break them (37: 16–20). These gestures could hardly have been bits of theatricality, if they were to arrest more than casual, or derogatory, attention. If they were to carry a message there must have been intelligible elucidation on the prophet's part.

But Ezekiel's own mental world was, in measure, theatrical, both his inspirations and his meanings becoming often more visual than verbal. The indescribable "chariot" betokened the divine *Shechinah*, the moving-all-ways, all-seeing "presence", which, for all its enigmas, could be seen visibly leaving the doomed city and Temple and going into exile with the people – this being the supreme disclosure in Ezekiel's theology. Other peaks of his visual drama are the "valley of dry bones" rising to new life (37) and the deepening river issuing from the threshold of the Temple and flowing into fertility and healing foliage. Such panoramas of hope have to be balanced by the meticulous priest-like concern the Book devotes to the measurements of the restored Temple. As a Jerusalemite travailing "by the waters of Babylon", a visionary returning – in fact or vision – to his beloved shrine, Ezekiel goes some way to reconciling the long contention between prophet and priest. His celebration of the doomed fame, the wide commerce, of Tyre is unsurpassed in its genre (26 and 27), sharpened perhaps by the inner soul-distress and perplexity of his own "chosen people".

It may be that one clue to Ezekiel, with which to conclude the present chapter, has to do with words as, in themselves, "centres of power". It stems from puzzlement around how acts and dicta as bizarre as his could "signify", the more so when, often times, there seems to have been no audience or, if audience there was, how could it wait around for the "meaning" of long drawn-out and highly artificial "dramas"? Did "signs" and utterances have some virtue in themselves aside from reasoned credence or rational persuasion? Might it suffice that a case had been stated, a promise pledged, a wisdom decreed? Speech is supposed to be honest at all times but when a speaker is put on oath a special weight attaches to the words. A bare liar then becomes more – a perjurer.

Similarly a curse or a blessing may be thought to effectuate what it contains by the very fact of its having been "enworded". Prophetic language contained many "Yeas" and "Woes" and "Hear this word . . ". By utterance, ground had been staked out, future invoked, spirits heartened, sinners charged. Did all these meanings have substantiation by virtue of their having been articulated in the divine Name and by the divine warrant?

If so, prophetic language is fulfilled, not in the crude sense which we have excluded here of prophecy as mere "foretelling", but in the potential of all meaning to bring itself home and "realize" itself in – to borrow a Quranic phrase – "the bosoms of men". If so again, the "sign" quality, to which all Biblical and Quranic prophethood lays claim and in which the "sign" word recurs continually, had necessarily, in both settings, to give way to total, spiritual, imaginative cognizance both given and received. Language remains the keenest of human mysteries yet its largest role is never surreptitious, mystical or random. "The weight in the word" is finally the summons it brings to mind and will, the cognizance – whether in bearer or hearer – that translates into obedience and personal surrender. Only so are prophet and language the antisepsis of the evil world and heralds of the divine righteousness.

# V

## Prophet and Situation

### I

That there is a situation in life crucial to the text on the page is evident in all prophethood. The place of "the occasions of revelation" in the task of exegesis has always been central in Qur'an studies. The "what" of meaning has always been required to turn on the "where" of locale, the "when" of time. The incidence of Scriptures, the birthplace or the call-time of prophets, the setting of inspiration – all these are manifestly vital clues for the centuries that read. How the contents gathered (if we may play on words) should govern what study gathers from them.

There is even a play on words in the Qur'an itself to capture this truth of things. Surah 106 has a single term to indicate one basic factor in the whole environment of Muhammad's mission, namely the caravans of Mecca in the management of the Quraish, its ruling tribe. In modern Arabic the same term can denote the way books come into being, namely by "composition". English, oddly, has the same double sense. As writings are formed into sequence and sense, so the Meccan merchants brought their commerce to rendezvous and shape.[1] Imagination could not have a livelier mental picture of the interplay between the central context of Muhammad's prophethood – he a Meccan and a merchant – and the content of the Islamic Book. It is the purpose of this chapter to explore in both Biblical and Quranic prophethood the controlling significance of circumstances, of scene and setting, in the coming to be of each and every text.

Surah 106 from which we take the token of a play on words is an immediate example of the task in hand. What is this *eelaaf*[2] (more strictly *Ilaf*) of the Quraish? We may translate:

> By the bringing to rendezvous of the Quraish, the gathering in convoy of

their caravans winter and summer. Let them serve the Lord of this house, who gave them provision of food against hunger and security from fear.

At once we are into the *mise-en-scène* of the whole Qur'an. These Quraish formed Muhammad's early entourage: they would become his harsh enemies and ultimately his conquest. The Surah, however, is capable of subtle other readings, and there are recent scholars who query whether Mecca's commerce was as widespread or as significant as tradition thinks.³ Should we read Surah 106 as meant to be continuous with 105 which rehearses the defeat of Abraha's forces that came against Mecca from the Yemen around the year of Muhammad's birth? Was that "the saving from fear"?; is *Ilaf* simply the foregathering of the trading caravans?; or is it the arranging of inviolate passage by buying off potential marauders or pledging them a share in the profits?⁴ Or does it have to do with the *haram* status of that central shrine, the *Ka'bah*, the "house" that was sacrilized in Quraishi custody as patrons of all foregathering pilgrims, albeit still pagan? In that way the lyrical Arabic verses are setting forth its true Lord, Allah, its transcendent "guardian".

However we resolve these possibilities the term *Ilaf* writes a physical, local history into the very fabric of the prophethood which addresses it. For these concluding Surahs of the Qur'an are invocatory and summon to gratitude, awe and right worship. Such was the interweaving of a situation and a scripture that has us borrow an accident of vocabulary around "composing" as being what both circumstances and writings do.

The situation factor runs, of course, through everything Biblical. It is important to appreciate that while Amos was brooding far away in Tekoa about the menacing rise of Assyria breathing down on Israel from the north, he was aghast at tidings of unholy luxury and blatant injustice darkening the scene in that same Israel. Putting the two scenes together ("Can two men come to rendezvous in the desert without prior plan?" 3: 3), he reads in their juncture the retributive purpose of God and thereby realizes that Yahweh presides in righteousness over history.⁵ The perception makes him a prophet and impels him into those "ivory palaces" with his reproach.

It has always been a cardinal principle of Quranic commentary that *asbab al-nuzul*, "occasions of revelation", are, after grammar and textual parsing, the first concern of *tafsir*.⁶ The meticulous gathering of reports from Muhammad's "companions" sprang in part from this principle. The Qur'an is not always forthcoming about "where" and "when" in the kind of direct detail we need.⁷ But the whole theme of its being "serial" or "piecemeal" in its "descent" pins attention on time and place. The identification of every chapter (except 9) as either Meccan or Medinan confirms the point, making the Hijrah, or move from the one city to the other, pivotal both to the Book and the story. It follows that the Prophet's *Sirah,* or life-story, from the first deliverance to his death at the Book's closure, moves in tandem with its contents.

This "situation about situations" seems to suggest the question why the whole should have been located in western Arabia in the 7th century of the Christian calendar. It is one to which we must return. Comparably, how ought we to understand the incidence of the great Biblical prophets from Amos to Zechariah in the period from the demise of the house of Omri to the rise of the Seleucids?

Those larger panoramic questions will, in measure, take us to CHAPTER IX and "Ongoing Finality". Intelligence with them will first turn on what justice we can do to the immediate settings and circumstances of private days and local years. Only in these did the long centuries have their school.

## II

It is at once obvious that perhaps half a millennium of Hebrew prophethood contrasts with the twenty-three years of Muhammad's vocation. However, the time-span of prophethood as the Qur'an sees it stretches back as far as Genesis 3, to Enoch and the patriarchs. With its own "minor" figures like Hud, Shu'aib and Salih, who have no counterparts so named in the Hebrew Scriptures, the Qur'an esteems all the figures down to Elisha as "prophets", while mysteriously excluding those whose stature we here have made sole referents to the Hebrew standing of prophethood. Those who, by this reckoning, are Biblically supreme, from Amos to Malachi, the Qur'an ignores (Jonah or Yunis is a special case).[8] It takes as "prophets" patriarchal heroes and exemplars whose histories lack either the historical under-writing or the articulate legacy of word and mission we are taking to be distinctive of the likes of Hosea and all who came in that broadly accessible tradition[9]

It follows that, while the Quranic perspective on prophethood has long antecedents, almost pre-historical, to its unique locale in Muhammad, this breadth of spectrum cannot well be brought into comparative study with the major Biblical tradition for which we have opted as authentic prophethood. Muhammad must have here an exclusive role.

This is the more appropriate in that the Qur'an sees all prophets previous to Muhammad – their "ultimate seal" – as in virtually the same setting as his own. The Qur'an's vision of a long sequence of "messengers" has them all engaged in a steady encounter with idolatry, rugged affirmers of the divine unity against all false worships and pseudo-divinities. The celebrated figure of Abraham destroys his people's idols and builds the true, pure *Ka'bah* in Mecca. The Biblical narratives of Noah, Joseph and Moses, in their Quranic shape, retain much of their Biblical aura but the consensus-significance is about divine unity. Though aspects of Hebraic "covenant" are present, including even the "holy land" theme,[10] the prophetic role more squarely fits the Quranic norm.

This situation is in line with the Qur'an's prior stress on the "covenant" of the good earth in the human custody of each and all people, on the Noahid rather than the Sinaitic with its exclusive, ethnic character. Throughout in the Qur'an Muhammad is fortified by assurances that the hostility he undergoes was comparably the lot of all his predecessors. That pattern of encouragement in adversity may well explain, in part, the very presence of Biblical parallels. For these largely come in the middle of the Meccan period when he was beset with adverse taunts and ridicule.

They required him to invoke the precedents whereby adversity signalled veracity inasmuch as humans always have hate or scorn for those who would accuse them. Muhammad's tribulations were the very mark of his authenticity, seeing that they incorporated him into a distinguishing tradition.

> Do not set up any other god along with Him. I am clearly warning you from Him. Comparably no previous messenger ever came to those in earlier times of whom they did not say: "He is either a sorcerer, or he is mad." Is this a habit they have passed down to each other?

This reflection (in Surah 51.50–52) is the more remarkable in that Muhammad, uncharacteristically, is speaking in the first person. His sense of long and honoured forebears belongs with the heavy incidence of hostility and rejection.

It was, of course, this situation in its deepening pattern through thirteen years that yielded the logic that prompted the Hijrah. It therefore underlies the entire historic polity of Islam. The world that is recalcitrant to words and exhortation must be called to heed by other means. There was, however, no precedent for Hijrah known to history in the wake of the things undergone by Hud, Salih or Shu'aib, nor were the vindications of Noah, Abraham or Moses of the Hijrah order.[11] The finality of Muhammad as "messenger" was matched by the originality of "the prosperity of God's servant".[12]

The ruling preoccupation the Qur'an has with the issue of plural, pagan worships, and with the steady asserting of the divine unity makes its thrust strongly adversarial. The mood is urgently imperative. The "bringing of good news" is a "bringing of warning". The second is more frequent than the first. The issue that is joined is inherently external in that it has to do with the party that offends by its waywardness and obduracy. In the interests of a profound and crucial positive it must adopt a negative insistence. The theme is "there is no deity except Allah" – to be repeated in the entire context in the like form, a decisive disclaimer in the name of a sure indicative. It follows that the outward accusation, with all its urgency, sustains an inward legitimation. It would hardly be otherwise where the very unity of God is at issue. To be the bearer of such a word, so vital and so far maligned by those who do not heed, is to possess an all extenuating mandate.

This Quranic *mise-en-scène* is in contrast with the Hebraic prophethood of the supreme centuries after the mere seers had receded into history. With them, for all the local shrines, the sovereignty of Yahweh is not at stake. His people are already in covenant and staunch in their land-sanction as divine ordaining of their ethnic destiny. The burden of these prophets concerns the dereliction of a vocation by which they are already theists in their own confident sense. This people, with their retrospect to exodus, are in trust with their own Sinai: they are no Quraish presiding over what still waits to be enlightened. The thrust of Hebraic prophethood is thus inward against domestic compromise and self-betrayal. "O Israel, thou hast destroyed thyself", is Hosea's cry (13: 9). When the young Isaiah likens his people to old-time pagans, it is in the keenest satire (1: 10) to drive home their apostasy. Apostasy only belongs in the Qur'an when the new faith, Islam, has been established. Meanwhile its hearers are *ahl al-jahiliyyah*, "the people of ignorance". The "ignorance" of which the Hebrew prophets accuse their hearers is not that of not-knowing: it is "ignoring", or disallowing, what they know too well.

To be sure, this quality of Hebrew Scripture is not without its temptations, but they are those of a wholly internalized theism where what is adversarial is also self-directed. Hence the frequent Biblical concept of "Yahweh's controversy" with the people and the strange contrast between the canny awareness of animals and the stubborn contrariness of Israel and Judah.

> How is the faithful city become a harlot? . . . The ox knows his owner and the ass his master's crib but Israel does not know, My people do not consider. (Isaiah 1: 21 and 3)

> The stork in the heavens knows her appointed times, and the turtle, the crane and the swallow observe the time of their coming, but my people know not the judgement of the Lord. (Jeremiah 8: 7)

With the dumb creatures there is an obedience which is non-volitional, whereas the human knows but will not fulfil, though the will is thoroughly informed of what is due. For it is a will steeped in a "knowing" long in hand and assumed in every prophetic appeal.

Muhammad's prophethood has to make its toilsome way against "established ignorance".[13] His immediate audience presides, to be sure, over Abraham's once-pure *Ka'bah* but does not know "whence it has fallen" in the wilful "exclusion of Allah" which it practices.[14] The place, like their hearts, is alien territory which God's apostle is summoned to re-possess in the true name of divine unity. He is his people's adversary in terms different by the very *sitz-im-leben* from those of Hosea or Jeremiah. This Mecca is not yet a Jerusalem. It may have had Adam's sojourn and seen Abraham's hallowing but it is still lacking its David and its Solomon, those architectural figures of its full destiny which only this prophet-herald to it, this Muhammad, is assigned to become – which he will become only in the wake of his primary prophetic task. That task lacks the people-background, the historic sense of destiny that every Hebrew audience enjoyed, to be addressed accordingly even in their worst apostacies.

Yet adversarial as the Qur'an was by necessity of its pagan context as Mecca framed it, that very quality of Muhammad's experience served to set for the Qur'an the puzzle of human obduracy. The confrontation in the name of divine unity being so rightly adamant, the controversy became the more exacting. That "they are saying . . . " "Say thou . . . " refrain in Muhammad's story, being so intractable, so prolonged, could not fail to arouse, both for him and for his disciples, the question: "Why are these humans so incorrigible?" "Why is the infallible word so far repudiated?" In their own different ethos, the Biblical prophets had faced the same painful perplexity. For them, thanks to covenant and election, it had a different ring. With Muhammad the near incomprehension, about how resistant evil minds could be, derived from the conviction of "the weight in the word" being its direct heavenly mediation on to his lips. How could it be that a truth so compelling, a heralding so absolute, could undergo the indignity of a reception so hostile?

"Oh my people", he cried, lapsing into direct speech, "how is it with me that I call you to salvation and you call me to the fire?" (40.41) Or, when Allah addresses him:

> If they be unbelieving of this word, you may well be consumed in pain, yearning at their lack of faith. (18.6)

There was only "grief" in laying siege to their incredulous hearts. Whether in Judea or the Hijaz, there was the same burden of an unheeding world. It might well spell bafflement about the efficacy of words alone, about the reason for the unavailingness of preaching.

One result of that perplexity in Muhammad's case was the conclusion that – words failing – resistance must be subdued. Resistance in Mecca's case was founded on the vested interests of pilgrimage and trade, both of which wre rooted in paganism. These, having no mind to yield to words, needed to be forcibly overcome.

But, even as and when that conclusion was reached and implemented, there remained the spiritual problem of why evil could be so entrenched, why wrong refused its own verbal correction. It is surely in response to this riddle around humankind that the Qur'an falls back on the formula: "In their hearts there is a sickness." The theme is frequent.[15] Jeremiah (17: 9) came to the same conclusion, and linked "disease" with "self-deceit". "Who can fathom the heart?" he cried. The analogy may leave us wondering, then, about "wilfulness" seeing that "disease" is not voluntary. Yet the sense of something deeply awry and perverse about humankind is crucial to the Qur'an. Those who, in the West, have wanted to suggest that Islam lacks "a sense of sin" misread its text. It is vital not to overlook or discount the significance of the thirteen long and arduous years of Muhammad's solely verbal vocation. In that measure, he shared the lot of all prophethood whereby its content incurs its cost.

What is at stake here calls for separate study in CHAPTER VII. Presently, it is the emergence of enmity as the epicentre. What the musician Verdi called "the ugly part of humanity"[16] comes into disclosure precisely where truth presents its challenge. There is a malice latent in humanity for those who would reform or caution it. As Al-Busiri, the poet-devotee, had it in his celebration of the Prophet:

> His cave was light with winds
> And concepts of truth and good –
> Stoniness to the infidels.[17]

Where exhortation is unwanted it works like provocation. Its being fit for acceptance spells it being open to reviling – a state of things implicit in that other Quranic concept of *zulm al-nafs*, or "self-wronging". "It was their own selves they wronged" is the steady verdict of the Qur'an about the heedless Meccans.[18]

The wrong Muhammad saw as done to Allah by diverted worship offered to pseudo-deities did not admit of any concept of Allah as vulnerable, seen as a truth, by paradox, about omnipotence. It was for Christianity to take that step as one for Islam urgently to repudiate. Yet the reality was there in the experience of God's agency, the prophets. In his Meccan precincts Muhammad was no less party to it than spokesmen in Jerusalem. *Shirk*, the cardinal sin that "associated" Allah with pagan objects of trust or worship or alleged existence, violated the rights of the one true God. The human capacity to do so was the ultimate measure of human wilfulness and the surest factor in the very necessity of prophetic mission.

The Qur'an, then, stood in its own terms at the heart of the human predicament. The encounter of Muhammad with Mecca "places" the ultimate dimensions of prophethood as radically as any, if the vagaries of a crude paganism are rightly measured. The sort of pluralism and idolatry the Quraish observed may seem a far cry from a sophisticated modern world. We must return later to how superficial that verdict can be seen to be. For idolatry has many breeds. Here it suffices to have the perspective we have reached on "situation" as Muhammad found it. The generations that listened – or failed to listen – earlier to Yahweh's spokesmen had quite contrasted "occasions of revelation" from those of the Qur'an but the disparity, to which we must now turn, had to do with the same fundamental burden of the wrongness of the world and, thereby, with the destiny of prophethood to be the touchstone of humanity under God.

## III

There are two central denominators of Biblical prophethood in the world of its great centuries. They belong together. The one is the precariousness of a "chosen people" at the hands of "unchosen" ones who possess supreme power. How were they to read the situation? The other is to relate, from within exclusive peoplehood, to the significance of other nations under the rule of Yahweh who has now to be seen as universal and yet distinctively possessed by the one people alone. It may be said that, for all their splendid eloquence, the prophets never resolved that second perplexity.

The obvious crux of both dimensions of prophetic situation was the exile. For exile, "hanging harps on alien willows" and "singing a Hebrew song in a strange land", arguably undid everything that covenant meant. It spelled absence from the land where covenant belonged. For land, by entry and by right, was the very token of covenant. It threatened also to undo history, inasmuch as history had been the score from which all songs were sung.

> There is a history in all men's lives,
> Figuring the nature of the time's deceased:
> The which observed, a man may prophesy
> With a near aim, of the main chance of things
> As yet not come to life, which in their seeds
> And weak beginnings lie entreasured . . .
> Such things become the hatch and brood of times . . .[19]

The Hebrew mind was always in retrospect to Moses, Joshua and David through whom their "main chance entreasured" mighty origins. How could these seemingly miscarry in "the hatch and brood" of heathen powers? Hebrew prophethood faced – in the unique idiom of its own provenance – the justification of Yahweh. It was their version of the moral problem of human history.

They resolved it by shaping the mystery into self-accusation. That was their glory. The sense of the covenant was vivid enough to trust that calamity must have a moral meaning and that, far from betraying their divine relationship, seeming undoing was, in truth, its sacred fidelity.

The insights begin with Hosea and Amos. The former, the only prophet to the Northern Kingdom preached in the context of war between the two kingdoms – Israel under Pekah and Damascus under Rezin – against Judah, who countered by stealing some of Israel's territory – all under the shadow of the Assyrians who depopulated Damascus and divided the Aramaean lands, and also reduced Pekah's domains in Israel. Through the long tyranny that preceded these events and the near anarchy that followed, Hosea's oracles of judgement read the scene in firmly moral terms of retribution and Yahweh's tender paradox of continuing love.

Amos, though lacking the tenderness of Hosea, had no less a moral message. He read the Assyrian menace through the turbulent decades around his Book in grim terms of requital of the moral decadence, whether Israel's or Judah's.[20] "The day of the Lord" which complacence read in the prosperity that changing vicissitudes allowed meant, for Amos the curbing time of divine nemesis on the wrongs of society, the exploitation of the poor, the excesses of the rich. But it is also in the oracles of Amos that we find the prophetic spirit deeply exercised about the significance of heathen nations. On the one hand, they emerge as punitive agents of Yahweh's justice, yet their brutality, their ruthlessness in mass slaughter, and their enslavement of the conquered are squarely under his indictment. He demonstrates a new awareness that even *the* Exodus may have its counterparts in Yahweh's inscrutable, but always moral, will.

In his later day, the original Isaiah[21] carried forward the themes of Hosea and Amos. The implications of his vision we have traced already. Nowhere does moral indignation rise higher than in his chapters 1 and v.[22] Adversity and prosperity alike are interpreted as charged with moral meaning. He, too, wrestles with what to make of pagan sovereignty that both serves as "rod of Yahweh's anger" (10: 5 and chapters 13–23 – all "oracles against the nations") and stands condemned by His righteousness. The contrast here with the Qur'an is complete. For history outside the Hijaz rarely figures.[23] It was both local circumstance and the absence of ethnic covenant that explain why the Qur'an has no need to arraign the nations. Their occasions come in the expansion. Meanwhile Muhammad moved in his own "inviolate land".[24]

From Hosea's day in the last dark years of the Northern Kingdom to the prophets of the exile of 597 and after, "the weight in the word" has to do with the inner reproach of "the elect nation" and the riddle of pagan "Gentiles" (to use a later term) and their ambiguous place in divine economy. The brief Book of Nahum, for example, a series of short poems, joins Judah's sure salvation (1: 15) with almost gloating fervour at the assured overthrow of Assyria and Nineveh, closing with an ironic dirge (2: 1–13 and 2: 18–19). Nahum's Yahweh is at once commanding the storm clouds, earthquake and famine, to requite the long ravages committed by his people's foes. "Upon whom has that wickedness not passed continually?" (3: 19). Somehow, even total Hebrew exceptionality learns to find neighbourhood in the enormities commonly befalling Assyria's victims.

Zephaniah's situation is comparable. He renews Amos' version of "the day of the Lord" and sees Jerusalem's disasters as meant for a school of penitence, while oracles reproach the corruption of priests, rulers and "prophets" alike. With Habakkuk the outward scene has changed but the twin moral abides. Preaching just before 597, Habakkuk is in dialogue with Yahweh about the pagan powers and, as we saw earlier, is summoned to unfailing trust. His final chapter is an experience of theophany, a near-mystical celebration of divine Lordship. We are anticipating the deep personalism of Jeremiah and many a psalmist. But there are warnings, too, for the neo-Babylonian power liable to the same illusions of grandeur that had undone the Assyrians.

## IV

The twin situation of Hebrew prophethood as to moral self-reproach and unhallowed heathen powers reaches its fullest height and depth in the prophets of the exile, in the later Isaiah(s), in Jeremiah and Ezekiel. With them the double issue finds its most moving voice. For the forfeit of the land spells the utmost predicament of faith. Jeremiah and Ezekiel rise to the answer by the letter to the exiles to settle (Jer. 29: 1f), the gesture of buying the field back in Judea (Jer. 32: 6f.), and the vision Ezekiel saw of the very "Presence" going into exile with the people (Ezek. 10: 18f so that what "departed" was what he "saw" by the river in Babylon). The Yahweh who can forsake the Temple and migrate with exiles into "foreign" territory spells the doom of the simple tribalism in which Yahweh-faith had first had its birth. Yet the people-nexus remains.

It remains, yet deepened and chastened into the perception of a suffering servanthood – the vision that feels towards the Messianic dimension of the salvation that "election" has always presupposed but which adversity has so far tragically denied. Prophethood knows this supreme "weight in the word" in the harsh implications of exile and, more intimately, in the costliness of Jeremiah's burden, wrestling with this growing sense of truth.

Thus the contrast with the Quranic situation is complete, yet, potentially, fit to be aligned, if only in that being a prophet to the Meccans was also a taxing experience of truth as painful issue, of truth itself at risk with its own meaning. There was a point in the Qur'an when the growing belief of some was urged on others as reason for their faith too. Pagans replied: "Shall we believe as the fools (*sufaha'*) do?" to whom the text responds: "Is it not they who are the fools? But they do not realize it" (Surah 2.13). "Who has believed what we are learning is the case?" was the question in Isaiah 53: 1. We have seen elsewhere how incredulity often waits pityingly on new conviction. The early Christians knew this only too well. It was the same with the dawning meanings of Jeremiah and Ezekiel. "How can these things be?" had to be asked about the conclusions they were coming to, in reading with Yahweh's eyes the meaning of their exile.

There is here no suggestion that the situation, in Surah 2.13, is other than remote from the foolish argument against the folly of faith, as we find that situation in exilic prophethood. But even remote analogies can be precious in the appreciation of significance.

It is noteworthy that the careers of both Jeremiah and Ezekiel belong with the Jerusalem Temple and the waters of Babylon. They dwell both in the sanctuary and the exile. Ezekiel seems to hover, perhaps only mystically, between each locale and he builds place-sanctity meticulously into his vision of a holy future.

We have to conclude that it was the mingled courage and pain of this double situation which generated the visionary hope of a "David" to come, better and surer than the symbol-king whose name embraced all that land, liberty and identity had once meant and ought yet to mean again. Meanwhile, land-forfeiture, stealing from the heart the self-assurance land had always under-written, occasioned a new awareness of the world at large, of peoples and cultures among whom Hebrew fate was now cast and from whom, if at all, Yahweh himself must contrive the rescue of his "chosen". Must not his doing so, however strenuous the hope, involve him in positive dealing with their heathen wills and hearts, while hitherto they had only been "rods" of his retributive anger?

It is right in this way to read the mental situation of the great Isaiah of chapters 40–55, whose invigorating poetry breathes both dimensions – a prospect of salvation and a sense of the wide world, of nations at large of whom, beyond Hebraic covenant, Yahweh must be no less cognizant. The intensification of special identity, as exile prompted it, began to reckon broadly with the great human dispersion.

"Comfort ye, comfort ye, my people", opens out into "Listen, O isles, to me." The prophet, formed from the womb (echoing Jeremiah's sense of meaning-in-life), learns that:

> It is a light thing you should be My servant to raise up the tribes of Jacob and to restore the preserved of Israel, I will also give you as a light to the nations that you may be My salvation to the ends of the earth.[25]

"Isles" seem to have fascinated this preacher. There were none in his native Judea/Israel. They represented the utmost of things and peoples far away.

To be sure, an ambiguity hovers around his celebration of this world-wide-ness. Was it that "salvation afar" would be no more than universal acknowledgement of the recovered destiny of Yahweh's own?[26] Such a climax deserved inclusive salutation, if only that the singular people's restoration might picture alien "kings for their nursing fathers" whose it would be to "lick up the dust" of holy feet (49: 23).

These vivid hopes of a glorious future for Judah and Jerusalem, somehow calling "all to the waters freely to drink", will need the compassion of some "Gentile" ruler, some "Cyrus" with Yahweh's "anointing" to that end (45: 1). Yet its ultimate secret will be the living faith "kept at cost" under adversity. That "cost" of unyielding trust in Yahweh alone ensures that tragedy is outlasted by fidelity. Only the trust that does not capitulate to wrong and evil lives towards salvation. It is in that sense that "only what is borne is borne away", only what holds out in pain holds on in hope. We are only lost to hope when we decide that we are. The faith that abides faithful is the clue to a future's salvation but such faith accepts to suffer.

Was it not by a logic of this order that "the suffering servant" theme of these Isaian chapters came to birth? That mysterious figure might be the whole nation, but only under that aura. More likely, it could be those within the nation representative of the whole but only in minority sharing of that vision. Or, more likely still, "the servant" would be the quintessential "prophet", seeing that fidelity under duress, and private bearing of a people's sins, had long come to light as the ultimate dimension of prophethood – of prophethood that finally fulfils itself, not in words and utterance, but in personality and life.

The literature of scholarship and controversy about the identity of the Isaian "servant" is long and inconclusive.[27] Mystery attends the meaning and contention becomes unseemly. But, given the "lamb" imagery of Jeremiah and the whole logic of his career and his "Confessions", it is fair to conclude that "the servant" takes us to the full measure of "the weight in the word". What in New Testament study has been variously called "the Messianic secret", would seem to have earlier disclosed itself, via Jeremiah, in the perceptions of this anonymous "Isaiah".

Could it be that more than the Jeremiah paradigm is involved and that this "Isaiah" is himself, in Babylon at least, a potential source of the "servant Songs". There are pointers strongly to this possibility. His superb literary style – unsurpassed throughout Biblical Hebrew and sustained through great adversity[28] – is evidence enough of a powerfully poetic mind. His strophes draw him in sympathy toward Cyrus of Persia, whereas he is ardently defiant of the Babylon he inhabited. This may have made him suspect as potentially seditious in the very fervour of his Jewish hopes. There is perhaps a hint of this in the one "Servant Song" where he abandons third person language ("He was despised...") and assumes the "I" word in:

> The Lord God gave me the tongue of one who has learned that I might know how to speak to the weary a word in season... He wakens my ear to hear...
> (50: 4)

The immediate sequel (vv. 5–9) makes clear that, in his own person, he underwent scorn and persecution.[29] Is he then the "Servant" speaking?

Either way, what emerges, as ever in prophethood, is the pain that belongs with the word.

It may even be that the vulnerable situation in which "Isaiah of Babylon" found himself explains his otherwise strange anonymity. For if his deliverances among the exiles excited official suspicion his hearers, in their very acceptance of his "comfort", would need to have been his "cover" of protection. Be that as it may, we can realize how the inner burden of his own prophethood became a clue to his theological perception of the long-suffering of Yahweh. Nowhere is this more clear than in the Lord's "dialogue" with His people where "You made Me a burden-bearer" takes us to the heart of divine compassion (43: 24b). Lordship thus vulnerable to human sin was at the heart of the Isaian perception and the supreme lesson of his own vocation.

## V

Prophethood moves into a lower key with Haggai, Zechariah and Malachi. They are lesser folk than the great Isaiah of the exile. Outwardly, it might be thought that their situation is a happier one. They are back in Jerusalem with returnees from captivity and occupied with the restoration of the Temple rites. They have, perhaps, one thing in common with "Isaiah" namely a liturgical bent, but theirs is a sober, even pedestrian, hymnology suited to their ecclesiastical mind. The stirring universalism glimpsed in the exile gives way to a prosaic pursuit of exclusive identity, vested in renewed ritual and repossession of territory. "Light given to the ends of the earth" passes into aliens needing to come among Jews and "take hold of their garments' hem" (Zechariah 8: 23) The master-wall builder, Nehemiah later busied himself constructing the defences of Jerusalem and hardening those of Jewish identity by repudiation of mixed marriage and the rejection of all things non-Jewish. Prophethood is again reading the divine will among the constraints of political ambition. There is an air of defeatism around the community, oppressed by slow and unpropitious progress. Haggai can only encourage Zerubbabel, "God's signet and servant", who seems a potential "Messiah", but is destined to disappear from history, leaving no trace. In "a day of small things", calls to zeal and discipline and purity of heart are all that these messengers can contribute, poised as they are between fear and hope.

The intensification of racial privacy and the emergence of Messianic "agency" concepts in would-be political terms tend to romanticize Jerusalem's future (Zech. 2: 1–5). There is a symbolic coronation (Zech.

6: 9–15) – perhaps even an actual one, but only vainly asserting the lavish predictions with which the Book of Haggai closes (2: 20–23). Intimations of dire things impending are turned (e.g. by Joel 3: 9–25 and Zech. 14: 1–19) into the deep irony of roles reversed, the mighty subjugators made to come as captive suppliants at the mercy of Jerusalem.

The undated Book of Malachi – perhaps contemporary with Nehemiah a century later than Haggai – repeats the rebuke of alien peoples but summons "the priests of Yahweh" to cleansing and a righteous ritual. Yet for all its concern with covenant status, it breathes the magnificent universalism of 1: 11 with "the Name of the Lord of hosts" "great among the nations" and the theme among them of "a pure offering". But the immediate hopes are religio-political whereby "the wicked will be trodden down" (Malachi 4: 3) with Zechariah's famous "scroll" searching out all thieves and liars (5: 1–4). The short Book of Obadiah, in this late hour of Hebrew prophethood, has two old-style oracles against Edom, the traditional enemy.

If one were looking for a Quranic parallel, one might broadly find it in the realization all "messengers" undergo concerning the evil hardness of the obdurate world, the negative capacity of human history in frustrating godly hopes. That which in Mecca prompted the policy of Hijrah in quest of power turns these last prophets of the Biblical Canon to Zerubbabel and Joshua, the High Priest, in intensified covenantal self-scrutiny and amendment that might give substance to the religio-political dream. It leads Malachi to adopt a sort of people-dialogue concerning Yahweh's ways – how have they "robbed Him?" "In what have they erred?" "What good comes of godliness?" and – through them all – "does Yahweh love His people?" Islam too, though differently, was in such self-interrogation about immediate history in the last pre-Hijrah years.

Analogies have to be cautious. Yet, with or without the comfort/problem of Hebraic covenant, all prophetic "word-weighing" wrestles with the viability of hope in a stubborn world and, thus, with the mystery of its own mission. The last yearnings at the Canon's closure in Malachi 4: 4–6 are for an Elijah redivivus, by whom "fathers and sons" might be reconciled and the ultimate "curse" lifted. Hebrew prophethood gave way to apocalyptic – as in the second part of what is now Zechariah (chaps 9–14) or it sought comfort in the sober realism of the Wisdom writers or submitted to the melancholy muse of Qoheleth, the Preacher in Ecclesiastes.

## VI

That final clue in Malachi 4: 5–6 concerning what is at stake between the generations, "fathers and sons", shows Hebrew prophethood at its closure still peoccupied with its ethnic anxiety, its self-awareness as being Yahweh's "one and only people". That core of the Jewish psyche was, and is, the dominant "situation" in which all else is located. The prophets never attained to a sense of single humanity duly shared by all peoples – a humanity surmounting the tribalism that made "Edoms" and "Gentiles" of other territories and other folk. We have to wait for the John of the Book of the Revelation to find "standing before the throne peoples, tribes, languages and nations" from the whole width of the earth.

Nevertheless, that ultimate inclusiveness needed first the private world Jewry believed it had with Yahweh. The intensity of that perceived identity was the womb of the new thing and Christian inclusion its progeny. Zechariah 14: 9 and Malachi 1: 11, as it were, reported it afar off in their dream of his Name one" and "a pure offering among the nations to the greatness of Yahweh's Name". Could peoplehood under God have been universalized if it had never known and told itself in the first terms of "the seed of Jacob"?

It follows, however, that there is one further question to ask about the situation of Hebrew prophethood. Was it truly the territory of final monotheism? If the One God is mysteriously understood as distinctively the patron of a single people, are they not rather monolatrous and not monotheist? Monolatry is the exclusive acknowledgement of a particular worship without disavowing other deities feasibly concerned with other peoples. Hebraic Yahwism (or Elohism) had not begun with any such disavowal. Indeed, something of its "holy war" ideology passionately presupposed the reality of other deities – patrons of alien peoples.[30] When the prophets came to comprehend the all-inclusiveness of Yahweh's sovereignty they still retained the special patronage He had for their unchanged "elected" identity. Thus it could be said that they continued to be monolatrous in their sense of inalienable specialness, while becoming splendidly monotheist in their recognition of One "whom the heaven of heavens could not contain". Theirs remained a fervent emotional faith in a singularity of divine covenant while becoming a resounding confession of all-embracing Lordship.

We do not need to conclude that this strange disparity suggests the ultimate failure of Hebrew prophethood. The reason why we do not has, again, to do with situation. That cherished unilateral possession of

Yahweh, reciprocal to being Yahweh-possessed, belonged with geography and history. As small territories situated in the war-path of great empires, Israel/Judah had massive reason to read their environment as one of menace and jeopardy. Located between the famous rivers of their "middle region", they were the battleground pawns of the powers of the Nile, of Tigris and Euphrates and of lesser enemies, Scythians and Medes. Manhandled by the Sennacheribs and the Tiglath-Pilesers of their world, they had ample reason to intensify their will for celestial patronage and to make absolute the reciprocal bond they had with Yahweh. Hence, in psyche and cult alike, their passionate devotion to worship and to identity as one equation.

Was it not in this sense that land-possession, Temple worship, exile and return, with the long defining retrospect to Exodus and entry, became the mental situation making prophethood the thing it was? The contrast with the situation inside the Qur'an was complete. The rivers of the Islamic Scripture are the streams through the gardens of Paradise. No Nile, no Tigris flowed imaginatively through the fears of the Quraish. Arabia, as its own language loves to say, is "an island", of the Arabs to be sure but not Arabs in dire emergency in the face of mighty alien empires. Their menaces came from within their own feuding tribalism, their ideals of manly revenge, of *muru'ah* and kinship pride. What bearing power in Ethiopia or in Najran might have on the peoples of the Hijaz bore no resemblance to the mortal perils Assyria and Babylon meant for Jewry in Jerusalem. To the north-west and north-east the peninsula of Arabia was buffered against Byzantium and the Persians, whose sovereignties held little conscious threat for the Quraish.

A certain Arab ethnicism is present in the Qur'an if only from the Arab identity of the final Prophet.[31] Arabness has the honour of sponsoring the ultimate monotheism but ethnicity is not its crux. Arab particularity in Muhammad is understood as "a mercy to the worlds". Whatever their migrations into or within their peninsula the Hijazis of Muhammad's day cherished no God-sponsored retrospect to a defining Exodus and have had no pilgrimage with a Sinai en route.

Yet, intriguingly, there is something akin in the issue that divides monolatry from monotheism. The former, among some tribes, or by familiar wells and oases, may well have been the case. There are gods and goddesses mentioned in the Qur'an – the famous three, Allat, Manat and Al-'Uzza in 53.19–23, Sirius as a star worship in 53.49, sun-worship in 41.37 and (in Sheba) 27.24. Worship of Allah could well have been conceded to Muhammad by the Quraish (monolatrously by him and his followers) provided that their own worships were neither maligned nor denied. The historian Al-Tabari tells of a meeting among the Quraish in the house of Abu Talib, Muhammad's uncle, when they said: "If he will stop insulting our gods, we will leave him with his god." Abu Talib reported this to Muhammad and counselled him:

> Son of my brother, this delegation is the most representative of the tribe to which you belong. They are only asking for justice by demanding that you stop insulting their gods and in exchange they will you to worship yours in peace.[32]

But Muhammad was not sent, as he believed, to affirm the mere existence of his "Allah": his mission was about Allah's *sole* existence. In reply to the Quraishi readiness for compromise, he told them they must say just one sentence. It would make possible the subjugation of all the Arabs and ensure their mastery elsewhere. They asked to know what the sentence was. He gave them *La ilaha illa-Allah*, i.e. the *Shahadah*, "There is no deity except Allah." This they would not accept.

It is noteworthy how, according to Al-Tabari, Muhammad linked this uncompromising confession of divine unity with the unification of the tribes. "As in heaven so on earth." Unify your worship and you end potentially competing patronage of human division. Arab tribalism was chronic enough in its disruption of human community but monolatry there, or plural worship, had nothing of the sanction that history and geography had uniquely bestowed on the religious experience of the Hebrews and their prophets. Yahweh and their situation were for them one experience. Conjoining "God *and* His people" was the story of their shared history, with the prophets its interpreters and thereby His mentors.

But beyond such social gains from a monotheistic faith, why need it matter now – for us moderns –that Muhammad repudiated all idolatry? Are we not all too sophisticated to worry about such themes? cynicism asks. Since Nietzsche, all theology has been a thing for museums. Whether "one God or many" seems an outmoded issue in a secular age. Can it still be significant that Muhammad refused all compromise with the Quraish? They might even have emerged from that conclave in Mecca as advocates of passive co-existence and optional believing.[33]

Hardly, for idolatry is by no means a museum relic. We may no longer manufacture what we worship, as stone-masons, goldsmiths and carpenters once did. Nor can we ridicule these in the simplistic fashion of Isaiah, or Muhammad or the psalmist, that is, by poking genial fun. Our modern idolatries are more subtle, more malign, more inwardly corrupting – the *idolas* as Francis Bacon called them[34] – of the market-place, the counting-house of private or public mind. These are far less readily identified as monstrous than the physical emblems of pagan cults, far less easily destroyed. For they exercise a tyranny that disguises itself as an empire or a liberty. Their subtlety takes captive the human spirit. Their authority defies dispute unless we are resolutely set for the only authentic worship that hallows all our situations in a due and ordered universe of meaning.

If that conviction dispels all sentiment concerning the present irrelevance of the prophethoods we have reviewed, in their personal, rhetorical and situational quality, there are many other questions about their finality. How we measure the continuity of their significance, both Biblical and Quranic, in the light of the closure of their story and their texts, must await CHAPTER IX. Meanwhile there are the themes of conscience and suffering and of how all belongs in the nature of God, the one Sender, to make the "weighing of the word" complete.

# VI

# Prophethood and Conscience

## I

"The law and the prophets" are frequently paired in the Bible. For their partnership is fundamental to the entire history.[1] Prophets are persuaders to the law's observance, recallers to the law's authority, mentors of the law's fortunes in the flux of Israel's history. Moses, "the man of God" at Sinai, is their great progenitor. Their writ runs in the path of his, though – as we discover in the temper of Amos or Ezekiel – the ultimate quality of prophethood is far removed from the thunder of Sinai, while the obscenity of "the golden calf" gives way to more subtle miscarriages by later Aarons.

It would seem that the Islamic counterpart of "the law and the prophets" would need to read: "The Prophet and the Shari'ah." For law in Islam stems from the text and exegesis of the Qur'an of which Muhammad was the sole recipient. Though carrying a similar divine Imprimatur, the Shari'ah did not come in tablets of stone, carried down from volcanic heights to a people in wilderness transit to covenantal destiny. It came in sequel to a steady creation of an empowered *Ummah* via Hijrah from pagan adversity. The one common factor was the intention for a people's future.

Muhammad's centrality in the earth-coming – if we may so speak – of the Shari'ah belongs not only with his unique role in the *Tanzil*, or "handing down" of the Qur'an, but also with the *Hadith*, or Tradition, which sought to re-possess and perpetuate the example of his personality and his *Sirah*, or prophetic career, as a further clue to the divine mind for the behaviour and ideals of the community that resulted from his mission. That *Ummah*, in turn, through its due consensus, reached by the *Ijtihad*, or legal enterprise of its qualified *ulama*, would enlarge and adjust resulting law, always in ways considered congenial to the prior sources in

Qur'an and Tradition.[2] The long story of Islam's jurisprudence is duly comprised in "The Prophet and the Law".

This inverse order of the Hebraic and the Islamic is the clue to many duties of the combined study we have in hand. One common theme which it proposes for us is that of conscience. For, in either case, law – divinely given and grounded in sacred source – would seem to obviate any necessity for conscience or even arraign it as unwarranted individualism pretending to possess a better wisdom than divine writ. Who are private believers to prefer their own inner counsels to divine truth? Would it not be well for them to heed the psalmist's prayer: "Keep thy servant also from presumptuous sins"? not the least of these being the notion that one had a better ethic than Qur'an or Bible could teach and underwrite.

Yet in the psalmist's own context there is another prayer: "May the ... meditations of my heart be acceptable in thy sight". So presumably he is right to have them? Yet, this second prayer may still be in the idiom of the first, as a plea to be duly submissive in "what the breasts conceal".[3] Here we have the whole question about living *under* God and yet also living *in* a self. For the strange truth is that the greatest Biblical prophets found themselves, in the name of what can only be known as private conscience (albeit divinely inspired), remonstrating with the very institutions of law itself. "Law and the prophets" proves, with an Isaiah or a Jeremiah, to be a very uneasy formula. Biblical messengers have much more to do than echo Sinai. They must become accusers of the very status it enjoys among a treacherous people. If "the fear of the Lord is the beginning of wisdom", the continuing of wisdom is to interrogate the fear of the Lord.[4] Is it guilty, bigoted, bland, slumberous, proud or devious? "Law and Prophets", "Prophet and Shari'ah", are only sufficient in the divine economy if "conscience through prophethood" is inherent in their meaning.

# II

It is noteworthy that law, not least ritual law, often exonerates rather than indicts. In the ancient story of David and Bathsheba and his murder of Uriah nothing roused his conscience until the appearance of Nathan the prophet (2 Samuel 12). No doubt he assumed some Israeli version of royal prerogative. Sacredly sealed kings could be above the moral law. The story of Nathan may be read as an early augury of the prophetic role in far more complex and subtle arenas of monarchy under God. Biblical prophethood in its finest hours must be seen as the authority of conscience in the corridors of religion.

It has often been remarked that there is little doctrine of conscience in Judaism and Islam. There is no classical Hebrew word for the concept and the Arabic term *al-Damir* does not occur in the Qur'an. Reasons are not far to seek. One is that the moral connotation of "conscience" often blends into "consciousness" in a more general sense, where what is radically ethical readily elides in each and every culture. Another factor is more incisive, namely that "sacred law" pre-empts or deters the exercise of conscience and so tends to its dormancy. Ruled by inclusive and authoritarian law given in revelation, any countering impulse can seem at best a false liberty, at worst implicit blasphemy.

Doubtless the sway of the sacred *may* coincide with what, in other settings, conscience would both approve and demand. David, with King Saul in his power in the cave, and with much accrued reason for revenge, nevertheless refrains from violent act, the point being that Saul is "the Lord's anointed" and so properly inviolate (1 Samuel 24). Such happy aligning of the duly ethical with the strongly sacral may well transpire and no prophetic conscience is required. But the sacral, defiling and distorting the ethical, is all too often the liability in religion.

In that realm due obedience to God's law must be brought. The divine thing must be heeded without debate as to how validly divine it was which some internal exercise of private conscience might want to ask. In the face of Sinai or Shari'ah, much courage there needs to be before believers arrive at thinking that conscience is, or could be, "the voice of God". In extreme terms it might be judged a deification of mere man. Or, conversely, can, or should, any believing theist see, in obedience to God, a sacrifice of personal conscience? If so, should the sacrifice be made, with what protest, or refused, with what result? "A poor man thou shalt not favour in his cause", says Exodus 23: 3. Initiatives of human compassion are not to enter into the loyal implementation of Torah. Ritual purity on the Jericho road may preclude due rescue of the stricken wayfarer.

Civil law in the secular world is familiar enough with issues of equity in which the rigours of statute law and judicial process have to be queried or waived in the interests of a more loving justice. In these familiar ways it is clear that law ought to be eminently revisable in loyalty to its own moral significance – a significance of which it is guardian and servant. Yet where law, as in Torah and Shari'ah, draws its entire content and its proper sanction from revelation of divine will, its responsiveness – even its responsibility – to such ethical accounting is halted or hobbled, by what is held sacrosanct.

The issue has been evident enough to secular thinking. It is indeed a prime factor in the secularizing of modern society, eager for a de-theologizing of the human scene. A deep irony is at once evident. To recognize that systems of operative law and the ethical norms of a society have to be subject to judgement higher than their own is to return them to religion. For acknowledging such criteria is precisely what being religious means, namely the will to enthrone the right absolute.

That will itself, however, has to be right by an ever critical quality in both its convictions and its submission. Thus religion, like law, in its order as structure, code and culture, has to be always in the care of conscience and of conscience in perpetual repair. It was the great prophets from Amos to Malachi who filled this role in the Biblical tradition. For they had their prophethoods within a long established theism, possessed of a divine Torah and sanctioned by ethnic covenant in territorial pledge, menaced by the flux of marauding empires.

The incidence of Islam in history was in sharp contrast. Muhammad's prophethood transpired, having no such retrospect but inaugurating in itself the theism it served. We must, therefore, look differently for the role of conscience in its Islamic incidence, aware of the contrasted *mise-en-scène* from that of "the goodly fellowship" of the 8th to the 6th Biblical centuries. Its role was evident in the vocation of the Prophet himself and emerged beyond the closure of the Qur'an in the struggles all religions have with the thrust of their own momentum. Of these Islam had its own peculiar version, given what conditioned its origins in Mecca and attended its massive expansion and its encounter with cultures of whose criteria of faith and society it has been scarcely aware in its own *manzil al-wahy*.[5] Moreover, the insistent nature of its demand for "submission", turning on the temper of its anathemas in face of idolatry, left no room for the exercise of private instincts.

In this context of prophethood as conscience there is a factor distinguishing the Qur'an from the Biblical scene, namely that the Hebraic role of priesthood was a dimension entirely absent from the ethos of Islam.[6] The frequent Biblical tension between the priest and the prophet is unknown to the Qur'an. It was a tension arising from the ethical, urgently set against the sacral when the sacral, as we have noted, conspired against the ethical, or when ritual claims superseded or ignored moral demands. Examples belong with the themes of CHAPTER V. So sharp did the issues loom that prophets had passionately to rebuke "vain oblations" and even questioned the divine warrant for the whole Levitical and sacrificial system. Priesthood retaliated in more vigorous assertion of holy legitimacy in all its works and ways.

Conscience in Islam did not have this lively controversy with the sacral patterns of its own vintage. For these were of its own adoption within its own prophetic milieu.[7] Whereas Biblical prophethood emerged long after the Mosaic and monarchic establishing of a covenantal people and so had a long retrospect of the givens of religion, the singular prophethood of the Qur'an coincided with the coming-to-be of its own defining forms of ritual. Thus its conscience could be – for the most part – absolved from a religious introspection of its own, its moral energies being occupied with the accusing of paganism.

Nevertheless, there were issues of conscience arising from its own assurance. One notable example is in Surah 80, entitled "He Frowned", where the opening concerns a rebuke to Muhammad having to do with a "frowning" reception he gave to a blind enquirer whom he should have welcomed as warmly as any attractive and able-bodied recruit. Believers were also required to examine their conscience when a *fitnah*, or "test of will", came where the very love of wives and children suggested reluctance for the dangers of necessary combat in the cause of Islam.

Moreover, if Islam lacked all priesthood with its liability to ritual alibis when ethics intervened, its characteristic emphasis on law played something of the same role. For law was "its earliest activity and most highly developed expression rather than . . . theology".[8] And legality can be as fruitful of casuistry and evasion of the good as can the claims of things sacrosanct. Law also finds the sacrosanct – or should we say the prescribed – congenial.

# III

The Hebrew prophets, to be sure, had their external anathemas – witness the sundry "burdens" of Amos, Isaiah and Nahum, and the rest. These "heathen" may have had something of the place of a Biblical "Quraish", though in the idiom of imperial threat, not that of urban enmity. Yet there is no mistaking the priority of domestic accusation. Amos, for example, only chastened Edom and Damascus in order the more pointedly to turn the tables on Israel. In any event, the rebuking of the nations belonged with their being "the rod of Yahweh's anger" against His covenant people,[9] making it plain that their recruitment as such meant no exoneration of their crimes.

Thus the external chargings against the nations only served to intensify the arraignment of the prophets' own society. Their story must be seen as a sustained explosion of individual conscience against collective community. We have seen in CHAPTER III, in the several "call" narratives and in the private courage – and tragic isolation – of the spokesmen, how deeply personal their vocation and their ministry. Disciples, to be sure, they may have had, to preserve their words and "bind up the testimony" for the future. Else, otherwise, we would have no ken of them. But the words, and the onus, were theirs alone. Religious literature has no more concentrated register of the gift and practice of personal conscience than here in the Hebrew prophets.

Its intensity is the more proven by the fact that it tells against the most entrenched public "values" and assured "inviolables". It is even ready to disavow Sinai, to disown the whole mythopoeic story of Joshua's "priests" with their feet in Jordan, to return an enlanded people to the wilderness as their true being, to see the mysterious *Shechinah* leaving holy city and holy land, to assure the exiles in Babylon that their "good" is there – and Yahweh too. They can interpret captivity as vocation and discover authenticity the more from the forfeiture of land and ephod and shrine. "The one people", by prophetic vision, can be "no more the people", as long as they "forsake the Lord" inwardly in their hearts. The unfailing covenant – paradox though it be – is no sure perquisite.

The preceding chapters on personality, language and situation have sufficiently documented the central quality of passionate conscience, sobering, chastising, retrieving and disciplining a wayward Israel and Judah through more than two crowded centuries. They were centuries lived under sustained threat of foreign domination, laden with perennial fears, and fraught with domestic anxieties needing to be steadied by stout-hearted patriotism. Instead, the prophets, out of their perceptions of conscience, read the future as belonging only to repentance and submission. Thus they came to be seen as traitors or apostates and were afflicted accordingly. When in their final generation in Ezekiel, they were called to face and interpret the ultimate negation that – by other lights – the Babylonian captivity spelled, their heartening appeal, we might say, was to the conscience of Yahweh Himself, responsive to a people's "refining in the furnace". Throughout, prophetic conscience had been a human replica of the Lord from whom it came. It had been, we might say, the inter-association in Hebraic terms between the Muslim *Shahadah*'s own unison of God as One and of a prophethood conjoined.

There may be those who say that, since defeat and exile happened, both in Samaria and Jerusalem and since rehabilitation on return proved so precarious and short-lived, the whole saga of prophetic conscience was no more than a noble gesture. To suspect so would only be part of a larger issue, namely whether conscience, leading to penitence, can ever be the concern of the state and the political order. So much we might conclude from the necessity in Israelite and Judaic monarchy to deplore and decry, and finally to anathematize, the likes of Amos and Jeremiah. Centuries later, Machiavelli was realist enough to understand that "princes", while they do well to have mentors and "mirror-holders", these – in the end – can only sustain and not subvert the power-order. *Raisons d'état* must always override *les scrupules de conscience*.

If he, rather than the Isaiahs of the Hebrew world, has the realism, then something like prophetic (i.e. a critical, personal) conscience must be looked for in Islam in the individual Muslim, guided by the submission he brings to the reading of the Qur'an and the Tradition and the mind of the community. Muhammad's own prophethood being final and uniquely his alone, Islam does not offer the "fellowship of prophets" with the "conscience-panorama" we have just studied. The criteria of the role of conscience for Muslims will have to be drawn from the sources the Islamic norms afford.

We have noted elsewhere the absence from the Qur'an's perspective of those prophets of the Hebraic mould. It was to their sense of conscience and its cost that so much is owed. Moreover the extra-Biblical prophets present in the Qur'an are largely assimilated to the Qur'an's own situations of contra-pagan witness. They are not confronting Yahwism, a self-compromising theism against which conscience has more exacting, more subtle, dealings. Even so, Salih, Shu'aib and Hud exemplify qualities of conscientious tenacity in face of the hazards all prophethood risks. Stonings and conspiracies of intimidation are their constant menace. The narratives, however, do not comprise the sort of sustained, explicit and highly articulate conscience found in the deliverances of an Isaiah. Nor are their sufferings related to God in a way comparable to the anguish of a Jeremiah. They are more elusive as prophetic personalities in the knowledge we are allowed of them.

Accordingly, the conscience Quranic prophethood educates must be traced in certain salient themes of the Qur'an itself as these bear on the personal liability of Muslims. Of immediate significance is the sharp individualism of the believer's standing. The emphasis falls on personal liability in that God calls none to account except for their own deeds. In respect of responsibility and guilt "none are made to carry what is not their own".[10] It follows that a sense of vicarious involvement in collective wrong – one of the basic features of Hebraic prophetic warning – is often precluded. It is true that this factor works both ways. Ezekiel had to warn his hearers that exoneration could not be claimed by association with famously righteous communal figures. He insisted in a quite Quranic way on individual reckoning.

Though Noah, Daniel and Job be in (the city) they shall deliver only their own souls by their righteousness.[11]

The aura of such prototypes could not avail for lesser folk pleading their fame. It could only serve the more sharply to incriminate defaulters idly invoking it.

Whether for merit falsely thought accruing, or for guilts somehow escaped, alibis in ethics are firmly denied in the Qur'an. The private self of each and all is the separate sphere of decision on Judgement Day, the assize for what "their own souls have forwarded" to it through mortal time, the very limbs of each self corroborating the ledgered account when "the books are opened".

This rigorous Quranic individualism in respect of evil and the ethical order leaves at issue the collective or communal aspects. On the one hand, a strong personalism in the things of conscience may sharpen individual reckoning with what corporate society transacts. On the other, it may have the contrary effect in confining what the individual is liable for and exempting the body politic from feasible private protest. This is the more likely when the political realm has been constituted precisely to embody the moral mind of the religion.

There are instances of both features in the Qur'an and the Tradition, perpetuating Muhammad's prophethood in the alerting and transacting of Islamic conscience. One immediate example is the abhorrence of infanticide that finds voice in Surah 81.8–9, when, in the great reckoning, "the infant (fem.) buried alive is asked for what sin she was slain". Here, surely, a personal indignation takes form in public protest. A religious conscience indicts social wrong.

In Surah 93 the personal experience of Muhammad at the early onset of his Qur'an-experience yields the moral logic of social concern.

> Did He not find you an orphan and gave you shelter?
> Did He not find you lost on your way and guided you?
> Did He not find you destitute and enrich you?
> So then, do no wrong to the orphan,
> The suppliant do not turn away
> And make the grace of your Lord your constant theme.

The Qur'an's steady insistence on our human custodian-status in the nature-dominion its frequent doxologies celebrate means that consciousness itself, moving in the realm of the senses, has to be moral conscience concerning wealth as duty and wonder as worship. What is ethical comes into its own through what, in the active sense, is theological, namely being God-aware in every human context. The practice of the good is made to turn on the habit of reverence.

The institution of Zakat, stemming from Muhammad's prophethood, embodies the same theology of society. It enjoins the regular payment of alms whereby the wealth of some is related to the poverty of others within the *Ummah* of Islam. The right to say, and think, "mine" about private property is conceded but on condition that it incurs a social claim upon its ownership – a claim which must be acknowledged and discharged as a religious duty. In that sense, private conscience is taken over, via a public institution of society, so that – while remaining a personal deed – it becomes also a collective law.

Here, it might be said, we find exemplified the genius of Islam and the achievement of the Prophet in this realm of conscience. Together these created an orbit, a regimen, in which ethical responsibility, vested indeed in private selves, was nevertheless discharged in a framework of institutionalized order and practice. Latent, then, was the issue whether, and how, private conscience should, or could, ever decide and act counter to that prescribing institution.

A stark instance of the issue might be symbolized in the laws of the Qur'an concerning "the spoils of war". As the title: *Al-Anfal*, of Surah 8, martial booty becomes a considerable theme of prophethood after the Hijrah. There are careful provisions about its distribution. These require discipline and system in allottings and claims, obviating unseemly strife and cupidity. The Quranic equivalent of "spoiling the Egyptians" is thus far morally regulated.

But what if a private conscience were to call in question such seizure and/or the campaigns that made occasion for it? In effect, the option would not exist. For the legitimacy of the collective "cause" of Islam excluded or over-ruled it. It would be no more in the purview of a private Muslim to be a pacifist than it was for Arjuna, in the opening of the Bhagavad Gita, to opt out of the "fate" of being a combatant. A conscience that thought to contradict the logic of the collective will could enjoy no such freedom. Indeed, even the impulse would need to be known for an "apostasy" if pursued or to be suspect as a hidden *nifaq*, "hypocrisy". The collective had the right to exclude it from feasible thought. Even so, outside its esteem of its own warrant concerning "fighting in the way of God", the Qur'an has a lively conscience about the lust of warring *badu* for ill-gotten booty. There are few occasions of indignation in the Qur'an more moving than its lament over the "despoilings" of tribal raidings.

By the snorting war-horses that strike fire with their hoofs as they storm forward at dawn, a single host in the midst of their dust-cloud. Man is indeed ungrateful to his Lord. He himself is the surest witness to that fact. He is violent in his passion for wealth. Is he not aware that their Lord knows them through and through on that Day when the tombs yield up their dead and all men's hidden thoughts are open knowledge?[12]

Quite evidently, Muhammad's prophethood registered a profound distress at this dire aspect of his environment and that, precisely for this reason, conscience approved – indeed demanded – the kind of solution that warfare against the Quraish intended. Why be satisfied with precarious "months of truce" if an over-all pacification could be had by well contrived belligerence? Private conscience going along with that, might feel itself innocent. But what if not? What if the precedent of assumed innocence in a collective wisdom should extend to everything such pragmatism might implement? Ought not conscience to be always alert to the possibilities for its own subversion by the blandishments of power?

# IV

What is at stake here is gathered into one of the Qur'an's most comprehensive concepts, namely that of *zulm*, and, more especially, *zulm al-nafs*. The term, with cognate verb and participles, has to do with conscience more squarely than any other in the Qur'an. It denotes "essential wrong", any manner of violation whereby "right", "what is due", the "true and good" are flouted, ignored or denied. It takes foul and ugly shape in political tyranny, commercial extortion, moral turpitude and personal ill-will and deed. The idea of "self-wronging", doing despite to one's own human meaning, means an inner betrayal of what conscience should be as the mentor of the total self, self-liable and self-aware.

Muhammad Kamil Husain, in a perceptive study of *zulm*, identified the claim of the collective, Islamic or other, as the field where personal conscience had most need to be on guard against special pleading or expedient case-making which if heeded, would pervert the mind. He read Quranic, and all other, conscience as requiring a steady vigilance to detect and reject all counsels of collective expedience. He saw that humans will do in the name of "community" what they would scarcely do in their private souls, or what their private selves would approve only when subverted by public clamour and institutional claim.[13]

*Zulm al-nafs*, as a central theme in the Qur'an, at least means that the self has, and must exercise, an individual liability which it violates if it surrenders it into other hands, however sacrosanct or authoritarian these may be. Such is human conscience – the inalienable dignity and elemental truth of human being. In this sense, we are all existentialists, personal self-accounting being ineluctable. As we have noted, "the last Day" in the Qur'an stands by this quality inherent in our mortality.

Doubtless, others in Islam would want to demur at Kamil Husain's measure of what *zulm al-nafs* implies. They might plead that the Qur'an would have us rather see the Islamic faith-system as ideally structured for our human nature so that conformity to right need be no existential crisis or unremitting labour of conscience. Instead, it becomes a submission to norms and laws over which we have no need to agonize because they are divinely given both in code and in rite for our due and placid habituation.

So much might be concluded from the *fitrah* on which God shaped our human nature as suited to, and devised for, Islam, with Islam, in turn, as apt for our identity, in body and soul.[14] Much in the religious psyche of Muslims might be claimed for that view. Muhammad's prophethood inaugurated the religious and the human in mutually congenial definition. The very struggle in its origins and the vicissitudes in its sequel might be read as calling that confidence into question. Yet, for many Muslims, a consenting rather than a distracted conscience marks the relation of the self to the *Ummah*, the private to the collective.

Perhaps the alternative is put too simply. It might be tested by the familiar division in Islamic ethics of five categories – the absolutely enjoined the omission of which is guilty; the desirable yet not absolutely prescribed; the neutral area; the reprehensible but not categorically forbidden; and the prohibited absolutely, the performance of which is damnable. The first and last here in measure do the work of conscience for it, while the second and fourth plainly engage a well-tutored conscience. The third would seem to be the free zone of conscience. The *hudud*, the "boundaries" we may not "cross", are "givens" for the faithful, for the most part, in all but the central area of the "issue-less".

Yet, salutary as the categories are for moral awareness, there are still open questions around what modern writers call "conscientization", or alerting to how far we have been "conditioned" by the plausibility context or the "colonizing" of the mind by sundry "imperialisms", political or doctrinaire. Seen this way, will any realm be "neutral"? There must remain throughout some sense in which the self is the arbiter of its own trust.

That it must be so springs not only from the theme of *zulm al-nafs*. It is implicit in another basic emphasis in Muhammad's prophethood, namely *ikhlas*, or "sincerity". Surah 112 links this ethical vocation squarely with the doctrine of divine unity. Repeatedly the Qur'an calls its people to be *mukhlisun lahu al-din*, "sincere before God in religion". Such "sincerity" demands an inward mentor. Without alert conscience, privately vigilant as well as publicly addressed, it would remain impossible. *Ikhlas* has to do with subtle factors that elude bare legislation. It needs to take guard against what authority itself may enjoin.

For a right allegiance may be wrongly motivated – right, that is, in its obeying but wrong in its intentions. The Qur'an itself detects a possible quality of "bad faith" or, at least, "insincere faith" in some occasions of *islam* itself.[15] This is the more likely to happen when what is personally incurred has been institutionally enjoined.

## V

It is clear that, however real the will to integrity, private conscience is always a relative tribunal. There is much mystery about moral choice and intention, if we recognize that the personal self, the ego, is for ever liable to self-deception, fantasy and inner-strife. With this in view, Islam has stressed the critical role of *niyyah*, or "intention", in all ritual acts under "the Five pillars of Religion". One must with inward deliberation "intend" the *Salat*, the fast, the alms-payment. One could hardly set out on pilgrimage unwittingly. This emphasis has very broad implications for the role of moral conscience inside performative consciousness of identity fulfilment. *Niyyah* can thus be extended to every area of ethical activity, social, sexual, commercial or political, and "intention" necessarily presupposes a circumspect awareness of issues latent in every situation. It can also offset the subtle trends whereby contemporary society is liable to read selfhood and its behaviour as hostage to sociological, or even genetic, conditioning effectively exonerating it from authentic liability. On such grounds any will to sincerity becomes a delusion and "intention" a misnomer.

Against such "alibizing" of personal being the Qur'an is decisively set. The central concept of *islam*, not as arbitrary or bare "surrender" but as consciously willed and sustained "conformity", necessitates the lively personal equation. The tendency to see "overpoweringness" in Allah (which sprang from the passion for unity against pagan pluralism) must not be allowed to obscure the basic truth that it takes a free self to be a *muslim* self. For what is compelled is not surrendered. What is sought from the autonomous cannot be had from automata.

This fact of the Islamic situation may often have been obscured by the debates around determinism and free-will but these, in turn, had their impulse in reservations about divine magnanimity with humankind or in improperly abject notions of human standing before God as not truly *khulafa'* as His "viceroys".

However, the innate institutionalizing of all things in Islam – ritual, social and legal – as well as its concept of Scripture served to diminish the scope that could be permitted to personal *niyyah*. One important example here is the notion of *ra'i*, or "personal opinion", in matters of law and interpretation. Many legists frowned on it as a dubious quantity. Or its exercise was severely limited by doctrines of "expert" qualifications requisite to *ijtihad*, or "enterprise", in the understanding of what Islam said, meant, required or allowed.

The long debates over *ra'i* not only led to the divergence of the Sunni Schools of law but significantly inhibited the appeal to conscience over and against establishment mind. Authority is always liable to foreclose issues it is loathe to face. Doing so takes refuge in the prohibition of "laic" ideas. The *Shura* or "counsel" which Surah 42.38 declares is the *amr*, or "imperative practice" among Muslims,[16] cannot be understood as a sort of universal plebiscite. "Counsels" are best authentic when only expertly, or cautiously, reached. There have been very few Luthers in the story of Islam, men or minds ready – and by the ethos warranted – for inclusive questioning of what traditionally goes. What examples there are have been sharply disowned or achieved only at the cost of deep suffering.[17]

Even so, the great themes of the Qur'an concerning *zulm al-nafs*, *nifaq*, *kufr* and *ikhlas*, "self-wronging", "hypocrisy", "giving the lie" and "integrity", all make conscience requisite and have to do with its deployment or suppression.

Therefore, it may be in no way remote or inventive to draw a final significance about conscience from the very incidence of the Qur'an in and to Muhammad's prophethood. On the traditional view of "inspiration" he had no personal part, no conscious input, in the structure and content of the text. He could only receive it in passivity both of mind and will. There is no need here to revert to the theme of CHAPTER V. Yet, even so, there were real issues of conscience in that experience. One among them bears tellingly on religious integrity everywhere. In Surah 20.114 comes the command to the Prophet: "Do not be precipitate in respect of the Qur'an before its revelation is determined for you." Rather, in words that follow he is to say: "Lord increase me in knowledge." Surah 75.17 reminds that is for Allah to take care of its accumulation, or "gathering".

Muhammad may well have been in personal tension around the

sequences and the intervals of his experience of *wahy*. For it was implicit in the Book's nature that it could only come to him "at intervals" and "piecemeal" (17.116). A gibe of his foes had been that if it was authentic why could he not have it all at once. Aside, then, from the issue of his immediate conscious involvement in the content, there was certainly this implicit moral task in its incidence, namely patiently to await its mediation despite the suspense entailed. Suspense, in far less loaded situations, is always a test of character. May it not be that this inward dimension in Muhammad's prophethood was in mind when he was warned about "the weight in the word"?[18]

Yet, if being "hasty" or "impatient" had no place in the prophetic vocation, still less was there any place for presumption or, in presumptuous terms, for the intrusion of personal conscience. That theme can well return, in conclusion, to the principle as stated by Ruhollah Khomeini. It governs both the reception and the exegesis of the Qur'an.

> No man has right to legislate . . . Whatever he formulates will be nothing but an academic exercise. Reason dictates that man is subject to no command except that of God who possesses the universe and the creatures in it.[19]

All, then we can do is to recognize the divinely infallible as the due mentor and monitor of our human obedience. Was it not precisely such a notion of an unquestioned writ in cultic religion that the Hebrew prophets, Amos and his peers, were minded to deny? Has the "reason" that "dictates" to us the divine "law and order" no capacity – by its "rationality" – to ponder what "dictation" might mean to its own integrity? If not, will it not be categorically against itself so that it subverts even the duty it fulfils? Conscience, it would seem, must become the vigilant guardian, for truth and love's sake, of the moral interrogation of religions – the more absolute these, the more urgent that vigilance. Prophetic conscience, Biblical or Quranic, is at the very heart of religious formation both historical and perennial.

# VII

# Prophethood in Suffering

## I

There are few more graphic images in the story of prophethood than that of the dancer Salome presented with "the head of John the Baptist on a dish", he having been summarily executed in prison at the grim wish of her mother, Herodias, whom his preaching had "sore offended". Fascinating to many a modern poet or musician it may have been, but few have paused to savour the enormity. Flaubert's *Salome* forgets the very name of the man whose head she dances for, while the poet, W.B. Yeats notes her

> receiving the prophet's head in her indifferent hands and wonders whether it was not, in reality, the exaltation of the muscular flesh and of civilization perfectly achieved.[1]

"All the prophets prophesied until John", the Gospel observes (Matthew 11: 13). His being "more than a prophet" in no way diminishes his prophetic significance. His brutal doing to death was no small part of it. All the elements are there in the callous Herodian guilt, the hapless exposure of the victim to conspiracies of evil and the cruel distortion of all values in the passions of lust and power. Here, in its direct evidences, was that "contradiction – the *antilogia* – of sinners" which a later writing identified as the core experience of Jesus himself in the antecedents to his crucifixion (Hebrews 12: 3), the dark reaction of society to the accusing word.

Such was the perennial hazard of the prophetic vocation. The "situations" studied in CHAPTER V have been ample proof of how ever present the logic of pain and heart-break was as the inner "burden of the word" through the long prophetic cycle. The point of this chapter is to take its relevance further as the evident seed-bed of Messianic hope and – in "the fulness of time" – the Messianic achievement realized in the New Testament. For the hope was born out of the seeming failure of the spoken thing while the achievement came in how the Cross of Jesus took up, and finalized, the vicarious principle that had always belonged in the vulnerability of the greatest prophets.

We see them vulnerable in a strange reversal of the imagery present for many centuries in the pillory – that ingenious institution of English penal law. It made the culprit stand erect with head and wrists clamped at shoulder-height in a wooden beam, suitably holed to accommodate them. Thus immobilized in full public view the victim endured the hours or days of the sentence, the cynosure of scornful eyes, the target of abuse, of brickbats verbal and physical. The pillory was designed to administer in disagreeable terms the opprobrium of society. As a punitive device its crudity might be considered well deserved. It combined an unhappy retribution with some hope of salutary correction, society the meanwhile indulging both its laughter and its spleen. Prophethood was too often a story of the pillory but in totally other terms. A hostile society impales its righteous mentors, holds its seers up to scorn, imprisons them in its long contempt, makes them the butt of its impenitent glee. It frustrates their liberties and maligns their ministry, recruiting public clamour to their tribulation and contriving ridicule to their discredit.

This "pillory" situation is graphically captured in a passage in the Wisdom literature from the period between the Testaments. It looks eloquently both backward to the likes of Jeremiah and forward to the experience of Jesus. In The Wisdom of Solomon (2: 12–24) a society takes stock of itself and opts for hedonism and a ruthless pursuit of gain and pleasure, careless of justice and compassion. In this mood it conspires with anger and enmity against "a man of righteousness" whom it finds repugnant to its ways and motives. What he represents, silently if not vocally, rebukes them. As one they sense, and resent, the explicit charge against them which his integrity signifies. His very presence, leaving them without excuse, becomes hateful to them. They know him sent "to accuse their very thoughts", "his ways being of another fashion".

In their self-exoneration, they reach for vilification, disputing his claim to be "the child of the Lord", and disavow his entire validity. As we have seen in all the foregoing chapters, resistance to things said passes into disparagement of the word-bearer. The tension, born of obduracy and hardness of heart, mounts into the final irony.

> Let us examine him with despitefulness and torture that we may know his meekness and prove his patience. Let us condemn him to a shameful death.

Even ill-will – in the end – must take the integrity of the reproach it knows full well into the cognizance of inevitable crisis. Then Gethsemane is in the making and the issue passes into the judgement of heaven where, against the grain of their own vindictiveness, the ungodly must consciously leave it. Accordingly, it is about the prophets, as Surah 2.87 observes: "Some of them you said were liars and some you put to death." Had the old story of Joseph and his brothers somehow unwittingly anticipated this drama? "This dreamer comes ... we will see what will become of his dreams" (Genesis 37: 19–20). They do so by a vengeance which knows well enough "what it does" until the far future opens their eyes from a long blindness.

## II

The relationship is well captured in how the schemers in Wisdom 2: 16 echo uncannily the words of Isaiah 53: 3: "We are esteemed of him as counterfeits" responds to: "We esteemed him not", only that the latter, once a truth of the situation, is said in penitent retrospect. Prophethood incurs the "disesteem" that social falsehood has for a prophet's "disesteem" of society's evil patterns. There is an intense personal cost in this reciprocal situation. For it is so unequally joined – on the one side corporate vested interest and the weight of a prejudiced tradition, on the other the embattled protagonist of the unwanted divine claim.

"Hero", however, would not be fit language for that prophetic role, despite Thomas Carlyle's notion to include "the prophet" in his lectures on "the heroic role in history".[2] The Biblical prophets are in no way Promethean, breathing a defiant challenge against implacable fate. Courage and tenacity are part of their destiny but a sense of frailty, humility, even worthlessness, is inseparable from the trust of divine words. Reticence, protest, self-doubt, even self-excuse, we have seen to be implicit in the onset and the continuity of vocation. Hence the sharp individualism we have had reason to note through their whole story, spelling an intense loneliness. "I sat alone because of Thy hand", cried Jeremiah (15: 17). Ezekiel is made to "eat the roll", the very text he has been given to speak (3: 1f.) – an analogy almost too graphic in its crudity to make the insistent equation between the task with the text. Diet has sometimes been a metaphor for duty but nowhere so taxingly as then.

In one of the rare incidents when the Qur'an-reader is allowed to visualize Muhammad in the act of preaching, listeners are found stealing away out of earshot, finding commerce and the market more congenial (Surah

62.11). Thus to be "left standing", isolated by unconcern, abandoned by disinterest, may be cited for a parable of the deeper reaches of rejection and deliberate ostracism as inseparable from prophet-experience in the obdurate or unheeding world. Issues are unequally joined between "the voice of one crying" and the indifferent collective.

Ostracism, in the Greek mode, at least meant that the inconvenient voice in the senate was banished into long exile where, presumably, accounts stood closed. The isolations of an Isaiah or a Jeremiah were of another order, malignity and intimidation in an unremitting encounter with court and society. To be sure, the Bible-reader is aware of "Schools of the Prophets" and of clusters of "disciples" but either these belong to the early days of seer-dom, or did little to mitigate the acute distresses to which major figures were exposed. In the case both of Jeremiah and Ezekiel loneliness invaded their very domesticity, the former forbidden to marry, the latter bereaved.

Personal privations, for all the bitterness entailed in the soul, doubtless were as grist to the mill of prophetic meaning, even as Hosea's marital betrayal (given the validity of our earlier "reading") served to tell, perhaps even to initiate, the heart of the message. That fact, however, in no way lessened the pain and its incidence. It only meant that suffering was the matrix of prophethood both ways – as both the whence and the whither of its personal cost. Where, as notably in Ezekiel, the "sign" quality of private experience takes a vital part in the message, the price is paid, whether the "sign" be deliberately contrived or whether things costly to endure are recruited into meaning.

The suffering equation in Biblical prophethood can be measured also by reference to the array of "powers and principalities" – as Paul might have called them – with which its mission found itself at odds. These were the formidable factors of institutional pride and national identity. Covenant, election, the nation, the Temple, the sacrificial system, even Judaic exceptionality itself – all had to be challenged within the onus of the prophets' charge against the falsehoods these enshrined and which tradition stubbornly perpetuated.

Amos challenges the uniqueness of the Exodus, reminding his hearers of divinely ordered migrations of Philistines and Syrians. It is because he cherishes the valid meaning of Israel's historical vocation that he shatters illusory readings of its covenantal status. His clarion call to social righteousness demolishes futile fantasies of self-standing "holiness" blandly read into covenantal mystery. His denunciations of privilege are as vehement as Jeremiah's famous "Temple sermon". Hosea visualizes "the wilderness", a primal experience long antedating the prestige of land-entry and Davidic "kingdom", as the authentic to which Israel must penitently return – not in fact, since history is irreversible, but in soul and mind.

"Who has required this at your hand to tread my courts?" is the query of Isaiah 1: 17, disavowing, both rhetorically and ethically, the whole Levitical system of "burnt offering and sacrifice". "The vehemence of his comparison between "Gomorrah" and the "chosen people", his denunciation of the prayers of those whose "hands that are full of blood", are the clearest index to the pain and danger entailed in such spokesmanship. Establishments hold no mercy for those who passionately disqualify their self-repute and take apart their crooked psychic satisfactions. In their encounter with the big battalions of crown and priesthood, the prophets were steadily exposed to charges of wild provocation, madness, fifth-column conspiracy and even treason, operating, as so often it fell to them, in circumstances of political menace and national disintegration.

The intensity of these confrontations and hence the anguish of the personal (in prophets) ranged against the institutional, no doubt stemmed from the fact that both parties drew their warrant from divine mandate. There is very little of the idea of "natural law" in the Hebraic tradition, though nature is God's realm and appeal to its constancy is frequent.[3] Otherwise, all is "theological" in its ground and standing. Thus the prophets, who stood in their sense of divine mandate for their mission, found themselves contending against publically perceived divine sanction in the themes of their reproaches and their denunciation. We even find Isaiah (50: 6): "I gave my cheeks to them that plucked off the hair", voicing his suffering in an echo of the tradition according to which the priest of Marduk ceremonially treated the king this way in an annual "renewal" of royal power. Nowhere is tension so exacting as where protagonists, prophets and powers-in-place, claim divine authority. There was an exquisite irony of pain in a personal conscience summoned to expose the "taking of the name in vain", by organs of its hallowing. The "holy" did not cease to be authentic destiny when it was normally defiled.

Thus compromised readings of "inviolate land" or "divine peoplehood" or "unfailing royal seed of David" required to be denounced while what could be legitimate in their significance remained the cherished heritage of the prophetic mind itself. There were times in the experience of each apostle to apostates when that supreme paradox proved almost insupportable. "Casting down", in Jeremiah's idiom, was decreed in any "building up". The painful participatory emotions around the burden of national forfeit is clear enough from the degree to which liturgies of celebration figure in prophetic language. It is as if love is being immolated in the necessities of truth.[4]

Yet, within the cultus and belonging with the nation, the heart of prophethood was the personal equation with evil, corruption and social malaise, these weighing on conscience in the ways explored in the previous chapter. Readers can resort to the Biblical Psalter to experience this dimension of distress and sorrow of heart. For so much of the Book of Psalms mourns and grieves from within the souls of prophets.[5] By the same token, their inner travail presupposes the entire tradition they must accuse, its norms, ideas, sources and affections. They are on the wrack of their own heritage in the terms of their own honesty.

This is very different, in its existential perturbation, from the shadowy precedent of the patriarchs of whom Martin Buber made so much as allegedly providing precedent for prophetism.[6] From Amos to Ezekiel, being "men of God" was happening, not in the dim partriarchal mists of idealized history, but in the harsh realities of ascertainably desperate history. As hinted in CHAPTERS III and V, any psychology of prophetism – were we to approve one – would have to be preoccupied with a deep inner quarrel between compulsive meanings and resistant moods. "The weight in the word" holds down the crisis in the will.

## III

The suffering that spells being vulnerable entails being vicarious. The two words inter-depend. Before moving to what the inter-play signifies via prophethood, for Messiah and God, let us take a final measure from Jeremiah and Ezekiel of the suffering we study. For they each coincided with the direst circumstances of the prophetic story, namely "the Lord's anointed", Jehoiakim, going into exile, and the very *Shechinah* forsaking the Temple. Were exiles still "the people of God" far off in Babylon, away from "the promised land"?

Characteristically in his "Confessions", Jeremiah cries: "Do not be a terror to me!" "They have dug a pit for his life", plotting against his soul, with "deadly plans" (17: 14–18 and 18: 19–23). The word "is like a burning fire" in his heart (20: 9). His pain is the languishing of the covenant in the morass of corporate folly. He must symbolize impending judgement by the foregoing of all marital bliss, "putting an end to the sound of joy and gladness" (16: 9). He is caught in the old gibe of: "Where is Yahweh's word? Let it come true if it can" (17.15). He is "sick at heart" with the stress of events, precisely because he feels himself in a strange liability not merely *for* Yahweh but *with* Yahweh – an awareness which only intensifies the heart-ache in his perplexity. For that intimacy, making him vicarious for Yahweh, deepens the mystery of his apparent abandonment to solitary tribulation. When he is forbidden to make intercession it almost seems that the same God who commissions him demissions his proper hopes. By his very vocation he has been privy to the divine mind, "standing in Yahweh's counsel", like all his fellow messengers. Shrinking from what he cannot renounce, he can only deplore that ever "his mother bore him" (15: 10). His whole personality conveys to theology the ultimate interrogation of God implicit in being made thus divinely vicarious in the midst of a "chosen" and wayward people.

In differing idiom the problem is remitted to Ezekiel. Consider his situation. In some respects, as we have seen in CHAPTER IV, there is something very Islamic about him,[7] yet, with national ruin, exile and despair, the contrast is complete. Political chaos surrounds his whole mission. Jerusalem is in peril. There is the first deportation. The Zadok priesthood to which he belonged is aborted. Harps hang silent on foreign willows. Does he make a visionary journey back to Jerusalem to wrestle with the mystery of a sanctuary at once inviolate and deserted? It needs "the spirit to make him stand", after the prostrating question about the Lordship of the inviolable now traduced by pagan power. The very "dumbness" that afflicts him yields the supreme paradox of prophetic utterance. The futility of mission seems to be sealed in an awareness that people will not repent. In any event how, until a far-off Cyrus, will any repentance avail? Warning the heedless and impenitent makes his duty his futility. He may find solace in robust oracles against Tyre as well as a rich role for his rhetoric.[8] But he is finally thrown back on a visionary future in which his assurance takes refuge in meticulous priestly prescripts for its incidence, while leaving his prophetic ministry in the enigmas of his puzzling personality. Are the curious extravagancies of his manner a right index to the perhaps unhinge-ing travail of his spirit?

We cannot tell. What there is no mistaking is the burden of his task, the onus in his experience. Throughout, for him, his predecessors and his heirs – Haggai and Zechariah and Malachi – after the return, is the condition of being, in some sense, proxy for God, Yahweh being "the Sender" and they "the sent". It can hardly be that this inter-play of roles, of ends and means, ceases or is annulled when tribulation presses. Indeed, when the obdurate society oppresses the spokesman it is because they are saying also: "Cause the Holy One of Israel to cease from among us" (Isaiah 30: 11). There is mutual rejection in which both prophet and Yahweh are decried. "Let both get out of our way", is the inclusive cry. When Yahweh is said to cry: "My heart is pained, 'broken', for them", is there not an echo of Jeremiah himself urging repeatedly his own heart-break in the same context? At least as a concept in relation there is no sundering either from the other. They are a single divine–human answer to the wrongness the sentness confronts.[9]

It is this association of the divine and the human in the one purpose of caring for truth, and the cost of the caring, that leads the course of thought to "the suffering servant" of Isaiah 42 to 53 – a figure around whom so much scholarship has circled with widely divergent verdicts. That the image of an ultimate vicarious reality belongs with the climax of prophethood cannot be in doubt. However far in contention the significance of "the suffering servant" may be, any theology of divine "sending" must take us to a theodicy of sequential suffering.

It is necessary first to ask in what sense the things prophets undergo can ever be other than tragic, can they ever yield what Psalm 34: 27 mysteriously calls "the prosperity of His servant"? For are they not, manifestly, the accompaniment of failure, of verbal frustration? Jeremiah's "pain is perpetual" because his pleas are unavailing. He is even so warned from the beginning, yet the paradox of preaching has to be lived through, "a wound unstanched". How is this situation to be "taken into God", as its essential architect, the seat of the sovereignty which the whole experience must radically implicate?

The figure of the "scapegoat" comes readily to mind. It was Jews themselves who invented it. In respect of wrongness "off-loaded" on to innocent parties, it fitted the prophetic situations we have studied and deeply those mentors underwent it. But except in circumstance the "scapegoat" theme has no purchase on prophethood. To think it had would be to focus only on what sinful society does to its prophets, while ignoring entirely what they are doing for society. It is this, the positive, in their pain and travail that we are in search of, as ever being, however strangely, "their prosperity".

Here, too, the metaphors derived from animal sacrifice, and so often invoked to interpret prophetic suffering, fall short as grievously as the "scapegoat" imagery. They are true only circumstantially, never essentially. Jeremiah may aptly say: "I was like a lamb that is brought to the slaughter" (11: 19) and Isaiah 53: 7 echoes the analogy. But animal situations are totally void of the dimensions, the emotions, the realities encompassed in a preaching that suffers, a suffering that pays with the word. Metaphors never serve where their limits are forgotten. We must look for the servants' "prosperity" in other terms than the artifice of sacrifice, if ever "sacrifice" is to come rightly into its own. The cost in prophetic travail is far removed from what can be signified by an altar ritual where dumb animals are immolated. In those terms, there is nothing less like a lamb than Jeremiah when he borrows the analogy.[10]

For, at the heart of all prophetic mission there is a dimension of divine intimacy, of being attendant in "the Lord's counsel". These servants of the word are God's *awliya'* – as the Qur'an's term has it – and Psalm 116: 15 is sure that "grievous to the Lord is the death" of such "His friends".[11] It is this kindred experience of God and "His devoted ones" that we have to comprehend, if what is "grievous" is somehow mutual.

This means exploring how prophethood fulfils the divine ends in the bearing of what "the weight in the word" requires its carriers to suffer. We can only trace the dimensions in which their double burden – speaking and suffering – "prospers" by starting with a negative. Thanks to their tenacious honesty, from which their travail stems, evil is allowed no exoneration. Wrong is not left to come to be assumed as right. Society, by prophetic indictment, is saved from a situation in which "anything goes". It is rescued from the ultimate shape of evil which would consist in its irreversible lapse into having wrong as its only quality, its unrelieved damnation. For evil is denied any final authority.

Therefore the good remains unsubmerged: it is not, we might say, "last-worded" by the vetoes of the Ahabs, the Jezebels, the faith-suborners, of this world. So much at least issues from the prophetic fidelity that has saved the day for goodness and truth, the travail that has kept the future open for their benediction. By faithful suffering the sovereignty of good is vindicated. By how prophethood has held its own faith in that sovereignty and loyally sustained it against all odds, it has ensured a place of recourse for penitence, for a society's re-consideration of itself. Evil men have occasion for their redemption from their former selves. Such transforming awareness of wrong is the beginning of salvation.

The cynic will note that this sequence is always precarious and holds no guarantee that it is bound to happen. That realization of being evil remains an open question is only part of the prophetic pain. It follows from the fact that good is never compulsive, from which its very aim to be persuasive springs. The two are plainly one. The pre-requisite in the overcoming of evil is that evil must know itself for what it is.[12] The conspirators we met in Wisdom 2: 21 at least came to know that "in their imaginings they were deceived". The actual sequel there is left to silence. What is not in doubt is that wrong was caught in its own image fully identified, deprived of all possibility of further self-deception.

That may seem a very minimal "prosperity". Elsewhere the saving potential is more explicit. Few passages in all prophetic literatures are more loaded than the transition, in Isaiah 53: 3 and 4, from "he was despised and we esteemed him not" to "Surely . . . (the word Handel's music made so hauntingly emphatic) he has borne our griefs and carried our sorrows". Incomprehending hostility passes into articulate conviction, turning on a single, dramatic "But . . .". Society incriminates itself only because it has been denied – in prophetically costly terms – the luxury of its own complacence, its corporate self-esteem.

The enumeration of the sequences of the servant's travail (vv. 7–9) are also a celebration of the terms of his fidelity. In both, the passage learns to trace the divine economy, the partnership between "the pleasure of the Lord" and "the hand" of His proxy in the living scene of history. What follows, by the analogy of a liturgy round a ritual, is that now alerted wrongdoers, duly self-convicted, may read in the servant's burden of word and travail "an offering for sin". Then "the prosperity of the servant" – being rightly identified for what, and how, it is – avails to "justify many".

Of what order is this "justification"? Not that they never sinned, nor that they are blandly exonerated, nor that some have escaped by accusing others, absolving the personal by deploring the collective. These would leave them still accused and hope forfeited. Instead – in the sense in which it can be so – their evil has been borne, undertaken, gathered into the vicarious vulnerability it shaped. Accordingly, via the penitence these evoke, its power over them is broken, its entail in guilt lifted from them by their "appreciation" of how it met its match.[13]

In such "justification" – not, emphatically not, of the evil but of the doers in this new perception of themselves – we can perceive a renunciation, a reversal, of the past. It is an attainment which bare preaching, mere exhortation, can never accomplish of themselves, seeing that its accomplishment turns on the sequence into vicarious pain and of pain into its full significance. Is not this how prophethood as verbal and confrontational points beyond itself to the ultimate "prosperity" of suffering servanthood?

But, it must be asked, can a future ever be opened in this way from a past of wrongdoing? Is not a realist moral order necessarily only punitive when it is defied? If we are not to condone evil, can it ever be as if it had not been – which is what redemption wills to hope – and find?

There is much that argues the answer must be No! For where there is guilt there is – elsewhere – injury, hurt, reproach and these, by their own momentum, can become implacable. History is full of what must be held to be unforgiveable. So Jewry must insist. So the Irish realize, musing on their own story. These may afford us pointed examples of what is everywhere apparent. W. B. Yeats wrote of his own society:

The Irish have suffered from the cultivation of hatred as the energy of their movement . . . Hence the shrillness of their voices.[14]

Musing on the Shoah, Jews and not Jews alone, would surely have to agree with the American Nathaniel Hawthorne in a different context:

After such wrong . . . there is no reparation . . . No great mistake, whether acted or endured, in our mortal sphere, is ever really set right.[15]

Both verdicts are somehow in line with the Hindu notion of the karmic "law" by which nothing is ethically reversible, nothing susceptible to radical undoing.

It is eminently possible to stay with a perspective that reaches only this conclusion. But, were we to do so, the question at once must follow: What then is the point of prophethood? Why stay, or pause, to accuse a world of inevitability in wrong? Much more, why do so to the point of desperate pain? In a world of karmic "law" prophethood would seem to have no place. May we not conclude that what cannot be retrieved has no reason to be condemned? Prophethood could make no sense except as a vexed dimension of unfailing hope.

That, it may be claimed, overlooks prophethood as, hopefully, preventive in relation to wrong not yet contrived. Prophets, as the Qur'an insists, are "warners", "reminding" of the "limits" round the good society. Karmic "law" would only come into play as and when they are maligned and go unheeded. True enough, but by the same token, are they not interrupting – verbally – misdeeds already *in situ* by virtue of the situation that called for their sending? No prophethood enters a *tabula rasa* or addresses a hitherto innocent world. If there can be point in their intrusion on an evil scene there must be point in its potential for correction. What is potential of correction – given the case we have made – must also be potential of redemption. We cannot postulate divine prophet-sending on a theology of ultimate despair. Yet fully to give the lie to despair is to recognize the partiality, given how the human situation is, of what only exhorts, instructs, and recommends. For these demonstrate their incompleteness precisely in that their due and worthy exercise carries those fulfilling it into the painful evidences of how unpersuaded humans can remain, and how criminally so. If there is hope in their preaching, there must be hope beyond it and through it in their travail and their heart-ache. Only in all three will they be "justified".

## IV

If, then, in terms of prophetic suffering, there is an authentic sense in which evil can be borne, it must follow that it can be borne away.[16] It is precisely this confidence which the New Testament draws from its perception of the logic, for example, of Isaiah 53, translated into the interpretation of Jesus' crucifixion. For purposes of such translation, the antecedents are the same – a teaching holding to its course in the face of "establishment"rejection, a fidelity to word holding firm as a fidelity into grief and death. Redemption becomes available for an evil-bent society, on condition of the price understood, in response to the penitence to which the entire story gives rise when its meaning is discerned and taken into heart.

It is this sequence from word to event, to event as suffering, from suffering to comprehension to forgiveness, that Paul tells in the use he makes of Habakkuk 2: 4 in Romans 1: 17. In the former passage, the puzzled prophet is assured that his "faith" (fidelity) in the pain of deferred hope will be vindicated, and meanwhile he is to trust. He will "live", i.e. survive and be "justified" by the divine pledge on which he relies. The "faith" and the "being justified" are entirely of him and in him as one personhood. With Paul it is "faith" (the act of trusting another) placed in the significance of the "fidelity" of Jesus in the event of the Cross that "justifies" believers who were not themselves party (as Habakkuk was in his case) to the constancy that underwent the suffering.

This Pauline citation (or misquotation) seems to beg several questions. Was there some sleight of hand in conjoining "being justified by faith" in these divergent ways? There are some who think so. For the meanings are clearly distinct. Yet we have seen, in pondering the Isaiah and Wisdom passages, that the realization of having been suffered for (on the part of a vocal[17] sufferer whose holding to truth at all costs has ensured the future for truth), if rightly acknowledged, aborts what would otherwise be the ongoing, clinging power of the evil and "justifies" the penitence that took it to be so. Evil could be overcome by good, precisely because good had not been overcome of evil. In seeing to the second, by his fidelity, the "sin-bearer" ensured the first for all who, by faith, could stand in it.

This, broadly, was the New Testament understanding of "grace" in sequel to the perception of how Jesus crucified had realized in an inclusive way what the precedents of suffering prophethood had foreshown. As hinted earlier, this perception suffered some obfuscation by being associated with metaphors drawn from ritual sacrifice, or penal process, which

– at best – could only dimly carry the meaning and – at worst – went far to distort it. It falls to a following chapter to study how this reading of the logic from prophethood to the Cross belongs with a final theology. Meanwhile here, it remains to explore the reading of "the suffering servant" on which we have proceeded.

There is, undeniably, a wide disparity of scholarly interpretation of the Isaian passages, the whence and how of the theme of the one – solitary or collective? – so "disesteemed". What is in no way in doubt is the reality of being loathed for a task fulfilled, of "acquaintance with grief" because of "the word's weight". All discussion has to proceed from that reality. That such "loathedness" is entirely credible with, if not inseparable from, all that we see concerning prophethood is evident enough. There is no question about the reality of the experience. But who is undergoing it, by what circumstances, to what end?

One can, of course, fall back on the conclusion that "only the inspired prophet can interpret the inspired prophecy". But to do so reduces all to pointless enigma. Meaning is not served by sheer evacuation, else why should what is there emerge to ask our comprehension? Or, as Martin Buber thought, is the anonymous writer proposing a mystery about some historical figure whose actuality is meant to be concealed?[18] But what is the point of an "actuality" like that of Jeremiah's "passion" (from within which the "servant songs" speak if they do not directly derive) if "what it conceals" is not to be reverently ascertained?[19]

Could "the servant's suffering" be a leprosy, actual or symbolic, a contagion from a sinful society to be "cleansed" by his "offering" as a moral ritual? Perhaps this meaning has to be read in a collective sense, representing either the exiles in Babylon or the "remnant" who remained in Jerusalem. Relations between these two parties were strained and contentious, and capable of yielding several versions of who was on behalf of whom in readings of Judah's fate.

Understanding is complicated by the variety of images employed in the text: "dividing the spoil", "seeing of the travail", "startling the nations", "the tongue of the learned", "with the rich in his deaths (pl.)", and "a light to the nations". Jewish nationalist, inclusive universalist, individual and corporate interpretations compete for credence, while scholars conjecture about things proleptic and retrospective in the purport of the texts.

It is no doubt salutary for a patient faith that due reserve should have to mingle with quiet confidence. Given the inclusive nature of the concept of divine "servanthood", it is fair to think the prophetic inaugural to the Messianic. For between them there is the continuity of divine bearings on human story, patterned in Israel/Judah as God's "pilot scheme" towards the open grace in Christ and an inclusive human peoplehood. If there is a culminating and decisive shape of divine relation to our human creaturehood, via proxies with divine mission, such as Messiah must be, then the antecedent prophethoods would surely indicate both its cost and its vicarious character.

In this way, Martin Buber was ready to allow the Christian identification (made in Acts 8: 30 and the Letters of Paul and Peter) of the servant as the Messiah as "approximating in the essential point" to his view of "the prophet's true intention".[20] Buber, however, queries this reading out of a sense that the Isaian and other passages cannot be seen as telling what could only transpire centuries later and be realized in a person only existing far out of contemporary Isaian relevance.

His hesitancy deserves sympathy, since prescience in Scriptures can be crudely invoked. The difficulty vanishes, given the clear continuity by which one experience anticipates the other. Could Messiah be found immune from what prophets had undergone, given that the single term "servant" describes each? What Buber calls "the awful fusion of all the evil in the servant's soul–body experience" comes very close to how the Fourth Gospel tells "the sin of the world". The New Testament would seem to be on firm ground in discerning clues to its own story concerning Jesus in the ultimate dimensions of prophetic experience. The Qur'an's own conjecture around the mission of Muhammad, earlier noted, belongs with the same theme: "You may well be grievously stressed in soul in track of those who believe not in this message" (Surah 18.6). Truth has to reckon with Gethsemane.

That Christian confidence – and its theology – belong elsewhere. Prophethoods are fulfilled in demonstrating how their content could be seen as climactic, as CHAPTER VIII must argue. Meanwhile, in anticipation of CHAPTER IX and the theme of a corporate Messianic community, it will usefully serve CHAPTER VIII if we note a broad Jewish dissent from the Christian progression from the prophetic to the Messianic.

It consists in reasserting the adequacy to human correction – and thus to divine purpose – of the verbally prophetic role alone. In this posture it may be said to share an Islamic mind-set. It suggests that the Jewish mind is disenchanted concerning the Messiah-theme, having been too long and too often disappointed in it. Insofar as a Messianic role persists, it is absorbed into the ethicism, the moral potential, of a "chosen people". Against original Christianity, writes André Neher, "the Jewish consciousness had to decide between works and waiting on the Lord", between man's liberty of choice and "the servitude of grace".

Seen as "servitude", any identification of Messiah-realized atrophies the people's will to be themselves their only "Messiah" and relegates to "heaven" the essentially human task of obeying "the law and the prophets". "Human society itself ... since Sinai, has held in its hands the silent keys of its own fortunes",[21] though only Jewry was present at Sinai.

This means, in effect, that society's hope is referred back to exhortation, guidance, appeal and warning. God has no more role in human affairs than their education. Prophethood need never have issued into the tragic. We can overlook the obduracies by which prophethood itself was repeatedly taken into tribulation. The Messianic dimension in history, which Hebrew prophethood itself engendered by its "weighted words", can be abrogated into a reversion back again to confidence in human amenability to language and counsel. But was it not precisely our non-amenability proven in how agonizing a vocation the likes of Isaiah and Jeremiah found themselves enduring?[22]

To ask in this way whether prophethood is finally self-sufficing as God's response and remedy in human history is to realize, via prophethood itself, that the answer must be No! Given that suffering prophethood duly and necessarily issues into vicarious redeeming, the urgent point about how any alleged Messiah in those terms, and in that sequel, finds continuity in ongoing history after the inclusive climax, is the task of CHAPTER IX. Then the Judaic identity of community in Messiah as the clue will come firmly into its own but in the different idiom the Christ-event ordains. Whether and how that event transpired take us into "Prophethood and Theology".

# VIII
## Prophethood and God

### I

The Islamic *Shahadah*, or Confession of faith, is the most notable instance of what grammarians call parataxis, namely the sequence of two sentences with no connecting explanation of why they succeed each other. Semitic languages, especially Biblical Hebrew and to a lesser degree the Arabic of the Qur'an, enjoy this usage and find it congenial. The opening chapter of the Book called Genesis is a prime example, with its numerous "ands" linking the long series of verbal statements. Hypotaxis, characteristic of Greek and Latin, is the contrasted fondness for explanatory, conditional and temporal clauses which elucidate the why and when of factuality.[1]

Strictly there is not even an "and" in the *Shahadah*. There is only the juxtaposition of "There is no god but Allah" with "Muhammad, the Messenger of Allah". What we might aptly call "a theology of parataxis" needs to be sought and found. In all such divine sending there is clearly "agency" at work, an "on-behalf-ness" between the divine and the human. What may it imply for our understanding of God that He recruits and sends humans in His Name? What must it mean that there is this human subsidiarity (to venture a contemporary term) in His method and intention? How do prophethood and divinity inter-relate within the absolute theme of divine unity? Beyond a necessary theology of revelation in the terms previous chapters have explored concerning situation, language and personality – these being on the human side – there has to be some inner divine meaning to the place of agency as necessary to the divine economy.

For necessary it must be seen to be, inasmuch as prophethood is a fact, and factor, in the activity of Allah. Messengers do not "send" themselves. Only in *not* doing so are they authentic. Yet, without them, there would be no divine tuition bearing on the temporal human sphere. Only in time can the Eternal have dealings with them. It would seem to follow that only in human terms can divine terms be comprehended by us, whether as revelatory or directional. For these to be had among us agencies that bring them are indispensable.

We put the matter in another way if we realize that what is Godwardness in us as humans (obligation, worship, reverence, submission or obedience) is reciprocal to what is manwardness in God. Indeed, this divine manwardness is the sum of what theology must mean, seeing that outside human relevance there is neither access to, nor significance in, the reality of God. It may well be intelligent and right to leave room for all that in God transcends what human-ness could ever comprehend in awareness or response. We could never confine God to things anthropic but only these can have conscious place in our theology. Prophethood is, manifestly, the effective crux of this situation. Messengers *from* God *to* us, interpreters of creation and mentors of creaturehood, are both the symbol and the point of this divine–human order in which we register their meaning and reckon with their claim.

For any and every theology, then, there is only this "God and . . ." situation. This versatile "and" word is crucial for faith, ethics and worship. It is always vital, seeing that only in "association" is God known.[2] So-called natural theology will locate the vital nexus in the created order and human rationality. Historical theology will find it in event(s) assumedly declarative – by voice or action – of the divine will and grace. Mystical theology will set it in psychic experience or illumination. But the "and" will always be implicit if it is not firmly explicit. Lear's haunting words about "unaccommodated man" ring powerfully for would-be theologians. For they must always find themselves "accommodating" God to where He, however mysteriously, "accommodates" Himself in the time of humans, their minds, stories, souls and wisdoms.[3]

In Hebrew Scriptures and Judaism, this "God and . . . " situation exists in "I will be their God and they will be My people". By a particular ethnicity, via "seed", "covenant", "land" and "election", Yahweh is found within human ken. He is domesticated in Israel with a paradoxical extension of meaning to all humankind, in the elusive category of excluded "Gentiles". "God and His people" is the controlling formula. The "and" situation in Christianity stands in Christian Christology, in how "God was in Christ" or, in the doxology-language of the Book of the Revelation to John, "God and the Lamb" on the single throne. There had been many foreshadowings of that culmination – as the early Church knew it – in those dimensions of personality and suffering we have studied in previous chapters as being inherent in prophethood.

The "God and . . . " formula for Islam is "Allah and His messenger." How does Islam understand the sequence in the two nominal sentences *La ilaha illa-Llah – Muhammadun Rasul-Ullah*?[4] A whole theology is entailed in an answer. Every instinct is insistent on absolute divine transcendence, on a categorical otherness between the divine and the human. Somehow, however, that vast divide has to be mitigated if ever law-giving and law-conforming between them is to transpire, if the transcendent is ever to be the duly worshipped. It may be said that Muhammad's being "sent" is precisely the satisfaction of that need, in the "Reminder" and the "Guidance" (*Dhikr* and *Huda*) which the Qur'an constitutes.

By that criterion of the sequence in the *Shahadah* the sentness in Muhammad's prophethood might be understood simply as the negation of pagan pluralism and the pseudo-worships of what is not God. Islamic thought and piety have never been satisfied with that minimal view. The "satisfaction" Allah finds in the Prophet as evident in *Tasliyah*[5] takes the relation of the Sender to the sent far beyond such a bare and limited task. So also do all the impulses of Muslim devotion to Muhammad and the intellectual celebrations of his status. The two clauses of the Confession demand a prophetology far more celebratory and luminous than a bare disowning of pagans and a simple assertion of Allah's Oneness.

What could such a prophetology be, what has it in fact been? How does the second statement of the *Shahadah* read back into the first? How does the first translate itself into the second? How is either the implicit clue to the other? Inseparable the two halves are. So Islam has always affirmed. Holding them together is a theological enquiry central to faith.

## II

It is evident that there has long been an instinctive Muslim reluctance for these questions. The Qur'an, in Fazlur-Rahman's phrase is, "the Command of God for man". We should desist from any effort to carry its "being given" into an ontology bearing on the divine nature. He continued:

> The Qur'an is no treatise about God and His nature: His existence, for the Qur'an, is strictly functional . . . because the aim of the Qur'an is man and his behaviour, not God.[6]

Yet he insists, further, that the Qur'an "works by its own laws which have been ingrained in it by God". This, he says, makes it "autonomous . . .

not autocratic, for in itself it has no warrant for its existence".[7]

It would seem, to minds outside the thought-set of Islam, that there is a dilemma here. Can Allah's ethical ground-plan for humankind, His essential imperative over the human scene, be at once a derivative entity having no "autocracy", and yet also an "autonomous" normative for human life? A revelation that is essentially didactic and educational must surely take its rise from a will that has the characteristics those commands and directives ordain and, presumably, cherish. Its actual derivation from the divine will – a position central to all Muslim obedience to the Qur'an – can hardly fail to be a sure index and clue to the eternal qualities of its own source. Nor, surely, can that divine source be neutral concerning the reception in human history of a "strictly functional" and yet "autonomous" Scripture acting as its arbiter over humankind.

On both counts, the Qur'an, as divinely "given" and humanly "meant", has relationship at the heart of its character. It is "relational" in that it prescribes behaviour and belongs with human language.[8] In mediating between eternity and time, between Creator and creature, it is set to bring heavenly discourse into human ken. Its vocabulary, even the very "Names" of God, draw upon human speech. Its ethical norms anticipate human conformity. Its whole incidence is to and for the human story. In those terms, it is right to say that it is "no treatise", but only in that it is no abstract product of philosophical enquiry or metaphysical speculation. But that – in this no-treatise quality – it is not "about God and His nature" seems quite false even to its "function". Despite the traditional demur Muslim minds have in moving from the will of Allah to the nature of Allah, it would seem that no Scripture having "laws ingrained in it by God" can be exempt from His nature. If demur stems from a fear of divine compromise with the temporal and the contingent the hesitation needs respect. Nevertheless, the reality in revelation itself must mean, either that the temporal and the contingent spell no compromise or that the compromise is welcome to a divine magnanimity – the magnanimity to which all things Quranic finally return. *Allahu akbar.*

We put the matter another way if we perceive the radical link between human creaturehood and human prophethood, the one being the audience of the other. "Messengers" would be pointless if humankind were not entrusted with the doing of the divine will, and the avoiding of the divine "forbiddens". That entrustment, according to Surah 2.30, is the clue to all culture in the tenancy of "the good earth" by its master-managers – the trustees that, by divine design, we humans are.

The passage in Surah 2.30 is crucial to all else. In conclave with the angels, Allah announces His intention to set "frail" humans over the creation He wills into being. The angels protest that humans are fickle, forgetful and potentially violent (just the very actualities the Qur'an is given, in due course, to correct and surmount). Allah, nevertheless, having His own counsel, rejects the protest and summons the angels, by prostration, to acknowledge the dignity of the creature. Reluctantly they do so – except Iblis, the arch-Satan, who is implacably opposed to what he sees as divine risk and folly. It thus becomes the aim and strategy of Iblis so to deceive, entrap and corrupt the fickle creaturehood that, by human connivance with his wiles, he can vindicate his assessment and demonstrate the divine unwisdom. The counter theme, then, of all moral theism, is that we humans attain to disavow the satanic disavower and so "justify" the divine wisdom – and mercy – in our critical dignity.[9]

Here, obviously, all prophethood belongs. It concerns our high estate; it rebukes our waywardness; it disciplines our frailties: it mentors our forgetfulness; it constrains our obedience. It thus monitors the whole human crisis. Hence, as Islam sees it, the long continuity of "messengers", so that "no people failed to have their own".[10] Hence also the concept of prophethood "sealed" in the inclusive "finality" of the Qur'an. If we were all puppets, no prophets could bring to us the tribute of their summons or their expectation. It is our creaturehood in Allah's creation that both necessitates and fulfils them.

If external nature, as the Qur'an insists, is divine handiwork, and if we in creaturehood are its appointed viceroys, or *khulafa'*, it can hardly be that this whole scenario constitutes only something "functional" about God and not something essential. If we have the whole universe in perspective and human history as a vocation under God, can revelatory "guidance" be only a coded blueprint and not a lived theology? The ends Allah has in prophethood are the one with the stakes He has in creaturehood. We must be ready to seek both between the two halves of the *Shahadah*.

## III

It would seem that we have to proceed to a Quranic prophetology via a theology of the *Shahadah*, from the aspects explored in previous chapters, notably the role of human personality and the dimensions of travail. There *is* the indubitable divine concern around the human scene. It matters to God that there be a human *islam*. Muhammad and the Qur'an are for Muslims the utmost evidence of divine initiative and solicitude. These, as we have argued, are in some sense definitive for theology. There is concerning God that which is sought and wanted from, and on the part of, humankind. Only so is any theology conceivable.

Much in Islamic thinking, with support from passages in its Scripture, leaves open the possibility that everything about Allah's human concerns is inscrutably immaterial to the divine will. This possible hypothesis of sublime indifference is perhaps needed to safeguard any suspicion of something, albeit crucial to mercy, truth and faith, as ever obligatory to God. But were this notion to be anything more than abstract theory, it would clearly signal the end of Islam.

Moreover, the Qur'an not only allows but requires that Allah be truly obligated. Any negligence or indifference towards us would deny the principle that "God has written down upon Himself mercy" (Surah 6.54) – a verse of great significance. Further, Surah 4.165 says that we "humans have no case, or indictment, against Allah, the messengers having been sent". *Hujjah 'ala* – "an argument against . . . " is a remarkable right for us to have against God. It would have been culpable divine default if no messengers had been sent. For to have left humankind in perpetual *Jahiliyyah*, or "ignorance", would have been a dereliction of divine duty. Without prophethoods granted us, Allah would have been unworthy of Himself.

Clearly then, notions of unobligated Lordship are ruled out. The blessed actuality of the "messengers" demonstrates divine Self-consistency. The two halves of the *Shahadah* have, therefore, to be understood as, somehow, an integral unity. But how?

Here it may be well to leave the *Shahadah* in view while turning back to the Hebrew prophetic tradition where divine "agency" makes for the theology subtly different from the Islamic. The antecedents in human creaturehood, though narrowed down into Hebraic "election", are the same in respect of responsible human "dominion".[11] However, the poetics of inspiration are different and it could be said that there is an intimacy, notably in Hosea and Jeremiah, round the personal instrumentality the human affords to the divine or the divine evokes in the human. This is distinctively Biblical.

It would be a delicate enquiry to learn how this Hebraic quality in prophethood relates to the meaning of Quranic *Tasliyah*. As earlier noted, the divine salutation on Muhammad and his being recipient of that benediction may be thought to correspond in some measure to the interplay, in things Hebraic, between what is both divine and human in the reality of commission and vocation. By Quranic lights, however, that interrelationship of God through agency and of agency for God, does not enter, as it surely does in Biblical ways, into the texture of the text and the experience of the spokesmen. The Quranic sense of the mediation of words, their "ingraining" (to use Fazlur Rahman's term) into a scripture does not yield deliverances like those of the yearning Hosea, the anguished Jeremiah or the unknown prophet-psalmists.

The *Shahadah* is far more reticent, perhaps deliberately so, about the wider bearings of its themes. "Yahweh and His Amos" or "The Lord of the *Markabah* and His Ezekiel" would be true enough but too terse to indicate in what the affinity consisted or how it came about. The life-settings were of course different, yet the rubric that runs through the Qur'an: "Obey God and obey the Messenger",[12] fits them all into a comparable frame,[13] the ground of realized agency, from God, for God and – in some sense – in God.

A striking passage in Psalm 27: 8 has the Biblical prophetology at its tenderest: "My heart said unto You: 'Let my face seek your face:'" or: "Come my heart has said: 'Seek His presence.' I seek your presence, Lord." That could fit the case of Muhammad, withdrawn to the cave on Mount Hira'.[14] It belongs with Amos scanning the horizons of his own generation's history. It certainly takes the young Isaiah into the Temple where his great vision ensues. This quality of attention does not anticipate divine commission in a way that presumes on it. On the contrary, it makes vocation possible and alone explains the sense of destiny so often enshrined in call narratives.

In all these ways the second clause of the Islamic *Shahadah* has kinship with Biblical prophethood but the prevailing Muslim view of *wahy* does not allow the "face-seeking" to "ingrain" the text of the Qur'an in the intimate way in which it informs the Biblical prophets. We are feeling for something wonderful, yet elusive, in how the reality of "situated personality" – earlier studied in CHAPTERS II, III and IV – can determine the Scripture and – in the prior sense of a rich word – "enthuse" the human persona at its heart.[15]

# IV

Perhaps it may help the course of thought here if we move from the idea of divine "agency" to that of "servant". The word is certainly central for the Biblical scene and entirely congenial to the Qur'an. Though *'abd* is readily used of any Muslim believer, it is eminently a title of the Prophet. Surah 2.23 has Allah designating him as "Our servant" in the very context of the Qur'an's eloquence as unmatched.[16] There is no doubt of the *Rasul* being the servant. That brings him, in vocabulary terms, right into Biblical terminology. It follows again that there is no doubt of the role of personhood. All that is at issue is the degree to which it penetrates the message-ing or participates in what the message brings.

There is no need to recapitulate foregoing chapters. The concern here is the theology to which they point. We have seen that when "the weight in the word", its summons to credence, its rebuke to obduracy, its entire "burden" borne to hearers, kindle encounter, inevitably the character and conduct of the prophet enter into the equation. His status is not only in question: his quality is tested. Personality has to "serve" ends – of patience, courage, and tenacity – which only *qua* "servant", and not merely *qua* speaker, the destined messenger can fulfil.

It may be argued that the Qur'an is susceptible of this measure of prophethood in that the theme of "signs", *ayat*, has so prominent a place. Every verse is an *ayah* as endowed with linguistic quality in "luminous Arabic" signalling the Book's sublime source. The same term, however, no less significantly, is applied to prophets in their very persons.[17] This Islamic usage has links, arguably, with – for example – the "signs" of Ezekiel and indications, noted in earlier context, of how the impact of messengers was sharply visual, even tactile, as well as vocal. Here, doubtless, belongs the definitive Christian aligning of "servant" and "son" – the two terms being synonymous in Greek. That culminating Christian concept of the Sonship of Jesus to God is in sequence to the whole Hebraic perception of prophetology as how a "vocal servant" may become also a "representing servant" by the logic that, in all "messenger situations", moves from word to sign and from speech to personhood.

It follows that the logic is eminently theological. To be sure, Islam repudiates it, but only for its understanding of divine unity as inspired by its properly urgent antipathy to plural worship. Right as a theology of unity is – and fully Christian – it need in no way exclude the life-dimension in which all merely verbal prophethood finds itself finalized. For the sequence is evident in the long story of Biblical prophethood, via "the servant" theme and its Messianic measure. Before moving on to where this takes us into the personal cost of prophethood (as where the "sign" quality is most expressive) it will be right to note how Muslim thought itself developed a "high" prophetology, alongside the exclusively verbal dogma of the nature of the Qur'an.

## V

The inaugurating command of the Qur'an is: *Iqra'* – "Recite!"

## PROPHETHOOD AND GOD

Muhammad was strictly enjoined to bring *al-balagh*, i.e. "verbal communication". Eloquence is the crowning witness to the divine status of the Book. Calligraphy devoted to letters and their script is the paramount art, just as "recital" in *Tajwid*, or "beautiful diction", is the high tribute to its "excellence" on loving lips. No one has ever had reason to doubt that Quranic revelation is a making "literary" of the divine mind, giving "Book expression" to what is manward in Allah. It is part of Islamic dogma that the Book, as "the speech of God" is pre-existent, and "uncreated", and, thus, in turn, "divine".[18]

Despite insistence on the simple human status of Muhammad, this faith in the "divinity" of the Book could hardly fail to engender, both from Sufi piety and philosophic speculation, a prophetology conferring metaphysical stature on Muhammad. The concept of "Wisdom" was readily to hand from the Biblical tradition – that emanation of the Spirit of God "entering into holy souls making them friends of God and prophets".[19] The term *Al-Hikmah* is conjoined with "the Book" as a title of the Qur'an (Surahs 2.129, 151 and 231, 3.48,81 and 164, 4.113, 5.110 and 62.2). Elsewhere it stands alone as denoting the Qur'an and/or its rank with all divine revelations.

*Hikmah* being a title of the Book, its human instrument could not fail to receive from due devotion an eminence of celestial identity, hailed by mystical piety in birth narratives, celebrations of miracles or holy chances attending Muhammad's ancestry, salutations of his birthday, or *Mawlid*, and prophetic anticipations of his time and task.

What piety could yield in this exaltation of his fame was readily elaborated by esoteric lore moving towards Muhammad's divinization – a development all the more remarkable in that it ignored or defied the Qur'an's own insistence to the contrary. Further, ethical philosophy, building on the theme of Muhammad as "the first of Muslims", yielded the concept of *al-insan al-kamil*, "the perfect man", embodying a divinized ideology of human behaviour.

Or, in the ongoing centuries of philosophic enquiry, thought on the divine agency in the *Tanzil*, or "causing to descend" on the Prophet of the heavenly text, refused to be content with a bare dogma that it was so. It was ardent to identify *Al-Hikmah* with some in-reading of the divine mind, whereby "the illiterate Prophet" could be paradoxically understood as endowed with supreme intellectuality. Theories of Muhammad's personhood sought to absorb, if not outdo, the Greek *theologoumena* and perceptions of indwelling divine *logos*. These could find some uneasy validation by extension of the Qur'an's own aura of divine "signs". If in extravagant ways,[20] it could also fall back on those allusions in the Book itself to Muhammad's crucial personal engagement with the content of the text. Had not Allah told him that He had "sent it down upon his heart"? (Surahs 2.97, 26.194). The heart, unlike the tongue or lips, is the place of intimate soul colloquy, of emotion and participation. Mechanical *tanzil* only by-passes the heart.

There was also *Al-Mi'raj*, the Prophet's mysterious "Night Journey" (Surah 17.1, where the "servant" word is crucial) and his rapture, or ascension into Heaven, for *Sharh al-sadr* of "the opening of the bosom", for "cleansing" and the "implanting of the divine wisdom and truth" in their ultimate and final shape. These passages – always in tension with the Qur'an's insistent on the "native", "normally human" messenger that Muhammad was seen to be – lent themselves readily to the all too eager speculative thinking of the Islamic centuries, not to be outdone by the intellectual explorations of mind and meaning they learned from a mediated Plato and a discovered Aristotle. The disquisitions, for example, of Ibn al-'Arabi proved the Islamic mind to be equal in ambition to any of the ancients.[21]

Yet was there only tension here with the Qur'an's categorically human prophet? The doctrine about his "illiteracy" in one sense almost invited a certain apotheosis of wisdom, once the intellectual appetite for speculation had been aroused in the Muslim *Ummah*. For, since the doctrine of "illiteracy" excluded normal "intellectualism" in the shaping of the Qur'an,[22] so that the contents could be the more infallible as being had by direct divine mediation of them, why should not wise probing into that "miracle" read it in sophisticated terms of hidden esoteric bestowal of a sort that would require abeyance of all that had to do with "common sense"? If the result was *Al-Hikmah*, in entire dissociation from normal powers, might that not indicate that *wahy* could be comprehended in theosophic terms? If, indeed, as "illiteracy" suggested, Muhammad was *nabi malgré lui*, "a prophet in spite of himself",[23] could not the whole be comprehended in philosophic versions of supernal wisdom?

Writers like Al-Farabi needed to relate philosophic ideas of the "active intelligence" to the orthodox faith about the Qur'an and, so doing, to bring to Hellenism an Islamic appreciation. Was he and were his counterparts, like Ibn Sina, in effect understanding "the (arch)angel" of Muhammad's encounter with *wahy*, in – for example – Surah 53 as having its *raison d'être* in some affinity between divine and human mind, the one activating the other in divine "intellection"? Orthodox minds, in for example, Ibn Taimiyya and Al-Shahrashtani, repudiated the idea, defending the classical dogma. So doing they paid tribute to rigorous conceptions of all divine–human relations, while their free-ranging adversaries proceeded upon a contrasted vision of the reality of God and of the nature of man, or expressed in cultural terms the distance between Greece and Arabia.[24]

Maybe, in practical terms, the difference matters little. Our present concern is the theology involved. How do "agency" and "servanthood" belong in the divine economy? How far does the human enter into the divine, the divine into the human, in the unmistakably joint enterprise of "being sent" and "sending"? The question points cogently to the whole Christian understanding of the Incarnation in "the Word made flesh". It belongs no less squarely with the Islamic conviction of a Qur'an mediated from eternity into Meccan time, from its *Lawh al-Mahfuz* (Surah 85.22) in heaven to its Prophet's speech (and mind?) amid the Meccan hills.

However we think to resolve the divine–human partnering what is plain is that the Islamic *Shahadah* is pointing towards a theology, a theology of things reciprocal between Allah and Muhammad. Doing so, it is akin to the deepest implications of Hebraic prophethood caught – as these were – in the same issues of divine/human interplay. Clearly we may reverse the repeated Quranic formula: "Obey God and obey the Apostle", to read: "Obey the Apostle and (so) obey God." Further, we could change the verb "Obey" and use the verb "Relate". For Islam, in relating to God would have us relate to Muhammad. In that enjoined relating to him we are duly relating to God in the terms that he comprises.

The heart of the Biblical, Christian, Muslim theology might be said to be asking what verbs can, or do, belong to the inter-formula present in all revelation, and, indeed, in all creaturely experience. Will the verb "know", for instance, hold? or the verb "find"? or "identify"? Certainly, in some sense, God will be thought on via what the prophet-connection, be it Biblical or Quranic, serves to indicate. In the case of the Qur'an, as we have seen, what it indicates moves all the way between God enlisting a final prophet prompted with divine words and God revealing through an emanation of cosmic wisdom vested in the words and in their bearer.

It may help the point, in parenthesis here, to note how the Christian credal phrase: "Very God of very God" belongs to the same realm of discourse. The clause is something of a Latinism in its use of "very", but it has in mind a very Muslim thing, namely the impression that saying: "to know Christ is to know God" is excessive, a going too far. The double "very" aims to intercept this dubiety, this embarrassed hesitation, as if to say: "Do not query what is meant: it is veritable. God has condescended to this disclosure of Himself in the person, the drama, of Christ. His doing so is entirely consonant with His nature." Thus the very form of the credal clause anticipates the sceptics in order, on their own ground, to reassure them. Such alertness to what wants to question it should always be the posture of a creed and belong with its task and with its shape.

"Very God of very God" is, of course, a long way in its confidence in a divine Self-revelation from the *Shahadah*. Yet the bracket (if we may so speak) of Allah and Apostle in the Confession is involved, by theological implication, in the same issue of inter-association. We have acknowledged many difficulties in bringing together Biblical and Quranic prophethoods as a common theme. Not the least of these is the way in which the Biblical ones point forward from the "servant" accent to the Messianic and, so doing, become the matrix prospectively of Christology in the meaning of Jesus. The Quranic prophethood moved forward into the Hijrah programmatically emerging from Muhammad's Meccan experience.

Prophethood, in the one case, points beyond itself and its education of humanity to the costly mystery of redemption. The other has no cause to point beyond itself, seeing that its words and message suffice, provided they be perpetuated in a community of obedience and ensured by the politics of statehood in their name. The two positions obviously turn on contrasted readings both of the nature of God and of the measure of the human predicament.

This brings us to that other dimension of "situated-personhood" which we noted in all the prophets, namely "the weight in the word" as what it cost to say it in the enmity of humankind.

# VI

Earlier chapters have sufficiently explored the hazard and travail inevitably attending on prophetic mission. The reader of Surah 36 is at once taken up into the irony of the herald "sent on a straight path" and how it immediately proves a harassed one, warning "heedless folk". The irony deepens in v.30: "O the anguish", or: "O the pity", about the "servants". These (*al-'ibad*) are usually taken to be hearers, the "bondmen" who never failed to mock and scorn a messenger. But "anguish" for the *'ibad* could be taken for the word-bringers. All turns on how we read the "anguish" noun, with its exclamation mark, *Ya hasratan*, whether as imprecation on the obdurate ("Woe be to the bondmen") or as a lament for the pathos of the messengers' rejection.[25]

Plainly there could not be the one without the other. The sequence in the Surah is painfully adversarial. Near its close (v. 75) Muhammad is told: "Let not what they are saying grieve you." That he was oppressively "grieved" in the pre-Hijrah scene we have fully documented earlier from the relevant evidence in the Qur'an. In Biblical terms also this reality of harsh experience is never in doubt.

The theological question, then, is how this nexus between speaking and suffering enters into God, or may it? There is no doubt of the suffering attending on the sentness, nor of that sentness returning into God. For no authentic prophet is self-commissioned. He preaches only because God wills to speak by means of him. His words are not his own, nor – in that sense – are his pains. They are not privatized into his individual experience as some accident of mere fate or retribution of bare circumstance. They come expressly in the discharge of his prophetic recruitment by God. As long as he holds to his mission they will inflict their cost. His only escape from them would be to cease the mission and abandon obedience to God. The more steadfast he remains the more vicarious he becomes. Inescapably, it is *for* God that he is vicarious.

It follows that there is no final prophetology that can lack a theology concerning where God is in the suffering of His "sent ones". The issue must be inserted at the hinge of the *Shahadah* and between its two halves. It dominates the whole Biblical panorama from Amos to St John. It inspired the early Christian Church to confess a "throne of God and the Lamb".

We have found ample reason earlier to realize that what "messengers" undergo at human hands is a condition of being vulnerable on God's behalf. Their coming and their speaking do not merely incur a hostility meant for God: there is a sense in which their vocal presence arouses it. For human perversity is not left in a limbo of non-accusation. It is confronted radically with its own image. "Troubling Israel" was the old gibe in the days of Elijah. Prophets are a "trouble" to their time and place – as Muhammad was in the disesteem in which the Quraish held him. "Untroubled" in prophetic terms society would languish in complacent self-approval and wallow in sins and untruths, the more rabid for remaining un-accused.

"Bringers of good" and "warners against wrong" thus encounter a wanton enmity. What contradicts evil suffers countering contradiction and the world is disclosed to itself in the exchange. Prophethood is simply targeted by the passions it incriminates. Its devotion to its mission is an expenditure both of courage and of grief. It measures the inhospitality of the world in "the bread of tears", "the treading of the winepress". All happens on behalf of God. Their vulnerability is His, inasmuch as their sending was.

The great Hebrew prophets, in remarkable honesty, wrestled in psalm and soul-search with this measure of their life-experience. It would seem that Muhammad also did in the deep antecedents of the Hijrah and the nadir of his story. Theologians too, in their own intellectual realm, must wrestle with it no less, if they are to retain any genuine faith in prophethoods from God and if they are to keep honest faith with their Scriptures.

Theology has no integrity here if it baulks the issue. There can hardly be any abeyance of the stake God has in His messengers when the earthly going is hard against them. His power, not to say His mercy, would be in radical question if there were any divine negligence of what the sentness is costing. Any desertion of their situation would betray the mandate which had entailed it. The divine enterprise in prophethood must surely be all of one piece as in the pursuing, so in the making and/or the breaking of God's servants. Must it not be that God is by no circumstance, no eventuality, "overtaken" in the inclusiveness of His will?[26] "Are not these things noted in your book?" the anguished prophet-psalmist asked (Psalm 56: 8). He yearned that "the tears" his calling cost him should somehow have significance for Yahweh. The incongruous imagery he used of a "flask" of the Almighty's to collect them only made the more vivid the intensity of his emotion.[27]

All that the sending of prophets signifies of divine solicitude for humans, their wrongs and destinies, is betrayed from within if the messengers are abandoned in their travail. The "burden" they have entered into requires to be known as "entering into God". So the deepest instincts of their Biblical story have ardently understood. Divine indifference becomes a contradiction in terms. For prophethood was never indifferently commissioned.

# VII

But has the theme somehow over-excited itself with this conviction? Muslims see it as a flawed logic. "O the pity of it about (My) servants" – even if referring to the prophets – does not mean that somehow Allah concedes that they are vicarious for His sake, or that, out of divine transcendence, He is identifying with their tribulations. In the brevity of the *Shahadah* there is no such inter-association.

Moreover, vindication of the messengers – but by other means – was, and remains, always assured to God's envoys. Doubtless, divine errands are greeted with enmity. Truth will always encounter contradiction. The vested interests of human selves and human collectives too readily hold it in contempt. But this situation need not be read as "overtaking" divine competence. Hebraic and Islamic instincts feel at once for God's interventionist action to vindicate and rescue what is at stake in the means He employs, the plans He devises.

The Pentateuchal writings are fortified by the idea of "elect" people, "elect" land and "elect" servants of Yahweh having "inviolate" status in which they are ensured divine protection foiling all that is adversarial. There may be hazards and trials but these call for the kind of endurance that has the pledge of deliverance, not for the patience that knows itself vicarious in unrelieved long-suffering. The surrounding pagans had notice served on them to appreciate the folly of threats against "inviolate" people. Consider the strange bravado of Psalm 2, reversing who needs to beware of whom.[28] Or note the warning in Psalm 105: 15: "Touch not Mine anointed and do my prophets no harm" – the reference being to patriarchs and people of Yahweh in their journeyings. Tenacity under guarantee is a different experience from that of long-suffering whose redemptive potential lies only in its own quality.

Each of those contrasted meanings may be read in the familiar Quranic phrase: *hasbuna Allah*: lit. "God is our sufficing", or: "It is enough that we have God." *Hasb* has the sense of "supplying that which no other can". Though not frequent in the Qur'an, it is said by the valiant (3.173) with the co-phrase: *wa Ni'am al-wakil*, "and the best of reliances",[29] in a context of battle and danger. It may thus be akin to the Hebraic theme of assurance concerning all dangers but it can also be read where jeopardy, as with the likes of Jeremiah, has no relief. Islam does not admit of the inviolability that Jewish covenant looked to enjoy. For its only covenant is the Noahid one of a dependable "good earth" and "the cosmic oath" which all humankind universally pledged.

The possible alternative meanings of *Hasbuna Allah*, in line with the Biblical contrast we have noted between the endurance of the ultimately inviolate folk and the vicariousness of those who suffer to redeem, are, however, generally resolved in the former sense by what the Hijrah made fundamental to Islam.[30]

That the emigration from Mecca to Medina, to mark the origin of the Islamic Calendar, belonged to antecedents of adversity is evident enough. Indeed, the entire logic for the Hijrah turned on the obduracy of the Quraish in their enmity to the steady preaching of the Prophet which they took as inimical to the vested interests of their paganism and of their trade. These were corroborated by the ingrained instincts of the *Jahiliyyah*, the crudities and malevolence exemplified in such as Abu Lahab (Surah 111) who enjoys the rare distinction of being personally named in the Qur'an.

The empowerment of Muhammad's message, following its (strictly) verbal non-success in Mecca, in terms of the ensuing city-state in Medina with its prowess at the Battle of Badr and ultimate re-possession of Mecca, initiated the Muslim mind into the due and proper amalgam of faith with power and of religion with rule. The story and the logic are clear enough and found lasting confirmation in the long centuries.

It is vital to see that development as on behalf of a preaching prophethood and for its sake. There would have been no case for, nor urge to, Hijrah had there not been an experience of unwanted witness incurring sharp adversity. The sequel to the Hijrah, in the name of the message that was made to resort to it out of deep rejection, can therefore be seen as the Islamic form of what Jewishness enjoyed in the bosom of inviolability, namely the God-ordained shape of its validation and of its security. Establishment in Medina can be taken as the Muslim experience of divine "election" into confidence and so a legitimated identity. In both cases suffering, in the cause of prophetic vocation, had no need to be taken further into some theology of divinely required vicariousness. Divine action, either in covenant or *Dawlah,* had circumvented any such need.

# VIII

Here, though, we meet an irony. As studied under "Conscience" in a previous chapter, it was precisely the Hebraic reliance on inviolable land, people and/or covenant that the greatest prophets were sent to interrogate and, at times, denounce. Isaiah's effrontery – as it might seem – in addressing Jerusalemites as "Ye rulers of Sodom, ye people of Gomorrah" (1: 10) or the boldness of Jeremiah's famous Temple Sermon (7: 1–4) are notable examples. The doctrine of an inviolable sanctuary was "lying words", falsely trusted by an evil people. The ultimate illusion would take the course of history to Masada. There the Zealots, deceived in their confidence in something finally impregnable (because it was still, barely, on the fringe of sacred territory) and on the verge of corporate suicide, were advised by their leader, Eliazar – according to Josephus – that they should have "conjectured at the purpose of God much sooner".[31] Their own forebears, the prophets, had done so six centuries earlier.

Prophethoods from Amos to Jeremiah that had been scorned or dubbed traitors for having exploded the myth of unconditional inviolate protection for the myth it was, could hardly have their griefs solaced by any such illusions. The idea that their suffering for the truth could somehow be dispelled by pledges about land and people, to ancestry or lineage, could have no place in any adequate theology. Nor could the God of their sending be understood aright in some theodicy of an inviolable people –

the very theodicy which His supreme messengers had disowned. We have to conclude that the divine stake in prophetic tribulation has to be seen as inhering in the divine nature.

If the Hebraic refuge in inviolability "heals the hurt slightly" (to take the language of Jeremiah 6: 14; 8: 11) so also does the Islamic confidence in the political Hijrah as the sufficient answer to the Prophet's verbal anguish, the final solution to human intransigence.

"Sufficient" and "final" are crucial words here. It would be folly to suppose that the "good" in ethics has no need of the "power" in politics. Society cannot subsist in any sort of inter-innocence. Human exchanges are everywhere depredatory and so vulnerable. There is a modicum of justice, righteousness, peace and order, which only power can induce and perpetuate. Islam is foremost among religions in embracing that truth.

But it is a modicum and no more. There are always "remainders" of wrong, anomalies of injustice, perversions of truth, which power – by its very nature and the means it uses – can never reach, can perhaps never even identify. Moreover, its own temptations will always beset its exercise, so that it is never the panacea reliance on it would like, or imagine, it to be. How often the inherent covetousness of power, its need to ensure its own survival, carry it into excesses that deny its own ideals. It is a too readily corruptible, pervertible a structure to be ever the inclusive divine answer for human society.

How clear it is that Biblical prophethoods could never lie in its lap. On the contrary, its structures – political and religious – were the steady theme of prophetic reproach. It was Quraishi power, prestigious and commercial and tribal, that most impeded Muhammad's message and effectively induced him, by its enmity, to resolve on a power base of his own. But when those power terms succeeded, as manifestly they did, they soon moved after his demise into familiar patterns of power-temptation. Three of the four "rightly guided Caliphs" were assassins' victims, as were several of their Ummayyad successors. There was the immediate *Riddah*, or pagan reverting, when tribes that assumed they had only "submitted" to the person of Muhammad, felt free at his death to resume the paganism a temporary vow had disowned. Surah 49.14–18 makes it very clear that there was political "surrendering" devoid of genuine faith and that "allegiance" was understood as "deferring" to Muhammad as a personal power-figure, on the part of the *Munafiqun*, the "hypocrites".

If, in these ways, power sullies and impedes its own best ends by the means it naturally brings to them, it constitutes no final answer to the dimensions theology must recognize in the reality of prophetic suffering – dimensions which must be seen to come fully home to the divine nature.

That, finally, is where Christian faith takes them in confessing "God was in Christ reconciling the world". Our study thus points beyond prophethoods to where Christianity drew its logic from precedents whose bearings may be read forward to the Cross.

There are first two tasks. The one is to think of "burden-bearing" on prophetic part as an experience of sharing in divine travail. The other is to consider the insistent veto, not only from within Islam, to any such reading of God in these "men of God".

In a striking passage in Isaiah 43: 24 – in line with the deep sense of divine pathos in Hebraic prophecy – there is a clear statement of the theology we are compelled towards in all the foregoing. It reads: "You hast made Me to serve with your sins." Whereas, in this prophet's view, Yahweh has not "burdened" His people with ritual duties, they have made Him "burden-bearer" by their wayward wrongs. He is "troubled by their iniquities". Could it be divinely otherwise if we reckon truly with the serious commissioning of God's prophet-agents?

The more urgently moral, the more searchingly spiritual, the more rigorously legal we acknowledge the spoken mission of God's messengers to be, as issuing from the divine Lordship, must not the exacting burden to them of those realities be seen also as significant for God? Otherwise is it not deceived and betrayed from within? No divine concern in the sending remains, in default of divine concern in the tragedy of being sent. A theology of prophethood has to comprehend all dimensions of the sentness, both call and cost, as being *in* God as His faithfully self-consistent enterprise. So the deepest convictions of Biblical faith have affirmed.[32] Where the *Shahadah* has simply juxtaposed the unrivalledness of Allah and the final prophethood of Muhammad, the peers of Hosea and Micah have felt their travail "entering into God" responsively to how God's purposes entered into them as "the weight in the word".

These things, turn, no doubt, on differing perceptions of the divine nature. They also turn on differing reckonings with human meanings. Is our wrongness only in broken law or also in fractured relationship? The profound ethicism of the prophets has concerned us under "Conscience", where we have seen how it passes over, either into eschatologies of judgement or anticipations of Messiah. For, by Biblical evidence as well as by Quranic doctrine, prophethoods end. They cannot be perennial. In what terms, then, is God's purpose in their sending and their ending most appropriately realized?

The question stays. Meanwhile, in present context, there remains the persistent perplexity, among Muslims and not Muslims only, about the meaning of divine identification with the tragic costs of the Word-burden in envoy-experience. Suffering, we imagine, must mean contingency which can never apply to *Allah al-Samad*, the "God whose resources are entirely in Himself" (Surah 112). Further, is not real pathos real limitation? How can Almightiness enter a Gethsemane? Or the eternal Allah be, as Isaiah thought, a "burden-bearer" in respect of us humans, creatures of His very will and awesome sovereignty? "Who is going to credit that kind of reporting?" Isaiah indeed asks (53: 1). That "very God of very God" of the Christian Creed itself hints, as we saw, at things that seem incredible.

That is not contingent which is inwardly ordained, nor is that limitation which has been self-prescribed. We have to take the issue of this divine "compassion" (in the full sense of an often diminished word)[33] into the very sovereignty which is supposed to preclude it. That ceases to be scandalous which is sovereignty's own magnanimity. Indeed, our forbidding it to God would be the supreme – and unwarranted – limitation, our denying to God the liberty of His own counsel.

What doubtless remains at stake is whether divine sovereignty has – or has not – this magnanimity, this expending selfhood, this condescending power. Were we to want, or think, the answer negative, why should there have been any envoys at all?

# IX

That they thought the answer positive was, on the part of the disciples of Jesus, the very making of Christian faith. It was, as they perceived it, the logic of what they knew as his resurrection. But, in the nature of the reality they underwent, they could only know it so in the aftermath of his Cross and Passion. It was conviction out of Gethsemane.

By that retrospect it was evident how the ministry of Jesus had fitted squarely into prophethood patterns. The word "prophet" belonged to him and was often used, as by the Galileans at his entry into Jerusalem, in salutation and expectancy. It was linked, familiarly – or perhaps sardonically – with Nazareth, his home town.[34] The Qur'an, too, readily affirms Jesus as "prophet" and associates *Ansar*, or disciples", with him, unconcerned as it seems to be about the actual content of his teaching.[35] Though, preparatory – in the Christian mind – to titles which leave "prophet" alone quite reductionist, the word is apt enough in every sense. It makes welcome common ground between the Qur'an and the New Testament.

It was precisely in the "prophet" capacity that the deeper dimensions appeared. For Jesus' ministry recapitulated the familiar features of rejection and antagonism. Out of these emerged the Messianic theme. All three Synoptic Gospels record the withdrawal of Jesus and the disciples to the remote territory of Caesarea Philippi at a watershed in the ministry (Matt. 16: 13–23; Mark 8:27–29; Luke 9: 18–20). The intent was to take stock of its implications and of its gathering sense of latent crisis. "Who are they saying I am?" Jesus asks. "What, my friends, is your reading of where we are and who I am?" Jesus seeks their mind, the public – and their private – perception of the course of things thus far. Situations pointing to suffering (as we have seen throughout) are the lot of all prophethoods.

What, then, of Jesus in his here and now? What for him in responding to situation defining vocation? Peter foresees a Messianic destiny with no mind for its nature. On both counts, the travail of Jesus only deepens but a Rubicon has been crossed. The ministry is resumed, only to intensify as it steadily clarifies the odds.

Most illuminating here is the parable of the husbandmen and the vineyard (Matt. 21: 33–42; Mark 12: 1–12; Luke 20: 9–19) The sequence of messengers is climaxed by the sending of the "son" – the only one who could present the claim of the vineyard's Lord in face of the usurpation explicit in the brutal dismissals of servants.[36] The import of the parable was clear enough and at once perceived by the authorities. Jesus implies that, while his ministry stands in a long tradition, it culminates in a more inclusive reckoning with human wrong – a reckoning which is also a more radical expending of divine concern.

The actual sequel unfolds and vindicates the point of the parable. Jesus is crucified at the hands of a coalition of human wrong, from which there has been no rescue either by evasion on his part, or by human refraining from the guilt of the deed, or by divine intervention to prevent it.

The broken disciples of Jesus find the bitterness of their experience in the pain of those three realities. The vivid passage in Luke 24: 13–32, so crucial to the self-awareness of resultant faith, is taken into the very crux of prophethood – the actuality of the tragedy the Cross spells the puzzle of its having been divinely allowed and the cumulative argument it shapes for fathomless despair.

These are the measures of the Christian realism out of which the Church was born. The links with prophethood are written large into the passion of Jesus – the passion which is seen to resolve the question that prophethoods, hitherto, had left puzzzlingly unresolved, namely whether the divine in the sending meant a suffering divine. The answer in the Resurrection was affirmative. The two disciples knew it so, significantly, in an "opening of the Scriptures" and via "the breaking of the bread".

## Prophethood and God

It is important to read what the evangelist confines into the space of a single day as the slowly gathering dawn of comprehension through post-Easter months and years. "All the prophets" – in Luke's phrase – had provided the clue by which, in Christ, the burden of their own mystery could be understood. They, for their part, had anticipated how the logic of their own perplexities would be fulfilled in the Christ whose Cross took it, inclusively and finally, into "the bosom of the Father". That language in the Fourth Gospel – a Gospel no less alert to the legacy of the prophets – shares the meaning of the Pauline formula of "God in Christ".

If, in the crucifying of Jesus, the enmity all the prophets experienced had proof of its utmost reach, then his mastery in love over that "sin of the world" gave evidence, in the very words it used, of God's partnering society. "Father, forgive them . . . " could be read as a divine exchange, if not of roles then of presence. To find "God in Christ" was to know "the Christ in God".[37] "Out of the depth have I called to You, O Lord" (Psalm 130: 1) had long been the cry of all prophetic experience. "Out of the depth" of his Cross and Passion Jesus had called on the Fatherhood of God. The plea of ancient anguish had found its counterpart in the reality of divine patience and grace. It stood clear that God was not merely in some tutorial relation to us humans, with His prophets as the pedagogues. His was decisively a relationship of seeking love and costly hope.

# IX

# Ongoing Finality

## I

"The world exists to end in a book", wrote the French symbolist poet, Stéphane Mallarmé, who thought that a book could finish what the world necessarily leaves incomplete. It could capture what time and history for ever left open in "the cracked tune that Chronos sings".[1]

Such imaging about the poetic word is a far cry from the Qur'an and from the prophetic tradition in the Hebrew Bible. Both these, however, are bound into the concept of an ultimate literature. The Qur'an's perception of a long serial sequence of "messengers and warners" involves a cumulative view of history past. But why should it come to a decisive end in the last of the series – the Qur'an itself? The question has concerned us elsewhere. It needs to be faced here with a mind also for the finalizing of prophethood in the Bible. There too the sequence seemingly ends, despite the prominence in the Christian New Testament of "prophets" among the "ministries" in the Church in several listings of "spiritual gifts". How that Christian feature must be read will come later.

We seem to be left with the assumption that what transpired between Amos and Malachi terminated, either by passing into Jewish apocalyptic or by culminating in the Messianic reality the Christian apostles identified in Jesus as the Christ. In that latter sense, John the Baptist was "the last of the prophets" precisely in being "more than a prophet". "All the prophets and the law prophesied until John."[2] That "until" would be the word also for the Qur'an, with Muhammad as its meaning. In either case, faith in a long continuity arrives at termination. "Would that all the Lord's people were prophets" is something we can no longer cry with Moses, except in the particular charismatic sense he intended (Numbers 11: 29). The Canon is hermetically closed and has been endowed with an irrepeatability enshrined as "Scripture" for both the Bible and the Qur'an.

For the Christian faith the logic of Hebrews 1: 1–2, is absolute. What was "sundry" and disparate "in past times *by* the prophets" yields to what is "spoken *in* the Son" with a perennial quality "the fathers" never knew. The Qur'an stands in its own different assurance as "the seal of the prophets". Islam is uncompromisingly staked on the finality of Muhammad as the consummation of all possession and exemplification of divine recruitment of prophetic agency. The "guidance" of history is complete and "religion perfected unto us" in *Al-Islam* (Surah 5.3).

To speak, then, of "ongoing finality" may seem like a contradiction of terms and of perceptions. Yet can finality ever be static? The very metaphor of "sealing", at least in the Hebrew tradition, intended disciples in a future for which the immediacy awaiting it was meant. "Sealing" in no way meant jettisoning or consigning to oblivion. It anticipated a future needing the relevance of what would then be the reality out of a past. Datedness, as we have seen in CHAPTER V, was inherent in any revelation at all, time being the condition of words in time. Finality must mean that settings are not limits nor locales prisons. Prophets are not hostage to circumstance: they enlist it for posterity.

## II

This issue of "ongoingness" has exacting dimensions for the people of both Scriptures and, in both cases, hinges squarely on the role of community. The temper of Quranic finality is the more adamant, containing – as it does – the paradox of a culminating sequence that cannot go further. It may be that, in the immediate context of the Prophet's closing years, the Qur'an's being utterly *sui generis* was urgent as an emphasis in view of competing claimants to divine *wahy*. It is clear that rival "prophets" were around to confront Muhammad's stature/status as Allah's sole mouthpiece. The very juncture in his person of text-receiving and power-directing meant that any would-be rivalry or challenge would need to pretend to the same capacity. That Muhammad's detractors were invited to "bring a surah like" the Qur'an has surely to do with this situation as well as with the credentials implicit in the Qur'an's Arabic quality.

But the Qur'an's finality – and its rigorous acknowledgement – were vital also in the aftermath of Muhammad's death and throughout Islam's expansion under the early Caliphs. It is clear from the traditional account of 'Uthman's veto on the multiplication of diverse texts of the Book that dangers lurked in diverse readings sponsored by different centres or engendered by political contention. By the same token, aspirants to prophetic status itself would be held the more treacherous and be the more vehemently denounced. In some measure, the very success of the Islam the Qur'an epitomized made for a rooted doctrine of its irrepeatable nature as the ultimate word of God. The submission of the *mu'minin* had not been only to "this man", whose death some in the *Riddah* thought had absolved all vows of fealty.³ It had also been to the whole, single volume of *Tanzil* "sent down upon him" – the volume which his death had left uncompromisingly complete. For there had not been, and never could have been, any other recipient.

These factors underlying and, in part, explaining, the insistent finality of the Qur'an differ sharply from the factors tending to a falling off of Hebrew prophethood in the sequel to Temple rebuilding under Nehemiah, the frailty of that enterprise and the emergence of the Maccabean zealotry and the Greek influences in "Wisdom" literature. Hebrew prophethood had never been in singular terms nor were its ongoings contingent on military success, expansionism and political hegemony. If we should speak at all of its "exhaustion" beyond the 4th century BC it had greatly ennobled the four preceding centuries. It could not fail of a future, a destiny which its own worth would ensure.

On one occasion in the frequent heedlessness with which Muhammad's preaching was disesteemed, the Qur'an (41.44) likened his people to "folk being called to from a long way off". The phrase could fit many in our contemporary world whom his Book is still summoning from across distant years and a far-off climate of mind. What then had a backward "seal" of completeness was also "sealed" for a forward empire of relevance. Such expectancy is implicit in all prophethood.

Or, Biblically, there is that elusive pledge about "the servant" in Isaiah 53: 10: "He will prolong his days and see his seed." Mysteriously "a progeny" awaits him – exegetes, translators, interpreters – through whom he will enjoy a risky perpetuity in times beyond his dreams and his control. For "In his hand there is a pleasure of the Lord" with intentions no bare life-span could embrace.

Futurity, then, was built into prophethood both Biblical and Quranic, and *de facto* has massively occurred. But *de jure* – as to validity and authenticity – how right has it been? How appropriate to origin and first dimension? And how, either way, are these vital questions answered, by what criteria and by whom?

## III

So much being at stake, it was proper, in the preceding chapters, to sift and measure the contributing elements – personality, language, situation, conscience, suffering and the God-relation. For all these deserve to monitor all present interpretation of the past. Any such control – if the word is to be realist – assumes the bringing of a present integrity. For, awesome as it must be known to be, the "prolonging" of prophetic "days" belongs precariously with the fragility of our reading custody. "Being dead yet speaking" turns on the audition of the living. If the divine Name can be "taken in vain" so also can the divine text.

This paradox of a decisively closed Canon meant as an ever-used Scripture, which obtains in respect of both Bible and Qur'an, means that it both regulates by its fixity and anticipates in its meanings. It both enshrines and expects. Its command is over minds on which it must depend if its authority is to avail. The old phrase about "people of a Book" has this strange double ring. Grammarians (in Arabic) would say that "Book" is "in construct" with "people" – a "possessed" with a "possessor". Thematically, too, and exegetically, it is given the "construction" its heirs make of it.

Thus the Jewish, Christian, Muslim doctrine that "Scriptures" are finalized – for ever inviolate and not subject to addition, subtraction, multiplication or division – requires that what they mean has no other resource but the receiving wisdom of their "people". It is noteworthy that when new religions emerge from old they invariably generate their own "holy writ".[4] Islam has always been watchful to denounce any calling into question of the Qur'an's finality.[5] It is, then, precisely in its closedness that a "people's Book" – Bible or Qur'an – is the more crucially left to its custodians, bound as these are to what it "binds", yet reading as they will, with them its opening.

Or, differently expressed, Scripture-Canons are quantitatively complete but qualitatively potential, seeing that inclusive meanings cannot be imprisoned in a shut place. The old phrase about "shutting to open" and "opening to shut" has its logic here.[6] What is "bound in heaven" waits to be affirmed on earth and meaning turns on the transaction both ways – in revelation and in readerships.

It may be wise, here in parenthesis, to say that we are beyond the crude "futurizing" that takes prophethood avidly as mere "foretelling" and then goes on to ask: "Did it happen as suggested?" and, if so, then the prophet is vindicated, if not, then he is belied. That limited notion about prediction has been relegated here to early margins in the real concern for witness and meaning, ethical and spiritual, the mind of God in verdict on the ways of the world. "Times and seasons" and calendars are one thing, righteousness, hope and the knowledge of God another. The "ongoing finality" that matters is not the sort that dating must disappoint or calendar-consulting distract. Nor does it belong with those manipulations of chronology that devise curious "fulfilments" over lapsing centuries that can bear only ingeniously contrived relation to the first – and continuous – moral context of the words.[7] The likes of Hosea, Jeremiah, Joel or Micah were not concerned when they told of judgement ahead or benediction beyond, with palm-reading notions of good, or bad, fortune, but with how "righteousness might roll down" like a river in flood, with how "swords into ploughshares" might be fashioned. Joel's "locusts" were not to be read as a soothsayer might: they made him a passionate preacher of repentance. Thus, again, the relevance of Hebrew prophethood for contemporary Zionism is not how it might congratulate itself on belated self-fulfilment but rather how it might heed for its own health the anguish of Jeremiah: "O Jerusalem who is there who will turn aside and ask how you fare?" (15: 5), or Isaiah crying: "Woe to them that join house to house and field to field, until there be no room, that they may be left alone in the midst of the earth" (5: 8). Prophethoods are only rightly finding perpetuity in the thrust of their own essential care for "justice, mercy and the love of God".

To this parenthesis there is one other point. Prophets themselves often emerged in the context of expectation. Their very sequence had a logic, like instalments, of others to follow. (It is this which makes finality a problem.) Moses came to be a progenitor in this way. His was a repute that prophets to be might emulate as the very impetus to their vocation. For, unlike priests, prophets are not born to office. They have to be "raised up", as the tradition of Moses exemplified. Deuteronomy 18: 15 became a significant verse in this context with Moses himself pledging (with divine concurrence – 18: 18) the emergence of one resembling him and similarly from the same kin.[8] Thus Moses came to symbolize the ideal prophet, though it is striking how far – in their indictment of law, ritual and covenant-illusion – Amos and his kin contravened much he was held to exemplify. Yet, as Hosea (12: 13) recognized the human agency in the Exodus remained unforgettable.

Of present concern is the way in which Islamic tradition has cited Deut. 18: 15 and 18 in authenticating Muhammad and, further, has taken the reference in John 14: 16 ("another Comforter") as a promise realized in Muhammad, in the manner of the Deuteronomist. The claim rests on a misreading of the Johannine term *parakletos* and its alleged consonantal distortion of another Greek word approximating to the Arabic meaning of *Ahmad* (or Muhammad).[9] By this reading Jesus also foretold the Prophet of Islam, further reinforcing Muhammad's likeness to Moses. That tallies also with the Qur'an's emphasis, noted earlier in CHAPTER III, on Muhammad's being "native" – as all prophets should be – among his own hearers. This was not only because, for Jewry, all "foreign" prophets were "peepers" and soothsayers, but also in implementation of the covenant with Israel. Only a Jewish spokesman could speak for the Torah God.[10] Islam required the same "nativeness" for its own different reasons, around the vital Arabicity of the Qur'an.

The immediate point, before moving to crucial themes on prophetic perpetuity, is to appreciate this Quranic view of a parallel of continuity reaching from Moses to Muhammad, even incorporating minor names who may well have preceded Moses,[11] but also ignoring all those through whom Biblical continuity passed – most significantly of all – from Amos to Zechariah. It will always remain a puzzle why the supreme prophets of the four great centuries from Hosea to Joel (Jonah being a special case) are totally absent from what perhaps we may call the echo-ology of the Qur'an.[12]

These points, however – to end parenthesis – are only incidental aspects, between heirs of two Scriptures, concerning their vested interest in certain specifics around finality. It is time to take up the main onus of "continuing weight in abiding word".

What after-life may prophethoods expect, what futures enjoy? In life there is nothing more "final" than the uttered word. It has gone beyond recall into the unpredictables, the fortuities, of a hearing and unhearing world. These, for all its ardour or authority, it cannot disabuse, if they abuse it. To protest against distortion will not be in its power. Only by a patient sufferance of risk and jeopardy may it take an onward course. "Unfulfilled intentions" there will be, like those of human misadventure, no less than the unintended "fulfilments" posterity will find. One might write of Scriptures somewhat as Ted Hughes wrote of "symbol": " . . . above all a vessel for interpretations: the reader fills it and drinks . . . Like the variety of potential readers, the variety of potential interpretation is infinite."[13] Or, if "infinite" here is too sinister a word, then "multiple" will suit. The old story of Moses, yielding to correction as to his own meanings in a circle of Talmudists, tells the same hazards meanings must run.

Good and sane hope in this situation lies in painstaking awareness of it and in a perception of the trust that prophets have placed in all their legatees. The ongoing of the one in the other may be studied here under three heads – the temporal, the textual and the testamentary. The first extends from the themes of CHAPTER V that had to do with the *sitz-im-leben* with which it concluded. How should the "whither" of interpretation ride with the "whence" of history? The problem was remitted from the earlier study of "occasions of revelation" as both Biblical and Quranic prophethoods knew them.

The textual factor in any continuity of meaning involves discerning the potential for development of allegory, the *double entendre* latent in form and vocabulary, the legitimacy – or otherwise – of insights only had from long retrospect. This malleability of texts to new readership poses issues as to discipline and consensus and is prey to unhappy exploitation. We have already noted that what is trivial, mechanical or merely ingenious, has to be firmly excluded.[14] But, equally, much central to Judaism, Christianity and Islam has turned on texts coming to mean more, or other, than their first origins could have held. The New Testament theme of "Christ in all the Scriptures" must figure strongly here, as will the elasticity of Quranic vocabulary.

"Testamentary" seems a valid word for the third aspect. If prophethoods spell legacies, "generation to generation", and these inherit their meanings, then the relationship is a kind of "testament", given and received. In Isaian terms, "report" is both "heard" and so "told", only taken in to be taken on. What, by the nature of its date and place, is bequeathed to other time and further place, is "testamentary" both from and to its destiny. The word captures both the role of lapsing years and the dignity of legatees and – if we allow the term – the heirloom of truth.[15] Both in respect of Biblical and Quranic prophethood we will find receptive community the ultimate factor in, and agent of, ongoing finality. The Muslim and Christian shapes of the communal role are strikingly different, for reasons, as we must see, deeply rooted in contrast around their Scriptural conceptions.

One imaginative route into our first concern over this "to-be-continued" issue around final prophethood – continued, that is, in right possession – would be to reflect on the "enmantle-ing" we noted as so vital in Muhammad's call. "Thou who art enwrapped", "thou who art enfolded" (Surahs 73.1 and 74.1) were real commissionings. We noted the "mantle of Elijah" tradition, the identifying "robe of office" to be assumed by Elisha. However we interpret its echo in respect of Muhammad, its heralding of the Qur'an, there is no doubting the imagery it bequeaths to our present theme. "Enwrapped" all generations are in their cultural attire. Few things are so dated as clothes. *Sartor resartus*, as

Thomas Carlyle had it, captures how times conceal themselves in the very garments by which they self-reveal.[16]

Garb, here, betokens all else about the flux of societies and the clues by which they transact comprehension. Plainly we are contemporaries neither of Isaiah nor of Muhammad. Only by an effort of will many are ill-equipped to make can we appreciate the antics of Ezekiel or kindle easily to the Sidrah tree of the Qur'an. Many of the imponderables of nature's threat to life, which, as with Joel's locust-plague, so moved the prophets to summon their world to penitence have, for us, been circumvented by technology. This should not mean that there need be no more penitents. It does mean that they must be had by a different logic. We find ourselves estranged by the Quranic theme of attendant jinns hovering round our personal wills. The ways are legion in which "then" and "now" are differently clad and, thereby, differently perceived.

Yet, in the original sense, there is no "unwrapping" the mystique of revelation. It has its house and home, telling the divine and the human in contemporary idiom and leaving ever present the task of reclothed significance. This means possessing anew the abiding themes, unforfeited because undiminished. The canonizing – both Biblical and Quranic – ensured the reservoir for all time. That was its role. But its role also was, in both cases, to deter deviance. Unclosed Scriptures would have invited addenda and addenda made for dangerous insertion.[17] In this sense, faiths via Scriptures are inherently defensive. Yet, if not crudely *about* the future, they are "bent *towards*" it. This paradox comprises the entire testing of faiths by their faithful, of the faithful by their faiths.

When the original Qur'an, in a crucial word, *tadabbur*, pleaded with its hearers for "reflection", for intelligent attention (4.82 and 47.24) they would have brought to it – when they heeded – considerations very different from those of a modern nuclear physicist or an oil engineer. They had minds more susceptible to the charm of their native speech and the prowess (*muru'ah*) of their clans than the case-making for a single worship. The demands on such *tadabbur* are more strenuous now but since the Qur'an is held to be still making them, response has to have its measure. It is not only that there are problems of historical criticism to which attentive minds must do justice, but also that theistic convictions at large have more exacting challenge than the 7th century could ever understand.

There are two grounds of confidence. The one is that Muslims have met the testings of time already in the middle centuries. The other is that there are broad and inclusive grounds inside Quranic perspectives adequately to encounter modernity and – as some perceive it – post modernity.

## Ongoing Finality

It is evident enough to historians that serious issues of faith which were only latent in the first world of the Qur'an had to be squarely taken up in the sophistication aroused by Islam's expansion into areas of the Near East which, though physically occupied and subdued, were more intellectualized by Greek and Christian inheritance and usages. Clearly, Al-Ghazali (1058–1111) in his *Tahafut al-Tahafut* and his *Ihya' 'Ulum al-Din* was engaged in a far more alert *Tadabbur* than Ibn Hisham of Al-Tabari.[18] He carried further the precedents of mental travail around theology set by thinkers in the 9th century and beyond, who had first taken the measure of issues concerning divine and human will, the Qur'an's eternity *cum* temporality and the Prophet's recipience in *wahy*.[19] These had never troubled the first four Caliphs or not in the same self-conscious terms.

Coming abreast of a faith's mental duties in that guise can well repeat itself when time and climate have again moved inexorably on and away from past securities of doctrinal formulation. The factors, technological and intellectual and social, obtaining in Islam's fifteenth century are vastly removed from those of the eleventh. There is no reason why the impulses, Quranic and spiritual, which availed for an Al-Ghazali in the crisis of his scepticism, cannot comparably invigorate the present age. Despite the sharp deterrents surviving into post-imperial time and the sundry tensions in Islamic nationalism, there is recognition of the mental labours obligating Muslims today.[20]

The key to hope lies in the basic Quranic emphasis on the divinely granted *khilafah*, or "dominion", humanity exercises as a trust from Allah, making humans liable, in the capacities of creaturehood, for the realization of divine purposes through a "submission" at once rationally free and spiritually due. It is a universally human privilege, not restricted in Mosaic terms to a single ethnicity. Otherwise it incorporates that same Biblical theme of a humanity commissioned into its own true fulfilment via its Godward obedience. It is a prescript, for ever elusive of realization by the forms and precepts of religion, yet for ever weighing upon them as a destiny that truly defines their human-ness. Only so does Quranic prophethood perpetuate its final meaning.

How the golden centuries of Hebrew prophethood "saw their seed" and "prolonged their days" in ongoing finality (though it could turn on that same vision of a guided human "dominion") is a different story. That they ceased in post-exilic history is clear, though the canonization of their texts ensured their currency – a currency surviving into times of Maccabean zealotry and the struggle with Hellenization and, later, the impact of Roman power. Quintessential to classic prophethood was the moral challenge to "chosenness" and "land-inviolability" and, thus, to the Hebrew psyche of Yahweh-bonding. We have seen how this ethos of an inwardly accused theism contrasted so sharply with the contra-pagan, outwardly confrontational ethos of the Qur'an in a theism of Arab genesis. It is not surprising, in the Biblical case, that prophets had their missions muted. The reasons lay in the growing claims of zealotry and then the loss of the Temple and the forfeiture of "the land" in diaspora. Inner accusation and moral scrutiny, after the fashion of the prophets, were foregone in the urgent impulse to close ranks, to replace the lost Temple by new devotion to Torah and synagogue. In due time, Talmudic lore and the mental ghetto became vital to preservation.

No comparable prophets arose in Mediterranean, Arabian or Egyptian dispersion, to rally the exiled Jews in the Isaian or the Ezekiel terms of the Babylonian and Persian exile. The sort of accommodation that Jeremiah's famous Letter had advised his readers to seek by eastern rivers was not concerted in Alexandria by Philo and his kin whose mental residence, as "men of Torah", was with Greek philosophy and its "wisdom". The translation into Greek, called the Septuagint, of Hebrew Scriptures had, with Philo, already prepared the way for a Jewishness increasingly focused on survival by adaptation to Gentile thought, entailing subtle compromises of the Yahwism the great prophets had loved and told. Thus their abiding legacy took form in Judaism in terms the Isaiahs and Jeremiah would have found hardly comprehensible. There was a reversal of Zechariah's vision of an enquiring world "taking hold of Jewish skirts" and saying: "Let us go with you for Yahweh is with you" (8: 23). Jews were now laying hold of the threads of Greek philosophy, finding divine wisdom in Socratic terms of rational logic in the external world and in the human soul.

Even so, it served to help preserve Jewish identity in the absence of the defining preservatives of land and Temple, via the abiding indestructibility of the ethnic. In broad terms the Messianic heart-beat of the great prophetic tradition was stilled in the abeyance of those defining themes. There were intermittent spasms of Messianic hope to relieve the torpor of the ghetto scene through long centuries but any prophetic "prolonging" in that idiom was tenuous indeed.[21] It remained so until revived in the political Zionism of Herzl, Jabotinsky, Ben-Gurion and Begin, where it stood most in need of the sublime ethicism of Amos, Isaiah and Jeremiah and the capacity of Hosea for divine pathos. Other aspects of "Messiah" belong with the section on "testament" when nascent Christianity took up the term. For the rest, Hebrew prophethoods, beyond mere survival, truly captured the centuries beyond them by their sublime moralism and and as the perennial scrutineers of the pride and folly of religions.

## IV

Caught up in these, the temporal aspects of what has to be "ongoing" from prophethoods are the textual matters, the potentials of rich vocabulary and the ambivalence of phrase and form. The endless liquidity of language is familiar enough through all literature. It becomes the more exacting for readers and believers when the literature is held sacred. For then the issues of word-meaning and interpretation acquire vested or partisan interests, liable to make them contentious. CHAPTER IV was occupied with "Language" in the context of vocation, situation and original significance. The task now is to reflect on what time does with all three by the way its passing affects what is subject to its flux and to the will of the generations.

Are there meanings, at first unrealized, that are legitimately located in the text? If so, by what criteria of "development" are they elicited and established as fit and right? There are notorious examples in the New Testament, the theme in Matthew and in Paul of "Christ in all the Scriptures", with its echo also in Luke (24: 25–6 and 32). The first, in telling of Jesus, makes frequent use of the formula "That it might be fulfilled." Paul says quite roundly: "That Rock was Christ" (I Corinthians 10: 4 recalling Moses striking the rock in Horeb). These Christian handlings of texts we better defer to the third section on things "testamentary". Judaism discounts them and Islam is oblivious.

The Qur'an's perhaps cryptic, but certainly significant, application to itself – or "something" in itself – of the phrase *Umm al-kitab* is a ready instance of the point in view. Surah 3.7 distinguishes between "verses categorical" and "verses allegorical". The former are (lit.) "the mother of the Book". "Essence" seems the likeliest English equivalent, "Substance", "foundation", "fundamental part", could serve. The fact of this distinction – as the passage is well aware – opens the door to diversity of reading, inasmuch as decisions have to be reached because, on its own showing "the Book" is not always categorical. Things "figurative" are present and, as such, subject to how readers see them and how they discriminate responsibly, as discriminate they must. The dilemma is no less present in the Bible, as readers of Jonah, of Daniel with the lions, or the "fiery furnace", have had to decide. Are they stories telling a meaning they readily suggest or are they miracle/facts over which we must puzzle to overcome a scientific scepticism?[22] If the former then we know what the *umm* within them is.

It is the incidence of this distinction pertaining so deeply in Scriptures

## Ongoing Finality

that transfers "the weight in the word" into "the onus on the heeder". What is housed in allegory will be definitive in import. Ezekiel's imagery of a river, deepening from ankle, to knee, to waist until full enough to swim in, conveys what is real precisely in being non-factual.[23] Whether or not Muhammad's "Night Journey to the farther sanctuary" (i.e. from Mecca to Jerusalem, Surah 17.1) is "history" or "symbol", Muslims have no doubt as to its being "real", as a dimension of his prophethood and of the Qur'an's credentials. In that sense, it is – in any event – categorical, yet deeply figurative.

It is noteworthy that prophetic texts leave the issue and the decision to the reader. Indeed, they could do no other. For any move to categorize would be the end of the distinction. And the distinction is clearly crucial. The Qur'an itself (3.7) warns against wayward play with the allegorical passages. Readers are put on their own mettle, as all are who must opt, for example, on the meaning of Hosea's being bidden: "Go marry a harlot", on Ezekiel's "eating of the roll", on Isaiah's "virgin-born" Emmanuel, on Muhammad's "two bows-length" vision of the angel. In all these, "substance" and "figure" in their apt way come together.

To be sure, the categorical sort may be recognized in legal or ritual directives in the Qur'an or in the Biblical prophets that use them. As such they are easy to identify. Even here, however, lawyers – for their own *raison d'être* – will find ample scope for debate. For even laws can resort to figurative terms that are capable of variant reading. Things allusive repose in plain commands. "Allah", for example, "has made the *Ka'bah* to be the sacred house, a holy edifice for mankind" (Surah 5.97). Why, then, is access to it denied to all non-Muslims? Or is *al-nas* (humanity) here to mean only Muslim humans and not (as it must mean in 114.1–3) all mankind? A large issue about any human ecumene turns on a single word in a context certainly categorical. Comparably, in many Isaian passages, as we have seen, the universal reach of Yahweh's "salvation" stays exclusively in Jewish grasp.

Perhaps it is fair to wonder whether the figurative and the symbolic in prophetic discourse invite the reader, in the ultimate reckoning, to enter, as far as may be, into the vision, the thrust of the imagery that originally found the words. If drama and literature work that way, then Scriptures also may break through the settings of their own time and convey their significance by new acts of cognizance and imagination in which they surpass themselves. The notion is, of course, suspect to rigorists anxious to keep exegesis on a tight rein and fearful of what may happen to their authority.

The poetry and discourse of Muhammad Iqbal (1876–1938) present the

149

Qur'an in a guise far removed from the meticulous margins of the old exegetes. It is confidently aligned with the *élan vital* of Henri Bergson and his "creative evolution". The Prophet becomes a paragon of dynamic personhood who, in effect, summoned his hearers to "exalt their ego so high that God Himself would consult them before determining their destiny".[24] As for *waḥy* in the Qur'an, he takes Surah 42.51:

> It is not given to any mortal man to have God address him except by revelatory inspiration, or from behind a veil, or by sending a messenger inspired by His leave with the revelation He wills.

In comment he writes:

> It is the psychology and not the content of the experience that is given . . . It is essentially a matter of inarticulate feeling untouched by discursive intellect . . . Inarticulate feeling seeks to fulfill its destiny in idea, which, in its turn, tends to develop *out of itself* its own visible garment.[25]

This is a far cry from classic Muslim account of how the very Arabic text of the Qur'an is divine speech. General Zia al-Haqq would not have seen it Iqbal's way, yet Iqbal became almost "the patron saint of Pakistan".

Citation here is in no way to deny Iqbal his Muslim right to read the Qur'an as he wills. It is to indicate how its content may yield to new measures and be infused with new perspectives. The principle that "everyday He (Allah) is at work" (55.29) means for Iqbal that "every moment the life of Reality is original, giving birth to what is absolutely novel and unforeseeable". The words recall both Bergson and A. N. Whitehead and "process theology".[26]

What texts mean and who is to say, as questions inseparable from the trust of faith, has taken equally venturesome form in the different idiom of Biblical commentary. What, for example, ought to be had from Isaiah's famous passage about the "maiden" bearing "Emmanuel" – a child to be significant for the young King Ahaz of Judah in the throes of a political crisis about which he was "unwilling to ask a sign". Isaiah volunteered one anyway. The passage (7: 10–17) had been variously read, long before the evangelist Matthew recruited it so boldly. Isaiah had a habit of giving his own children symbolic names. Was "Emmanuel", "God with us", his own child? Does *almah*, in the Hebrew, mean more than "a child-bearing woman". Why did the LXX use *parthenos* and not *neanis*? Did it intend a virginal sense? If so, why?

In what way would the child's birth and weaning signify to Ahaz? Not – *in situ* – as some far-future redeemer-king. "The arriving" to "eat curds and honey" suggests a time period in which the hostile coalition Ahaz feared would have crumbled, thus ending his faithless fears. Is that diet a sign of intervening poverty and privation or, by contrast, are curds and honey the food of small princes, denoting majesty? Given that the months from birth to weaning could suffice to prove royal fears groundless, could that be the crux of the sign? Or, might it be that something so elemental, so ordinary, yet always so miraculous, as childbirth – any childbirth – betokened the unfailing divine preservation of the universe? There is nothing more humbling, more re-assuring, than the maternal entrustment with infancy.

It was Matthew, none before him and none after until Justin Martyr, who glimpsed that idea and forthwith linked it with the (to be) Messianic birth in Bethlehem and the whole cycle of "virginity" in the origins of Jesus came into being, with none but imaginative warrant from what Isaiah originally intended. As long as the prophets hold such potential beyond their own reach to censure or control, the textual issue of things "ongoing" from their words will have this tangled future.

All words spell periphrasis, seeing that – as John Donne had it – "truth round and around must go", first circulating textually and then textually circulating in the currency of generations. The Letter to Timothy (2: 2–9) rejoices that "the Word is not bound".[27] Pundits, and maybe prophets, might wish it were. Are the latter rather akin to the playwright Berholt Brecht who, asked to provide an epitaph, proposed: "I made suggestions." There is always what Coleridge called "the nature of the imagery".

Fertile in this context is the vital dictum of the Qur'an (112.3) concerning Allah: *Lam yalid wa lam yulad*. How should it be understood, how translated? It is the central principle of *Tawhid*, divine Oneness, excluding all likeness or representation. "He does not beget, nor is He begotten." In the sense of *not* being in a change of contingency in which, *qua* paternity, the son displaces the father who gave him being, and that "father lost his", the words would be so obvious as not to need saying outside a benighted pagan context. But were the words designed to disavow Christian credal language which used the words "begotten of the Father" with the caveat "before all worlds"?

If so, the words "beget" and "begotten", used in both the Surah and the Creed, were at totally cross purposes. The Creed entirely agrees with the Surah in the Surah's intended meaning, which is to deny paternity to God. But "Fatherhood" might be something else, something like authorship, liability, care, love and education – none of which could be credibly denied to "the ever resourceful Lord" – that definition implicit in the Surah's own following word *Al-Samad* (which elaborates on the preceding phrase), meaning One who has all in Himself, but One who, precisely in that infinite capacity, initiates, from within Himself, enterprises of creation, providence, revelation and grace. For His eternal resources are not imprisoned in Him so that He is no master of His own will, no arbiter of His own ends – ends which might well spring from His authoring power, including the intervention in our history that Christians identify in the coming, by human birth, into human need and wrong, of Jesus as His Christ.

What unhappy misconstruings and contentious mischiefs turn on the sense of words, what miscarriage of metaphor! Much also in the realm of law in the "categorical" area is susceptible of textual uncertainty. The legitimacy, for example, of plural wives (up to four) can be nullified by a simple alternative reading of the single verb *ta'dilu* in 4.2. Meaning "do justly by . . ." or "treat impartially . . ." the word leaves open whether it intends material provision or sustained personal regard and affection. If the latter, plural marriage is ruled out since the proviso that allows it is unattainable.[28] Elsewhere, how far can analogy reach in extending from existing Quranic directives findings that might cover situations never envisaged in the 7th century? These multiply daily with great seriousness across wide spheres of technique and culture in which the concept of non-repugnancy to the Qur'an has to find its due authority.[29] The "occasions of revelation" through twenty-three years must cover "occasions of perplexity" after fourteen centuries.

Outside legal prescripts, it is easier, maybe, for both Biblical and Quranic exegesis to handle things figurative pliably and feel justified in doing so. For a certain permission so to do is implicit in the shape of the original text being that way. Was it that the "genius" of revelation, divine or human, intended to be allusive and to leave discretion to future minds? So much is implicit in the concept of "signs" – a term basic through all the prophets and crucial to the very conception the Qur'an has of itself.

Whether concerted after the manner of Isaiah and Ezekiel, or integral to the Qur'an in its given way of being "Qur'an", "signs" speak only into their interpretation, just as metaphors wait for, and wait upon, the cognizance they require. "The face of God", "the great throne", "Allah seated", "near as the jugular vein", "the heavens reared on unseen pillars" – all these are Quranic imagery, just as "the hand of the Lord", "Yahweh's arm", "treading the winepress", "the shadow of a great rock" are Biblical. This, throughout, is language seeking out imagination and demanding that it be vivid. All is a literature designed for soul co-operation that it may fulfil itself. The co-operation it solicits must find the response congenial to both text and heart, in a sort of inter-subjection, that has to renew itself in what can only be an ongoing task. That inter-play, reversing Coleridge's "Dejection – An Ode", has

> ... every hope from outward forms to win
> The passion and the life, whose fountains are within.[30]

Two notable examples in recent study would be George Caird's *The Language and Imagery of the Bible* and Fazlur Rahman's *Major Themes of the Qur'an*, both published in the same year. Caird explores the subtle relation of language to meaning, of idiom to thought in Hebrew, and the role of metaphor.[31] Given the entire commitment of the Qur'an to Arabic, there is no Islamic equivalent of the Septuagint's enrichment of Biblical study. Much of what Caird has to say about cognate forms belongs also to the power of Quranic diction. His sense of the potential movement, or "ripening", of meaning through the fertility of single pivotal words can be marked also as the central concern of Fazlur Rahman. Among them *taqwa* with its derivatives is paramount, and capable of incorporating profound present overtones of a "God-fearingness" braced by acceptance of increasing awareness of the sciences and of the fact that "the Quranic cosmogony is minimal".[32] Divine *qadar* in the Qur'an is in no sense a crude "fatalism" (a western error): rather it means

> that while God alone is absolutely infinite, everything else bears the creaturely hallmark of "being measured", i.e. having a finite sum of potentialities ... whereby it fits into a pattern.

That pattern is governed by the divine *amr*, the Creator's "command" by which all things have their being but which obtains perpetually in the outworking of their innate reality.[33] It is easy to glimpse how contemporary researches, and their "findings", can fit into this vocabulary.

Fazlur Rahman is equally resourceful in his study of *Al-Akhirah*, the Quranic term for "that which is the Last", in passages of "the future state" which are among the most problematic of "the figurative" elements:

> (it) is the moment of truth ... an Hour when all veils between the mental pre-occupations of man and the objective moral reality will be rent ... Every person will find there his deepest self.[34]

This reality of "end-values" lies behind the Qur'an's theme of what we "send before us" of good or ill, and the "weighing" of our deeds in moral balances. Fazlur Rahman holds that the whole purpose of the Book is to be prescriptive and imperative rather than to be "about Allah and His nature". His reading of *Al-Shaitan*, Satan, perceives an objectivity of evil, *taghut*, though "there can be no Satan independent of human nature".[35]

Under "Man in Society", Fazlur Rahman elaborates this theme of humans "corrupting in the earth", as moral declension through "hardness of heart" and "weakening of moral fibre" consequent on the negligence that prophets as "warners" must accuse. There is a "judgement which descends upon nations on the basis of their collective performance" – hence the frequent Quranic narratives about history's retributions on the tribes.

It is this theme of our human capacity for "transgressing the limits", for indulging in wrong by neglect or defiance of divine laws, which refers our course of thought back to the role of conscience explored earlier in CHAPTER VI. For though prophetic conscience from Amos to Malachi knew only too well how devious humans could be, it also came to know that law itself, in its very majesty as God-given, could generate attitudes that spelled exoneration or even licensed iniquity.

This is the supreme paradox of a theocratic ethics, of law which, precisely because it comes from God, circumscribes obligation to its precepts, implies exoneration as long as they are kept, and even makes its people myopic about how far they are captive to complacence and self-esteem. When such *fitnah* – to use a Quranic term[36] – is reinforced by concepts of inviolate covenant and election, the danger that conscience will languish is the more acute.

It is a further merit of *Major Themes* that Fazlur Rahman integrates personal conscience into the meaning of *taqwa* and understands *Al-Akhirah* as "conscience in final reckoning", "confronted with "the Hour of Truth".[37] He sees it as needing to be always under scrutiny from within itself. If this is so then Muslim conscience – like any other – cannot exonerate itself by appeal to a static moral orthodoxy, nor absolve itself from selfishness and pride on the ground that, within its given legal limits, it is "law-abiding".[38]

We have this way arrived at a point where finality, ongoing through textual insights ripening the sense, must take us into our third dimension – the testamentary. For it is just this waywardness of humankind that seems to make of each and every prophet vocation "an anguish of lost causes". Prophethood seems like a destiny in which "there is no discharge". Jeremiah conspicuously found it so. Do "messengers" not discover that their hearers are incorrigible? The social factors that needed their ministries of accusation and of exhortation combine to frustrate them. There is always a sort of "if only . . ." dogging their counsels and their pleas. "If only they would listen, heed, attend, submit . . ." all would be well. But humans prove non-amenable to truths that can only properly be persuasive and not coercive, if truths they are to remain. For they would be compromised, if not travestied, were they to turn on force.

It is this human situation, evident through Bible and Qur'an alike, which suggests a strange paradox, namely that prophethood would need to perpetuate itself either in the way it had long done, or in some alternative form. We are familiar enough with "serial" sequence, with how both Bible and Qur'an insist on a long succession in the prophetic way. Is that witness to fidelity or to futility? None could suffice beyond their generation. New generations required an endless repetition.[39] When it came that there would, could, should, be no more of them (in the Biblical way by faltering and subsiding, in the Quranic way by having Muhammad close the long cycle): their undying significance had to find another way.

They had to issue into custodial community, to entrust themselves to testamentary heirs to perpetuate their meanings in the world. In that shape their mission would continue by embodiment in "thought-schools" to which, in varying terms, they bequeathed themselves. We noted earlier the "sealing" of deliverances for "disciples", who would be heirs of their meaning, not as individuals purporting to emulate them but as communities holding their "testaments" – these consisting as the present possession of a closed past, something once historical and now bequeathed, both final and ongoing.

We need to study this communal custody of prophethood in its three dimensions in Jewry, Christianity and Islam.

# V

The Judaic is readily defined. For, via election, covenant and "the land", with the emotions of Exodus and "the wilderness", it was inherently communal from the beginning. It was by instinct and self-perception, an ethnic identity. Jewish birth was read as covenanted birthright as "the people of God". There were undoubtedly elements of Canaanite "national" dimensions in this ethnic monolatry.[40] The great prophets educated it into a superb moral monotheism, most notably Isaian in its articulation. But when, with the Deuteronomist, it became self-conscious in some measure about potential embarrassment in this congratulation and told itself that its vocation sprang from no merit or deserts, seeing in fact they were "the fewest of all peoples" (Dueteronomy 7: 6–8), the modest disclaimer in no way argued the extension of monotheist privilege to all the nations. The Isaian summons might call these to "look to Yahweh and be saved", but not to hope for incorporation into "peoplehood to God" like Israel, His chosen.

Hebrew prophethood in its finest hours lived and moved within the heritage of ethnic self-perception but only to call it into sustained ethical accountability. It made the aura of covenant the scourge of compromise and the spur to purity. In that double role, both belonging and reproving, it proved the strongest monitor of the meaning of elect privilege. As we have seen in earlier chapters, it accused the whole sacrificial system, called the very Temple "a nest of robbers", queried any "holiness" *per se*, and exploded the myth of inviolability. It wrestled with the paradox of an "election" that was both eternally ensured and morally conditional, of "the renegade Jew" who, though guilty, was still covenantally assured.

It followed that when Hebrew prophethood came to an end, either in "wisdom" lore, or apocalyptic pre-occupation, or in proto-Zionist zealotry, communal custody would take ultimate form via the synagogue, devotion to Torah and accommodation, in post-Titus times, to the exigencies of diaspora. These, by their very nature, and their urgency, deepened the communal factor and sustained it even through varying degrees of Hellenization. The scribes of the synagogue became the heirs of the prophets, the Talmudists their mentors – and all in the ethos of singular peoplehood.

The constant psyche of distinctiveness in that experience of being Jewish sadly only served to intensify into a pathos of its own. What it believed of itself determined what it had to do about itself, and what it did about itself made the belief the more tragically existential. The "Gentile" was needed to certify that a Jewish loyalty to Jewishness was consciously intact. Possessive and protective community were one and the same. The result was the ghetto as where Jewry could truly be itself, in its exclusively dietary, social, mystical and covenantal requisites. The ghetto in turn accentuated what these deployed, with non-Jewish society reciprocating in its rejectionist "imaging" of the separatism it perceived.

When the "Enlightenment" proved, or was seen to prove, a false dawn that had drawn Jewish communal life into external, "Gentile" venture and then betrayed it, 19th and 20th century "sons of the prophets" from among the Jewish community read their progenitors in terms of political Zionism. Ancient hope, sustaining ancient exile, could then be read as a long dormant incentive to recover "the promised land". Things Isaian became Herzlian, the visions of Ezekiel a programme for European diaspora. Twenty-five centuries of lapsing time and change could be digested as awaiting "auto-emancipation" at their close by pioneers from Europe making good the songs of exiles in Babylon.

The story has often been told and is apposite here as a vibrant form of "ongoing finality" "fulfilling the prophets". "The land", being "given", demands to be re-possessed. Its repossession is the long neglected clue to authentic Jewishness authentically recovered. Populating the land as a pre-requisite of possession, needs auspices which diplomacy may elicit and cajole. Secure populating requires political power, must attain statehood and sustain effective action *vis-à-vis* inevitable counter-action to be expected from an "existing non-Jewish population".[41] For "the land" is competitively loved and inhabited. In this way, by its reading of its prophetic "Writings" and the bitter logic of its long diaspora, political Zionism made itself the fulfilling community in what the classic prophets ultimately meant by "the territorial dimension" of what – in the long interim – had now become their Judaism. This transpired by the inner rationalizing, and nationalizing, of Jewish experience, *and* by the bitter malevolence of the "Gentile" world.[42]

Those writings, seen as under-writing these political Zionist intentions from afar and validating the shape of procedures, are believed in some quarters to have found their long-unknown, or long deferred, meaning. Resourceful communal custodians have taken up their promise and fulfilled their relevance. Prophetic texts find their realization in the State of Israel.

The question, however, stays. Could they approve? Or would they be "musing" "till the fire kindled" about what this Zionism might be doing to Zion?[43] Would Hosea, so deep a lover like any agricultural zionist of soil, of oil and wine, of sowing and reaping, of being Yahweh's "husbandman in husbandry", would he find some new "harlotry" in the moral morass of necessary statehood? Would Isaiah think again of his grim likening of his people to "Sodom and Gomorrah"? Might Micah wonder when armed settlements, like erstwhile swords, would give way to the ploughshares of shared tenancies of a land at peace? Had the other "Isaiah" no warning against the dispossession of the peasantry to make way for the elect? How might Jeremiah still be crying: "O Jerusalem, who is there to turn aside and ask how you fare"? Ezekiel dreamed he saw the *Shechinah* forsaking the city and going into exile with His people. Could he see the mystic "presence" currently returning?

These being the burdened questions of the Peace Movements in Israel, could these advocates of reconciliation be more surely "the sons of the prophets"? How to interpret things textual, tangled and controversial as it is, belongs still more squarely – as here – with the testamentary. How, in deed and truth, do the prophets have their heirs? For these, while needing exegesis, fulfil them only in life, in deeds and policies. Ultimately, the final legacy of the Hebrew prophets was their moral conscience, the demands of righteousness rather than the blue-printing of far off dispensations.

## VI

There is no doubt that the Christian faith was, in its very origin in sequel to Jesus' ministry, an "ongoing" of community with the classic prophets. Emphatically it saw itself that way – witness the very shape of its Gospels and its drawing on "proof texts" to sustain its case. It was an ongoing sharply contrasted with that of continuing Judaism we have reviewed and, no less emphatically, it was the work of Jewish minds and wills.[44]

The Christian "New Testament" and the faith it enshrined were clearly "testamentary" in the sense we have been studying as the third category of the future of Hebrew prophethood. But they were so from a sense that prophethood, of itself and by its verbal means, could never succeed. For its will to persuade, reform and vindicate "the weight in the word" simply by the "word's weight" ran into impasse. It encountered that incorrigible human-ness we have studied. It saw this conclusion of impasse, blockage and failure in the logic of suffering to which its costliest efforts led – the logic we have traced in CHAPTER VII.

It found that logic confirmed the way in which, after the Zechariahs, prophethood faded away or let its righteousness yield to the pessimism of writers like Qoheleth and the "wisdom" thinkers. It knew its days numbered in the trend towards eschatology, a futurism that decided to visualize interventionism from on high, rather than moral action in the present. It needed to wonder whether the very – and always urgent – repetition of "messengers" down the years did not argue the final futility of them all. Were they on a treadmill to immolation at the hands of human perversity? There was not a failure of nerve but rather an evident fragility of hope.

Hope would have to pass from the prophetic to the Messianic and perhaps that Messianic would somehow conform – in its being redemptive, not only verbal – to the paradigm of suffering so far personified in prophets themselves. Perhaps the image of "the suffering servant", drawn from what prophethood had learned of pain and travail, would disclose the secret of what, beyond prophethood and its word-reach, might answer the incorrigible world.

It is fair to hold that, in the bitter experience of those Jewish disciples of Jesus, his being crucified, clinched that "image" from both its angles. It stood as a definitive occasion, a total confirmation, of a world incorrigible in its enmity to divine word, as Jesus personified it, and it claimed the disciples' faith in its Messianic meaning by the terms in which he underwent it. It claimed their faith out of the deep abyss of their own failure to "tread that winepress" with him. Their dereliction at the crucifixion can be seen entirely in line with what we have learned of the near despair of prophets at the capacity of humankind to reject and despise. It was part of the meaning of resurrection that the disciples began to interpret the death of Jesus in these terms, to identify in it the Messianic actuality, and to read that conviction as calling them into sharing divine "peoplehood" – now re-read – as embracing all humanity on the single criterion of faith. As a later formulation had it: "His own received him not . . . but as many – not of blood, nor human birth, nor human will – as received him, he warranted as being children to God" (John 1: 11–12).

This Jewish-wrought perception of how prophethood found its future in community this way, and from these origins, at once Messianic and worldwide, was the making of the Christian Church, the testamentary meaning of how, and why, Jesus suffered, and how his "kingdom had been opened to all believers". That opening out of peoplehood under God to "whosoever willed" meant no Jewish forfeiture of its reality but only a widened sharing of it. Or it would only have spelled forfeiture if the loss of its first exclusivity had been read that way.

Has it not proved a sound verdict about Good Friday to know it as measuring, representatively, the wrongness of the human world? Did it not confirm how the prophets we humans need are less than congenial to our mind – indeed fit to be thus "despised and rejected"? It has been said that when "the Word was made flesh" the upshot in the crucifixion showed the enmity our flesh had to the Word and thus confirmed the inner travail of all truth-speaking.

> The Word's failure to inform the flesh (was) witnessed in the central symbol of the crucifixion.[45]

The "failure", though, is this way misread. Had "the word" only "been made speech, discourse, counsel on the lips", that negative verdict might stand. For all prophethoods suggest it. But "the Word was made flesh" precisely to lift the whole encounter of truth with humanity to another level, to locate it in a life and to have that life embrace in death the whole quality of the wrongness that would oppose it, and so bring into one climax the experience of all the prophets. Because "the Word made discourse", "the Word placed on lips", the divine will to be persuasive, could not, in those terms, suffice the incorrigible world, "the Word was made flesh" "in the fulness of time", so that in a life and in a death humankind might know "the power and wisdom of God" in finally comprehensive terms. This is the culminating meaning of "the Word made flesh", "dwelling among us that we might behold his glory". "Made words", "made sayings", "made guidance and counsel" – these had their long place in prophetic history moving towards what would vindicate them all by darkly confirming what they knew of hostility making for grief or failure, and suffering it in redemptive love.

Taught by the long tradition of the Biblical peoplehood to which they belonged, the disciples of this "Christ-in-Jesus" faith instinctively knew that community must be its mouthpiece and its perpetuation. Its ongoing finality would be in the society gathered into its meaning and pledged to its reproduction. These are the two salient features of the New Testament Letters – a new sense of the world as wide and includable, a lively realization that "the mind that was in Christ" had to be also in them. To know themselves divinely forgiven was to know themselves obligated to the practice of forgiveness. People constituted such by a divine redemption had to live as redeemers in their own immediate world. "As Christ suffered in the flesh, arm yourselves likewise with the same mind", wrote Peter in his First Letter (1: 4.1, cf. 2: 21–24 and 3: 14–18). Paul frequently makes the same association between the patience of Christ and the forbearance under antagonism of the Christian. He could even write about "bearing in the body the dying of the Lord" (Galations 6: 17). There was no mistaking what "the marks of Jesus" were, nor where they belonged.

This sense of things communal and personal echoes back in the Gospels also in the strange reminders about "bearing the Cross".[46] It was, however, only after the event that the disciples understood. Earlier they had only been baffled by those mysterious anticipations from Jesus of what he saw to be awaiting him.[47] There was nothing morbid or fatalist about those intimations of "acquaintance with grief". They stemmed from the gathering evidences of his immediate ministry as greeted by contention and ill-will. Those features tallied closely with prophetic disesteem in "its own country" – the "country" in Jesus' case being controversy around the Sabbath, authority, election and the "loving-kindness" of Yahweh. Did not all these bring a growing impression about a suffering destiny? Did he not consult his disciples as to what were the makings of Messiahship and its portents in surmisings about him which they were well placed to register (Matthew 16: 13–16)?

It all comprised a finality, a conclusiveness, ongoing in the convictions, the shape and the fidelity of a new open society in its meaning. It was "testamentary" in that the event generated the community and the community lived by the event. The "imitation of Christ" was at once its mandate and its vocation. Jesus had initially "called disciples to his company" in order to share his meaning in Galilee. He would continue to do so down the passing centuries. "Company" as a word derives from the sharing of bread (Latin: *panis*). "Bread and wine" would be the sign of how his finality would be ever renewed.

## VII

It remains for this chapter to study the testamentary dimension in the ongoing finality of Islam. As the prophethood to end all prophethood the Qur'an, as we have seen, was inherently irrepeatable. That fact only made the perpetuity it had to find the more crucial. The text itself would be the arbiter of its own future, the monitor of its own fulfilment. Other Scriptures could belong with its "guidance" (*huda*) only by how far they conformed to it. By completion, the final revelation must have all else yield to its norms and its criteria. The Qur'an held the ultimate responsibility as the inclusive last referent, "the Mother of the Book".

This supremely Scriptural dignity made community in its care the more decisive. For its due custody inevitably became communal. Muhammad had his "companions". These were aware of those *asbab al-nuzul* we studied in CHAPTER V, the points and places of his receiving his, and Allah's, text. Commentary would duly rely on their witness. Further, where the Qur'an had no directives for guidance in newly arising situations, they could draw on his example out of their familiarity with his *Sirah*, his prophetic years, and thus afford a further source of Shari'ah to extend, but not emend, the Qur'an. By the *isnad*, or "chain" of overlapping associates of theirs, other "informants" through more than two centuries after Muhammad's death could attest Muhammad's example, in lengthening reliance on the first ones, and so provide a perpetuation of law-derivation from the proven memory of how he had been.

Given, as sacred scholarship believes, the early canonizing of a single Quranic text,[48] the course was set for a growing custodial "ongoing" of the Qur'an and of Muhammad, in possession of the one and the emulating of the other. *Nass* and *Sirah*, text and biography – in the terms Tradition housed it – became the "guardians" of their human guardians, the mentors of the minds that served them. Those two "sources" of a right

Islamicity were supplemented by two other "means" whose exercise lay with the Muslim community. These were the *Ijtihad*, or "initiative" of experts in exegesis, traditional lore and *fiqh*, or jurisprudence. Such *Ijtihad*, round which there were long debates as to what "expertise" constituted and how it was accredited as being such, was meant to concert and sustain an *Ijma'*, or "consensus", of Muslims at large. When both mature expertise and communal mind had rightly availed in their responsibility, their "findings" could validly attain the status of sacred law, given consistency with the Qur'an and Tradition, as soundly innovative. Thus there was a principle of legitimate "development" of Shari'ah implicit, under due safeguard, in the community of believers.[49]

The ongoing-ness of original Islam had another vital agency in the caliphal Islamic state. Islam as crucially a political fabric, possessing "the political kingdom" as explicitly the accomplice of the rule of God, had been determined for Islam by the Prophet's own Hijrah from Mecca to Medina and his steady erection of a power base from which Mecca would be finally Islamized.

It is important to realize that the impulse to that emigration, interpreting the antecedent situation that induced it, was circumstantially akin to the decision by Jesus that he must prepare for suffering to have a climax. For the situation, in either case, was the sense, otherwise, of impending failure. Failure loomed sequentially to the evidences of rejection, the resistance to the spoken witness, the venting on the messenger of the unwantedness of the message. It is from the arguable similarity of the two situations around Jerusalem and Mecca that the contrasted sequels came – and came as hallmarks of the ensuing faiths.

In *Major Themes*, earlier quoted, Fazlur Rahman makes the Quranic case with his usual clarity. Urging that the Prophet is commissioned only as a "messenger", he goes on:

> Since this message is from God and is directly needed by men for survival and success, it has to be accepted by men and implemented ... If the message is not accepted and the mission does not succeed, then the preacher may have discharged his duty, but God has definitely failed and mankind is doomed. But if God's purposes are frustrated and humanity doomed, has the preacher "discharged his duty"? His duty is to *succeed* in implementing the message.

The logic of the Hijrah could not be better stated and he rightly adds: "This trend represents the basic thrust and the real élan of Muhammad, both inside and outside the Qur'an."[50]

## Ongoing Finality

The passage exactly summarizes the vital role of state and power durably "outside the Qur'an". It is through the crucially political organ of *Dawlah* that Islamic community gives ongoing finality to *Din*. Religion is perpetuated in the sub-sovereignty by which the inalienable sovereignty of Allah is to be implemented. The confidence that "implementation" can be this way is of one piece with how the confrontation between Muhammad's message and his setting is seen to develop and intensify. For the encounter, thanks to the Hijrah and its sequel, becomes increasingly physical and, at least on the Meccan side, conspiratorial. The Qur'an here is increasingly alert to *nifaq* and *munafiqun*, to "intrigue" and "dissemblers".

The term *fitnah*, noted elsewhere, becomes "sedition" rather than merely "what tests". Muhammad's message had always served judgement on paganism and its ways. The challenge-bringing he could not avoid in truth was counter-challenged by a popular, and "class" calculated, belligerence which was taken to require matching in kind, until it capitulated within those agreed parameters.

Capitulate finally it did. Then the mutual embattledness could end in Meccan submission – a submission which amply vindicated and acknowledged the means that had led to it. Islam remains entirely consistent with its origins in the long-range confidence it derived from them that faith is political and due power its apt instrument. The Prophet's ongoing message is rooted in his ongoing community fashioned – as well as dated – from the Hijrah. The issue of continuity was thus to be in the genius of the origins, as it had earlier, differently, been in the New Testament. By the Islamic criterion of "implementation", the "rapture" of 'Isa (Jesus) to heaven meant his not enjoying success in the Quranic form. On that account too, the supreme accomplishing of prophethood would be in Muhammad's form, giving another measure to how he proved to be the ultimate Prophet.

Thus far, though, we might have been supposing that Sunnis were the whole of Islam. For it is the majority "people of the Sunnah" whose shape of "ongoing" we have been outlining. The smaller Shi'ah segment of Muslims represents a partly different theory of how Muhammad's significance belongs with the ages. They saw the role of community needing to be confined within the esoteric stature of the masters of *Ijtihad*. These *mujtahidun*, in the Shi'ah tradition, unlike the "learned" of the Sunni quality, were mystically endowed with insights vital to the meaning of the Qur'an and to the obedience of the faithful.

These *ayatollahs* (lit.) "signs of God" acquire their eminence in this role by a gathered repute for piety and erudition. They exercise their role as legatees or representatives of "the hidden Imam", through whom they are linked to 'Ali, the fourth Caliph, cousin and son-in-law of Muhammad, and the first Imam. For the Shi'ah lay great store by the hereditary principle and the meaning – as they receive it – of Surah 33.33 in its marking of *Ahl al-Bait*, "the people of the house", as "immaculate" repositories of the "wisdom" of the Prophet. When the last named successor in the Imamate "went into hiding", and the vital succession could no longer be identified, "the hidden one" was to be awaited.[51] Meanwhile *ayatollahs* could speak in his name as in some sense enshrining his latent authority by virtue of their acknowledged stature in holy lore and life.

In this way there was a subtle difference both in the place of popular community and in the criteria of Qur'an study and *tafsir*, or interpretation. Whereas for the Sunnis the whole community of sound Muslims, with due academically learned guidance, could yield a concerted *Ijma'*, or "consensus", for the Shi'ah they could only properly submit to *ayatollah* minds.[52] *Tafsir*, in their sights, became *ta'wil*, the text – not in an open-to-all sense but by the insight into its secret of those gifted to reach it.

These significant distinctions between Sunni and Shi'ah Islam had much to do, not only with hereditary factors in the "possession" of Muhammad after his death and a different reception of the Qur'an, but with the Shi'ah experience of tragedy. Their history bore many marks of non-success, making them a fascinating minority verdict in Islam against the prevailing Sunni idea that "God's business must succeed". The logic we found expressed above by Fazlur Rahman could not tally with how "the partisans of 'Ali" were worsted in the quarrels that followed Muhammad's demise, nor with how 'Ali himself (on the Shi'ah view) had first been cheated of the Caliphate and then murdered in it, nor with how later his son, Husain was done to death in the massacre of Karbala'.[53] Caught in such victimization – and that by figures who had not even joined Islam in its hard pre-Hijrah times – 'Ali's partisans could not find God's vindication where the Sunni found it, in "manifest victory".[54]

They had to cope with, and somehow find a meaning for, outright grief and political disappointment. They did so in developing a theology of the merit of vicarious suffering – a merit which could be invoked as "atoning" for the sins of those who knew how to plead it.[55] In these ways the Shi'ah shaped a continuity of Muhammad's finality in terms significantly divergent from majority Islam. Those terms certainly owed much to cultural, ethnic and social factors from the wide physical expansion of Muslim faith but they sprang from subtle tensions implicit in the very nature, the historical context and innate assumptions of the Prophet's Meccan mission and its Medinan climax. The loved criterion of evident success could not enjoy a unanimous verdict even within Islam's own household. That it did not and could not is eloquent commentary on its finality.

# VIII

The old adage: "Call no man happy till he is dead" might suggest the dictum: "Find no faith whole and full while it is alive." To live is to outlive. To want security for its own sake is to forfeit the right to it. Faith and worship are staked on the believing worshipping community. So much the closure of Scriptures makes evident enough. Prophethoods ongoing are in the love, care and intelligence of the responsive people and the centuries they have possessed to be, in turn, themselves possessed by them. So much we have seen. This mutual possessing and being possessed means that what origins constrain, inheritance controls. It remains to see, in conclusion, how the founding characteristics of Islam and Christianity preside over this destiny for ever in hand.

An old Muslim tradition is sure that "there is no emigration after the conquest", meaning that "success has succeeded", that its political strategy has permanently ensured Islam. The renowned historian/sociologist Ibn Khaldun (who quotes the tradition) sees "the power of wrathfulness" indispensable "to help the truth become victorious".

> In the opinion of Muhammad all of this world is a vehicle for transport to the other world. He who loses the vehicle can go nowhere.[56]

Yet, what of another tradition that Islam, coming as a stranger, will continue as a stranger? There were those Shi'ah "emigrations" in mind and soul from the main corpus of Sunni Islam. In recent centuries there have been wide diasporas of Muslims beyond the extent of *Dar al-Islam* in classic terms. There are endless "emigrations" of spirit from the citadels of rigorous dogma. The very Caliphate had no fixed abode in place and time. Islam has effectively "migrated" out of the single *Ummah* into "nation-states". These, in turn, have diversely debated how their unison of state and faith should be conceived and achieved.

Continuity, then, can only be in those first constraining political terms if these are ready now for the present constraints of converging cultures, international law and global ethics. It is where the very genius of Islam is most realized conceptually that its deepest introspection belongs. The tasks of co-existence and inter-humanity are paramount precisely where the founding instincts were most assured because, in the there and then they seemed so thoroughly vindicated. Yet, even about that vindication, unanimity inside the Muslim community was early dispelled. That old debate about success and grief, about right of succession, about Scriptures and custody, which divided Muhammad's immediate heirs, belongs more squarely, more widely, with his heirs today. Or, differently expressed, if it is always post-Hijrah in historical Islam, it is continually pre-Hijrah in the soul. Either way, community was, and is, the die-casting of continuity.

It is the same for Christianity, in the distinctive founding idiom of the constraints that have been with us from the great prophethoods and into the achieved and recognized Messiahship of Jesus. Unless the writers of the New Testament had misled themselves – and they were the most intimate to their sources – what the prophets underwent in terms of divine agency drawn into vicarious pain pointed onward to "the Word made flesh". Whereas in early theophanies Yahweh "appeared" with a word and withdrew, leaving seer/hearer to heed and tell what he heard or saw, the great prophets came to embody the ongoing relevance so that the discharge of their vocation made them the very presence of a divine significance.[57] All this we have seen in full in previous chapters.

Thus prophethood anticipated an ultimate union of personality and word as one – and one in travail. God, to this degree, himself participated in human story. The "office (of prophets) increasingly invaded their personal lives",[58] and so became the vehicle of divine presence, with biography a kind of "God-event" in the idiom of a message given, a personhood engaged and a travail undertaken. The arguable inclusion of Yahweh Himself in all these is plain. Of Hosea, one writer says:

> The language intermingles the prophet's own experience and the theological word. The prophetic consciousness is inseparable from the lover's introspection.[59]

Hosea, Jeremiah, Habakkuk on his "watch-tower" – all, in their own idiom – "tell" in their persons what cannot be reduced to words in a statement. The "statement" is the agonizers, the sufferers, the burden-bearers they are. They are for Yahweh and thereby with and in Yahweh. Is not Yahweh then in and with them not only in their commission but in their commission's cost?

We have seen how, in this way, the Christ-event is wholly continuous with prophetic experience but in the fuller inclusiveness explicit for Christian faith in its reading of the Cross. The entire logic carries that understanding forward from "the goodly fellowship of the prophets" to the "apostles" of that Christ-event, "the Church that is Christ's body". Their Easter took them into the world where it is always Good Friday.

# Notes

## Chapter I  *Messengers with Burdens*

1. "Virtual" seems the just word here. For there are clear implications of the role of personality in the Quranic scene and these have been strongly developed in Islamic perception of, and devotion to, the Prophet of Islam. Moreover, it seems well to locate the Christian debate over the finality of the Gospel in Christ in this ultimate dimension, rather than in assessments that merely compare texts and teachings.
2. In James Hastings, *Dictionary of the Bible*, vol. II, London, 1898, p. 576. Cited from note 3 below, p. 17.
3. John Skinner, *Prophecy and Religion: Studies in the Life of Jeremiah*, Cambridge, 1922, p. 16.
4. But only for the reason that "servanthood" is seen as never the pretentious "Sonship" that Islam mistakenly attributes to Christology as the New Testament knows it. Ironically it is precisely a "Sonship" which achieves "servanthood" and a "servanthood" which only "Sonship" can bring that Christian faith has always understood. Surah 4.172 brings these two together, only sadly to divorce them: "Messiah will never scorn to be servant to God", implying: "He cannot therefore be Son." Paul in Philippians 2: 7 makes precisely the same point in the opposite sense, namely of "the Son who "does not scorn" to be the servant but makes himself of no reputation . . ."
5. "Inherent incompleteness" in that truths verbal do not prevail by merely being uttered, and "completion" in that something beyond the "education" prophets inculcate is crucially needed in and beyond the *antilogia*, or "contradiction" (Hebrews 12: 3) they undergo, i.e. either a Hijrah into power or a Gethsemane into redemption.
6. Mount Hira' had the cave in which, as tradition reports, Muhammad withdrew in meditation and where he received the first experiences of *wahy* or "revelatory-inspiration", that began the Qur'an on earth. This theme will recur in succeeding chapters. It was studied in some depth in my: *Returning to Mount Hira': Islam in Contemporary Terms*, London, 1994. Tabuk was the far point of Muhammad's military campaign northward in 630 following the capitulation of Mecca. The two points might be said to comprise the time-

range of the Qur'an at least symbolically.
7  The striking feature of the language of these prophets is its sense of emotions, in Yahweh, or grief and pain and yearning analogous to their own. See further note 17 below.
8  Surah 94, with its title of *Al-Inshirah*, may be read in terms of solace and succour in an "Opening of the heart" of Muhammad for a mission referred to in following verses as "a burden weighing down (his) back", and as a "hardship relieved by ease". There is also a hint in Surah 62.11 of the dismay experienced in seeing an audience drift away from his preaching in preference for trading in the marketplace. But the Qur'an has no place for anguished remonstrance with God as in the "Confessions" of Jeremiah. These are found, e.g. in Jeremiah 11: 18–23; 12: 1–6; 15: 10–21; 17: 9–18; 18: 18–23 and 20: 7–12.
9  The Jewish concept of "land-by-right", "the place of Yahweh's Name" is, of course, exclusively a Hebraic experience or pretension. It has no parallel in Islam. However, there is a sense of the status of *Jazirat al-'Arab*, "The Island of the Arabs". Surah 90.1 implies that "this land" is inviolate and Muhammad has the freedom of it. Mecca's sanctity was assured by virtue of Adam and Abraham, and its being the Prophet's birthplace and the final *Qiblah* of Islamic prayer.
10  It recurs continually in the Medinan Surahs. It resolves the two halves of the *Shahadah* into a unity of theological and political submission. See Surahs 3.32 and 132, 4.59, 5.92, 8.20 and 46, 64.12.
11  It is intriguing, nevertheless, that this title should be constantly present in the reference to Jesus. A "Messiah", however, whether in Hebraic or in Christian sense, has no place in the divine economy in the Qur'an, seeing that education of us humans, and exhortation, comprehends what Allah undertakes in respect of His creatures, i.e. "guidance in the straight path". Tradition, however, and the experience of the Shi'ah, make space for "future interventions".
12  It is in this sense that "reproach" in the Qur'an, where it is not externally levelled at resisters to the message, is internally applied to misconduct in the "cause", either by evasion or seditious attitudes. Either of these constitute *fitnah* (or "what tests") among Muslims after the Hijrah, or equally, the machinations of enemies to it. Cf. also *nifaq* and the *munafiqun*. "Hypocrites".
13  This seems to be the intended meaning in Surah 7.158, where it is twice applied to Muhammad. The plural seems to mean "non-Jews", i.e. people without Scripture. See fuller discussion in *The Event of the Qur'an*, London, 1970, pp. 61–3.
14  Hence the importance of the fact that Muhammad was "of the people" (another sense of *ummi*) and of the pagan accusation that his words came (seditiously for native usages) "from a stranger". (Cf. Surahs 16.103 and 41.44.)

15　The point here is of much import both for faith and for exegesis. The eternity of the Qur'an must be necessary if it is truly God's speech, since Allah does not "acquire" what He ever lacked. Yet the text is clearly, and necessarily, engaging throughout with times and places in temporal flux. Classical theology has insisted, against certain Muʿtazilites, that such problems must not be allowed to compromise the dogma of the Qur'an's "uncreatedness". However, in this century Fazlur-Rahman has argued that due recognition of the human part need not, and should not, damage what is *intended* in the dogma, namely the status of the Qur'an as truly from Allah. Others dismiss this view as jeopardizing that status by any concession to human factors.

16　The experience of "inspiration" in words and imagery has long baffled philosophers like Plato and poets like Wordsworth. The issue belongs squarely with ensuing chapters.

17　A notable example is Psalm 56, where verses 5 and 6 surely indicate a preacher vilified and harassed, rather than a David even in his "brigand" days. Then the writer asks God to take count of his tears. "Are not these things noted in Thy book?" It cannot be that the Lord who sends him into such costly ministry can be oblivious of what it means in suffering. Muhammad's pre-Hijrah feelings may well have been of this order but there is no psalmody around them.

18　Old Testament scholars, like Gerhard von Rad and H. Wheeler Robinson, have differed sharply over whether "prophecy" ceases when prophets speak to God, as in note 17, or whether, instead, the prophet then becomes sublimely more significant. See the former's "The Confessions of Jeremiah" in: L. G. Perdue and B. W. Kovacs, ed., *A Prophet to the Nations: Essays in Jeremiah Studies*, Indiana, 1984, pp. 339-47. For the latter: *The Cross of Jeremiah*, London, 1925.

## Chapter II　*The Casting, The Saying, The Weighting*

1　The phrase comes in the Joseph saga in Psalm 105: 18 (Prayer Book Psalter). The meaning is probably physical, "They put his neck (*nephesh*) in irons", but this in no way precludes the figurative sense.

2　Passages from Haggai 1: 1, Surah 7.158, Surah 46.9, and Amos 3: 1: We observe that Biblical prophets are normally named as the spokesmen of their messages. There may be anonymous prophets hidden in the editing of the longer books while the covering name of the first "Isaiah" conceals supreme, if unknown, figures responsible for chapters 40 following. Personal identity is always Biblically significant. It has to be noted that the personal name "Muhammad" occurs only four times in the Qur'an (Surahs 3.144, 33.40, 47.2 and 48.29. Three of these attest him as "the messenger", while 33.40 reiterates this with the sad addition that he "is not the father of any man among you." Surah 61.6 has the much debated allusion to one "Ahmad" whose coming Jesus foretold, the word being a synonym for "Muhammad". This misreads the "Paraclete" word in the fourth Gospel (see below, chap. 9, note 9). It may be that the Qur'an's departure from the Biblical norm of named persons in prophethood indicates that Muhammad's *persona* is totally taken up into his status as *Rasul-Allah*. The difference is a clue to many features both ways.

3   William Shakespeare, 2 *Henry VI*, Act 5, Sc. 1, line 36, and *As You Like It*, Act 1, Sc. 2, line 247.
4   William Bradford, Governor and historian, of Plymouth, Mass. in his *The Plymouth Foundation*, 1630. To be sure, only some of the New England pilgrims saw themselves a "apostles" to the "Indians", and in other ways too, the analogy does not fit. But analogies are sometimes useful in being less than readily obvious.
5   The issue will recur later. The strong individualism of moral liability in the Qur'an, the insistence that all guilt is our own and cannot be palliated or "forgiven" by arbitrarily assigning it to another, is true enough – and Christian. But this truth cannot be allowed to preclude the other truth that, "bound in the bundle of life," we are all vulnerable to what others do, how others relate, and that all this has to be "borne" and "taken", whether in resentment, sullenness, hatred, or in a forgiving stance, and love.
6   A. N. Whitehead, *Religion in the Making*, Cambridge, 1926, p. 26.
7   "Your sole onus is the message *per se*" is the clear directive to Muhammad, making him exclusively a preacher, a "word-bringer". See Surahs 3.20, 5.99, 13.40, 16.35, 24.54, 29.18, 36.17, 42.48, and 64.12. It is significant that there is no direct command in the Qur'an for the making of the Hijrah. The word in 72.10 has to do with courteously breaking off an argument. The cognate verb is frequent in description or narrative of the *muhajirun*, the "emigrants". All but 3, 5 and 24 of the above *balagh* Surahs are Meccan.

## Chapter III   *Prophetic Personality*

1   Margaret Smith, *An Early Mystic of Baghdad*, London, 1935, p. 184.
2   Inasmuch as he was a "herdsman" in Tekoa, depending on how we understand his "farming" and his "tending sycamores" (1.1 and 7.14).
3   This is not to exclude the metaphors shepherds yield to theology concerning pastoral ministry and going after "the one that is lost" with the potential cost of bringing it "home". However, the wayward son, in the three parables of Luke 15 about "lostness", needed far more subtle and painful "rescue" than a lost sheep and lost silver. It is about that waywardness in collective social form that prophets have their missions and their toils.
4   Though the last in the Canon, the word Malachi, meaning "My messenger", probably indicates that the text is anonymous. Jewish sources suggest "Ezra the Scribe" as the author. Otherwise the tradition of precise identification elsewhere is significant of the vital part played by personhood in all its fertility and relevance.
5   Attaching, that is, to verbs and prepositions. Hence the importance when, in translation, the English "you" is used rather than "thou", of indicating the

singular in direct speech to the Prophet, not for address on his part to plural listeners.

6   The only two occasions of this command to Muhammad are in the one Surah, 96.1 and 3. The command in 17.14 is to the unbeliever on Judgement Day: "Read thy book." In the plural the command in 73.20 refers to believers in their recital.

7   See below, and discussion concerning the personal part, if any, of Muhammad in the reception of the Qur'an – a discussion raised by Fazlur Rahman among recent scholars and rebutted by others as "an isolated case". See, for example: Ataullah Siddiqui, *Christian/Muslim Dialogue in the 20th century*, London, 1997, p. 161.

8   Throughout, study has to be alert to how the content of Quranic verses has to be taken with the inferences it holds for the actual encounter of preaching and communal reaction in the givens of the Meccan suqs and shrines.

9   Namely: "Your Lord magnify, your garments purify, shun defilement, give not with a view to self-increase and turn patiently to your Lord." The fourth one indicates clearly that Muhammad sensed the personal dimension in his office. He was keenly self-aware in its discharge, even if passive in its reception.

10  The significance of Mount Hira' for the antecedents of Muhammad's experience with the Qur'an is more fully studied in *Returning to Mount Hira'*, London, 1994.

11  *Tahannuf*, i.e. "following the *hunafa*'", is not to be confused with *tahannuth*. Among Quranic references are Surahs 2.130, 3.67, 4.125, 6.79, 10.105, 16.120 and 123, and 30.30. The plural occurs in 22.31 and 98.5.

12  There is a marked solicitude for orphans in the Qur'an. Would it be right to associate it with Muhammad's own father, 'Abdallah, having died before he was born?

13  In reference to the principle in all exegesis of *asbab al-nuzul*, the "occasions of revelation", as the points of the incidence, or "sending down" of the verses by which their meaning could be understood. See below, CHAPTER V.

14  The pagan charge that he had "heard it from an alien" had to be stoutly rebutted. For the meaning of *ummi* as "sent to a people as yet illiterate" in not having their own sacred text (rather than Muhammad's being totally without reading or writing skills) see discussion in: *The Event of The Qur'an*, London, 1970, chap. 3.

15  John Skinner, *Prophecy & Religion: Studies in the Life of Jeremiah*, Cambridge, 1922, p. 73.

16  Borrowing a term from 17th century England denoting those failing to conform to a faith and practice communally enjoined on them – in context here the issue of "the renegade Jew" – covenanted by birth but personally and morally an "opt-out" from its duty.

17  Scholars differ as to how to read the import of Hosea 1–3 and the prophet's experience. This proleptic reading seems the most authentic. See also chap.

4, note 28.

18 It is a pattern which extends also far into the New Testament. One of the differences between Hebrew prophethood and that of Muhammad is also evident here. The former arose within an established monotheism whose compromises it strains to reproach and correct, whereas the Qur'an belongs with the coming-to-be of an authentic worship in the context of an established paganism. The difference is profound, the strictures of the one being internally addressed, those of the other externally. If we think of "cleansing Augean stables", those of Mecca are its wilful *jahiliyyah*, those of Isaiah 1 are of a "chosen people" become "like Sodom and Gomorrah".

19 The references in Isaiah 44: 2 and 21, 49: 3 and 5 had to do with the "servant" vocation of Israel itself, as affirmed to the nations. They echo the concept of "the holy seed" which dominates Jewish self-understanding and extend it to the (should we say quite literally "embryonic") Messianic vocation.

20 The language in 20: 7 is violent in the extreme (cf. v.10). The Hebrew word has been rendered "enticed", "duped", "entrapped". Ideas of "conspiracy" and "subterfuge" are present but the surest imagery is that of sexual deceit and violation. See chap. 4, note 33.

21 Inasmuch as the text of the Book of Jeremiah has gone through many redactions and poses many issues concerning arrangement and exegesis it is hard to know how, precisely, these outpourings of the prophet's soul took literary shape. What may be owed to the Deuteronomic tradition? Did they somehow express the tragedy of a whole community puzzled by the seeming neutrality of Yahweh? There must, however, have been a commanding personality to have shaped even a partly artistic reconstruction. We can feel with the Jewish Rabbi, Abraham Heschel, that Jeremiah was truly entering into the pathos of Yahweh.

22 Amos 5: 18–20, where he reverses the popular notion of a day of Jewish triumph into a dire experience of their sins' requital.

23 For Habakkuk "The just man shall live by his fidelity" (i.e. the trustful will find their trust vindicated) whereas when Paul, in Romans 5 etc. borrows the phrase he has it mean: "By our faith (i.e. trust) in the saving Christ we will be justified before God." Paul substitutes Christ availing for us redemptively, where Habakkuk has the fidelity of the righteous man who patiently awaits what God will do.

24 See, for example: Andre Neher, *The Prophetic Existence*, trans. W. Wolf, S. Brunswick, 1968 and H. Wheeler Robinson, *Suffering Divine and Human*, London, 1940.

25 R. R. Wilson in J. L. Mays and P. J. Achtemeier, eds, *Interpreting the Prophets*, Philadelphia, 1987, p. 165. See chap. 7, note 7.

26 *Al-Kitab* and *Al-Hikmah* – "the Book and the Wisdom" are coupled together as titles of the Qur'an at least eleven times, and once with *Al-Mu'izah*, "the Preaching" (16.125). Elsewhere *hikmah* is used in a more general sense, as in 54.5: "Wisdom in all its range."

27 This "opening of the bosom" – or – we might say – "the exegeting of the heart" (*sharh* is used for what a reader must "draw out" from a text) means, in Tradition, the purging of what might hinder comprehension and then draw out the soul to its immersion into the truth. It is significant that *sharh al-sadr* is also applied to the bringing of any believer to the embrace of *islam*. See 39.22.
28 The strict sense of "mythology" is that of intimating meanings in the guise of stories. The *maulids*, or celebrations of the Prophet's "birthday" with recitals of Aminah, his mother's pregnancy etc. were devotion's way of stating faith about the Qur'an.
29 It is noteworthy that they did not, whereas there are two long narratives in Surahs 3 and 19 concerning the virgin conception of Mary and the nativity of Jesus. The personal references to Muhammad, as in Surahs 93 and 94, have to do with the incidence of *wahy* in his adult years.
30 See, for example: Michael Marmura "Avicenna's Theory of Prophecy in the light of Ash'arite Theology", in W. S. McCullough, *The Seed of Wisdom*, ed., Toronto, 1964, pp 159–78.

## Chapter IV  *Prophethood and Language*

1 Notably in *Ion*, para 534, with the notion that human awareness is suppressed when deity communicates to seer or poet. Elsewhere Plato sees an "out of mind" condition obtaining where inspiration is in flow. Centuries later, in the same tradition, Philo, too, thinks of the mind "evicted" by the onset of the divine spirit which occupies until normal tenancy is resumed. It is not suggested that the Muslim view of *wahy* stems from these ideas: it belongs in its own Arab realm of poetry and eloquence.
2 On the "poet" allegation see 21.5: 37.36: 52, 30 and refutation 69.41. The theme of the Qur'an's *'ijaz*, or "inimitably perfect Arabic", imbues the whole. See notes on "Bring a matching surah", below note 5.
3 Modern literary criticism moves from what a text kindles in a reader, so that – in measure – what it "means" stands in what readers, hearers, "take". The analogy can only cautiously be applied to Scriptures but it can obtain, especially if we remember that, in recital, the Qur'an is experienced as an emotion – always more than "information". Studious perusal is only part, maybe a minor part, of its impact. On the question whether texts can "mean" more than they ever originally "knew", see CHAPTER IX.
4 Nevertheless, with the Qur'an as well as the Bible, theses about "inspiration" dispensing with "authorship" that is clearly human have to acknowledge rich evidences of its presence. This, eminently so with the Bible, is true also of the Qur'an. See below.
5 E.g. Surahs 10.38, 11.13 ("bring ten"), 20.57, while 52.34 has "a *hadith* like it".
6 "For good" in being at home with each other: "for ill" in that as the proverb goes "honour is there withheld".

7 The point here is not simply that any Englishman will consider Shakespeare out of English inevitably reduced if not ill-served. The Qur'an's "native-feel" among Arabs is much more than a cultural indulgence in identity. It belongs with the very concept of *wahy* as that for which Allah opts, out of His own inscrutable will. In that way translators do not merely put at risk what is cherished: they question divine disposal.

8 The debate ebbed and flowed through the middle centuries. What was "God's" could never have been "acquired" and must therefore be as eternal as God Himself. Yet the Qur'an was also "in time and of time" and – as such – in some sense a "creature" time-wise.

9 *Islam and Revolution: Writings and Declarations of Imam Khomeini*, trans. Hamid Algar, Berkeley, 1981, pp. 393 and 391.

10 *Ibid.*, p. 392.

11 This necessary business with "words" should not exclude the element of "vision" as notably in Surah 53.6–10 where a visual scene had its part in the Prophet's initial experience. "Words", however, were the essential medium of what *wahy* brought as meant for faithful utterance.

12 A ready way of identifiying the poetry of the Qur'an is by using A. J. Arberry's *The Koran Interpreted*, 2 vols, London, 1955 (and numerous later editions) where he has arranged poetic parts in poetic form. The translation stays closer to the Arabic than English disciplines would allow but this was deliberate on his part. Hence the "Interpreted" in his title indicating, not a commentary, but a "rendering". He may also have wanted to qualify "the Qur'an", by the adjective, out of deference to the Muslim sense that only the Arabic version is "Qur'an".

13 As, for example, by the Palestinian scholar, Isma'il al-Faruqi. See his analysis of Islam's "concretization of absolute value which Muslims are bound to attain", in *'Urubah and Religion*, Amsterdam, 1962, pp. 200f. and (co-authored with Lois L. al-Faruqi) *The Cultural Atlas of Islam*, New York, "The Content", p. 114f. See also Fazlur Rahman, *Major Themes of the Qur'an*, Minneapolis, 1980., p. 74, on the "almost coercive" *sultan*, in the text of the Scripture, as "that which overwhelms without leaving any real alternative".

14 Cf. Isaiah 44: 9–20 and Psalm 115: 4–8 where a Hindu might well retort that "idols" given "mouths and ears" were never meant to "speak and hear". Semitic satire needs a keener insight when taken into Asia.

15 In the context of idol-making in the Surah this seems the right translation, though the phrase "and what you do . . ." (*ta'malun*) comes frequently in verses about Allah "seeing" and "observing" all our doings; 37.96 has been read as suggesting "fatalism" – as it might if "deeds" are meant rather than "things we fabricate".

16 Human *khilafah*, or "dominion" via the senses recording "what's there" and mind cognizing it with intent to "manage" it, is not shared outside the human realm.

17 The translation has been somewhat abridged (where indicated) – with apology – in order to bring out the fourfold domain of human "empire" as given in nature for responsible employ.
18 From Surah 96 onward ("created man from a blood clot . . .") through numerous passages marvelling at the mystery of the fertile womb and the "safe lodging place" that precedes birth and "processes" fertility. Note also the Qur'an's special interest in "orphans" and its abhorrence of infanticide.
19 The term *itmi'nan* here, and the cognate verb, is beloved of Muslims. The Qur'an distinguishes the self-reproaching soul from "the soul at rest" in remembrance of God (85.2 and 13.27).
20 The translation uses two English words, in three cases, to bring out the full sense of the Arabic. Allusive writing may well incite extravagant (lit.) minds and exegesis has always taken refuge in "God alone knowing". Cf. Ayatollah Ruhollah Khomeini in *Islam and Revolution*, trans. Hamid Algar, Berkeley, 1981, p. 375: "The sense I am discussing is possible, not certain and part of the possible meaning."
21 As, for example, in Amos 4: 13, 5: 8f., 9: 5f., and is not Isaiah 12 a "cultic song"? See below.
22 The puzzling passage in Surat *al-Ma'idah*, "The Table", 5.112–15, and the request of the disciples that Jesus "send down a table from heaven". It has echoes of the Last Supper, but maybe also of the feeding in the desert and, perhaps, the "manna" story after the Exodus.
23 Cited by Ayatollah Khomeini, *loc. cit.* note 20 above, p. 394.
24 For example, Surah 75.36 (a camel metaphor): "Does man think he is left untethered?" or 50.16 Allah as "nearer to man than his jugular vein". Or 23.67 where Muhammad's indifferent listeners are likened to "some chatterer talking glibly after nightfall". In these and many other scenes we are squarely in the setting which yields the analogies.
25 The sense of *theopneustos* in 2 Timothy 3: 16 where the "writings" in mind are those of the Hebrew prophets.
26 The use of one thing as symbol of another, as in "crown of glory". The Greek language may be supplying the term; Hebrew of the Biblical order knew well how to employ what it signified.
27 Amos prophesied against it but was a native of Tekoa in the south. Hosea's ministry belonged in the reigns of the northern Kingdom, from 743 to 724.
28 On this reading the command: "Go marry a harlot" (itself otherwise incongruous) must mean that only in the sequence of Gomer's infidelity he came to know what the impulse to wed her would eventually contain.
29 Cited from C. S. Lewis, *Rehabilitations and Other Essays*, Oxford, 1939, pp. 192–3.
30 Throughout the Judaic prophetic tradition it is never entirely clear whether "the ends of the earth" are incorporate in Yahweh's glory in their own right or only as tributary to that of "the chosen people". Even the famous Psalm 87 is capable of contradictory readings of how "foreigners" can claim

Jerusalem as their "birthplace". Ultimately monotheism is reduced to monolatry if the Oneness of God does not comprise the oneness of a common humanity. Only in being "equally" God to all is God "one" to any. See chap. 5, note 26.

31  He was due to be 74 years old on Good Friday, 1759 and, now blind, he had an intuition that he might die that day. He died, as he had wished, after several triumphant performances of *Messiah*. Seventeen years earlier, on completing the oratorio, his servant found him with tears streaming from his eyes. "I did think I did see all heaven opened before me", he wrote of the concentrated effort of authorship crowded into twenty-four days.

32  In CHAPTER V. Here there is no direct need to conjecture about the formation of his Book as we know it, nor disentangle narrative from poetry or text from source.

33  The language is almost violent. "You ravished me", even "you raped me", borrowing from the image of a naïve girl seduced by a cunning lover who disguises his real intentions until a point is reached where the victim has no retreat. The sense of having been inveigled into what, at the outset, he neither realized nor understood, is deep in Jeremiah's words from the soul.

34  This popular notion is a travesty foisted on to a greatly heroic figure.

35  How his "audience" would bear with him and wait upon his meanings through a protracted time is puzzling and attaches to many of his contrived "dramas". See below.

36  Cited like the adjacent passage in chap. 3, note 25, from ed. J. L. Mays and P. J. Achtemeier, *Interpreting the Prophets*, Philadelphia, 1987, p. 165. The writer is R. R. Wilson, and see, further, chap. 7, note 7.

37  Wilson's word in *ibid.*, p. 165. Rumi, in reference to Muhammad's role in the Qur'an, uses the analogy of a stone lion in an ornamental garden, through whose mouth a plumber has contrived a "conduit" through which the spring flows. For Rumi, see *Discourses of Rumi*, ed. and trans. A. J. Arberry, London, 1967, pp. 51-2.

## Chapter V  *Prophet and Situation*

1  The sentence avoids the word "authorship", i.e. writers "composing", in order not to violate the Muslim sense that Muhammad in no way "authored" the Qur'an, but that he received its contents by *wahy* in a way which, nevertheless, had to keep pace with events and "assemble" itself serially.

2  *Ilaf* transcribes what is written, *eelaf* what is heard. *Ilaf* might leave at risk the full wealth of the Arabic derivative.

3  See discussion in M. Kister, *Studies in Jahilliyah and Early Islam*, London, 1980, and *Society and Religion from Jahiliyyah to Islam*, London, 1990

4  The root yields the word *alf*, meaning "thousand" and *mu'allif* means an "author". Various shades of meaning to the word *ilaf* in the Surah have been suggested. They need to be read with the prefix *li*, with the sense of ". . . in view of . . . let them worship the Lord of this house". For "sustaining the

5  journey winter and summer"? For "organizing men and camels to do so"? For "putting together protective sureties"? In any event facilities of access and of travel were significant in the story of the rise of Islam.

5 The six cumulative analogies in 3: 3–6, which culminate in conviction as to divine action, all have to do with significant "coincidings" (the snare and the ensnared etc.) that justify this reading of Amos' sense of mission in the mutual incidence of these two realities.

6 There is technical discussion of it in Jalal al-Din al-Suyuti's *Al-Itqan fi 'Ulum al-Qur'an*, Cairo edn, 1931, vol. 1. sect. 9, pp. 48–58: ("Knowledge of the Causes of the Descent").

7 Thus not even the Hijrah itself has direct notice. However, the first defeat of the Quraish at Badr is noted as Yaum al-Furqan, "Criterion Day" in Surah 8.41.

8 Surah 10 is named for him but the data is limited. Moreover, the Book of Jonah is more the *story* of a reluctant messenger, than an encounter in real mission. It seems wise to read the story as an analogy figuring the whole people as fleeing from their covenant vocation, being "swallowed" in the dragon of exile and finally released, chastened and disciplined, to resume their original calling. The other lesson is that of a universal divine compassion.

9 With these we are surely in a different context from that of Moses wishing that "all the Lord's people were prophets" (Numbers 11: 29), namely ecstatics and soothsayers.

10 The words occur in the Qur'an (5.21) directing Moses' people to "enter on the holy land which I (Yahweh) have assigned for you".

11 This is striking in view of the Qur'an's insistent perception of all prophets preceding Muhammad to have had essentially one message and one comparable experience of opprobrium. Was the Hijrah eventuation part of the distinctive finality Muhammad possessed?

12 Echoing the telling phrase of Psalm 35: 27, with its Messianic overtones.

13 The classic term is *jahiliyyah*. We can consider it "established" in that it was sanctioned by the structures of tribalism, the custody of the Ka'bah and the commercial power-dimension of Mecca.

14 The frequent Quranic description of the Meccan pagans as living, thinking, operating *min dun-Illahi*, by deliberate exclusion of Allah from their affairs and their attitudes.

15 On some twelve occasions the refrain comes *fi qulubihim marad*, e.g. 2.10, 24.50, 33.32 and 74.31. They belong both to the pre- and post-Hijrah periods. The diagnosis of sickness ascribed to "dissemblers" and "refusers" of the message may arise from a sense of exasperation that men should be so witless or callous. It also springs from the urge (as in 74.31) for an unhesitating quality of "certitude" concerning what should never be in doubt. Ultimately, however, it is well to take the "disease" analogy to its radical depths, as in the sense argued here.

16 His verdict in commenting on Shakespeare's Iago.

17 Al-Busiri, *Al Qasidat al-Muhammadiyyah* ("Song on Muhammad"), trans. H. Howarth, *Images of the Arab World*, London, 1944, p. 132.
18 On "Zulm in the Qur'an", see M. K. Husain in *The Muslim World Quarterly*, vol. 49, no. 3, July, 1959, pp. 196–212, trans. from his *Mutanawwi'at*, Cairo, 1958, vol. 2, pp. 3–28.
19 William Shakespeare, *Henry IV*, Part 2, Act 3, Sc. 1, lines 75–81. Thus the present draws its logic from the past, the past informs the drama of the present.
20 In any event his oracles against the foreign powers concerned both and there were many in Yahwism who did not concede the division of the Kingdoms.
21 To hold the "unity" of all "Isaiah" from 1 to 66, as some do, must mean to recognize a certain growing unity of "discipleship" enshrined in "a goodly fellowship". Otherwise, the whole Book represents an anthology over some four hundred years. Its main divisions are 1–39, 40–55 and 56–66. Only the former belongs squarely with the Isaiah of Jerusalem. The latter two bear all the marks of exilic time and test. Yet there is a sense in which the vision of chapter 6 belongs to the end and a "whole earth" "full of His glory".
22 With the land as "vineyard" and the people as its "dressers" warranting the strong satire of the words. There is no parallel of a Qur'an "paganizing" Muslims in the way that Isaiah is ready, in his bitter rhetoric, to "sodomize" his own hearers.
23 The main exception is Surah 30's allusion to Rum (Byzantium) and the Persians in mutual strife (30.2). Surah 18.83f alludes to *Dhu al-Qarnain*, i.e. Alexander the Great. The entrustment of the good earth to humanity at large as the realm of Allah's wisdom and will, with the consequent human *islam* by which these are vindicated, against the wiles of Satan to disrupt them – this is the core philosophy of history in the Qur'an. It is explicit in the simple question: "Am I not your Lord?" (Surah 7.172)
24 This seems to be the meaning of the phrase in Surah 90.2: "The Land" is its title – Allah "swears by this land, this place of your security". There is, surely, more than the bare sense that Muhammad is "citizen" or "dweller" in Mecca. The pronoun is singular but the following clause: "by father and by fathered" implies the whole society, perhaps even all humankind – Mecca's environs as a paradigm of the earth (which we might associate with the point in note 22 above).
25 The "Comfort ye . . . ". is not reflexive as what "the people" must do to each other, but a directive to the messenger who has to "fortify their heart" with the pledge of the end of their travail. The wider vocation to "lighten the nations" clearly turns on the immediate promise to Jewry. It reads like an overflowing exuberance about their own destiny ahead. This new sense of "the nations" as somehow involved in benediction proved the seed-bed of Christianity.
26 As, for example, in the double sense of Psalm 87 which can be read as incorporating Egypt, Ethiopia and Philistia as the lands of "born citizens of Zion".

*Or* perhaps they are only being summoned to acknowledge – as aliens – a new royal succession in Zion which they would do well to recognize?

27 The Jewish writer, H. M. Orlinsky, for example, finds only foolish "eisegesis" in a "significance that only came in New Testament times". He argues that "only the nature and needs of Christianity after the death of Jesus" produced the idea of a vicarious sufferer. *Studies in the Second Part of Isaiah*, Leiden, 1977, pp. 11 and 13. There is also the notion that attributes the "Servant" theme to the influence of the worship of Tammuz, drawn from a Babylonian liturgy of the New Year. See H. H. Rowley, *The Old Testament & Modern Study*, Oxford, 1961, pp. 147–51. Others think that, in some way, the passages represent the self-interpretation of the exiles against non-exilic Jews regarded as inferior.

28 Sound echoing sense, verbal finesse and sheer rhetorical power make this "Isaiah" a towering literary figure, well able, via splendid A. V. English rendering, to inspire and deserve the haunting music of Handel.

29 The imagery of scornful spittle and pulling of the hair and the marring of the face passed into yet deeper history. The "learner" theme recurs vividly in respect of Jesus.

30 See, for example, the grim analysis in Gerhard von Rad, *Holy War in Ancient Israel*. trans. M. J. Dawn, Grand Rapids, 1991.

31 One fervent exponent of this Arabism was Isma'il al-Faruqi, in *'Urubah and Religion*, Amsterdam, 1962. The sub-title ran: "A Study of the Fundamental Ideas of Arabism and of Islam and its Highest Moment of Consciousness." His enthusiasm for that linkage has to be tempered by the "universality" that employs this "particularity". But see also a more moderate version of the same theme in the joint work of Isma'il and Lois Lamya al-Faruqi, *The Cultural Atlas of Islam*, New York, 1986, Part 1, pp. 3–69.

32 Abu Ja'far al-Tabari, an early historian of Islam (839–*c*.923), Vol. 23, p. 127.

33 F. Mernissi, who cites Al-Tabari, even makes this point in *Islam and Democracy, Fear of the Modern World*, London, 1993, p. 99. "The Quraish were for freedom of thought and multiplicity of gods . . . opposition to the One would forever have a negative colour."

34 Francis, Lord Bacon, *Novum Organum*, ed. T. Fowler, 2nd edn, 1889, Book 1, 39. These "idols" (*Idola tribus, specus, fori et theatri*) were not "literal", but notions where peoples, individuals, gossippers and word-spinners had their sundry "mind-sets" and verbal usages to which they paid unthinking homage.

## Chapter VI *Prophethood and Conscience*

1 As in Matthew 7: 12, 22: 40 and parallel passages, or "Moses and the prophets", Luke 16: 29 echoing Isaiah 8: 20.

2 According to Sunni Islam. The Shi'ah have a different understanding of Qur'an interpretation and of the development of sacred law. See below, pp. 163–4.

3   The phrase with which the Qur'an refers to human deviousness and guile. Cf. Surahs 3.118, 40.19, cf. 114.5.
4   "Beginning" in the sense of "essence", or "gist". Nevertheless the balance of the sentence is right.
5   Borrowing the title of Muhammad Husain Haykal's study of Islamic Pilgrimage and its setting. "In the Abode of Revelation", Cairo, 1938.
6   The word *kahin* occurs only in Surahs 52.29 and 69.42, normally translated "soothsayer". The rituals of Muslims are all personally performed so that the Hebraic idea of "the priest" or "the levite" does not obtain. The New Testament theme of the "presbyter" as "ministering servant" had no purchase in Quranic thinking. "Monasticism" was strongly condemned in the Qur'an (57.27) – *Rahbaniyyah* being a human invention for which Allah gave no warrant. However, 5.82 commends monks and priests (*ruhban*) as among those "nearest in love" to Muslims. Surah 9.34 gives a sharply contrary opinion. It is important to emphasize that the absence of "priesthood" in Islam in no way counters the truth that humankind are custodian "priests" of God's creation. That truth of our sacramental entrustment in the natural order is deep in the *khilafah* concept and the Qur'an's frequent doxologies.
7   Though many of the rites of *Hajj*, or Pilgrimage, like the circumambulation of the *Ka'bah* and the "stoning" ceremony, were taken over from pagan usages.
8   Borrowing the words of H. A. R. Gibb to state a familiar truism (*Muhammadanism*, London, 1949, p. 88).
9   The arresting verse in Isaiah 10: 5: Having identified Assyria as Yahweh's tool in the requiting of Judah, he in no way exonerates the heathen power from her own iniquities. Like Amos before him, Isaiah reads a moral sovereignty in the motions of world history.
10  The rigorous principle laid down, for example, in Surahs 6.164, 17.15, 30.18, 39.7, 52.38, 2.286 and 65.7.
11  Ezekiel 14: 14 and 18. In the pain and perplexity of their condition, the exiles were only too ready for sustaining reputations as their plea and psychic security, their land and temple being forfeit.
12  Surah 100. Pre-Islamic poetry also mourns and reproaches this aspect of Arabian culture. Such raiding was, of course, the plague of Meccan commerce with its exposed caravan lines north and south. "Ungrateful to his Lord" translates the emphatic *lakanud* "insensitively boorish", "one who registers no debt, no obligation", "a disavower of benefits". The sense comes very close to "conscience-less".
13  See his "The Meaning of Zulm in the Qur'an". *The Muslim World Quarterly*, vol. 49, no. 3, July, 1959, pp. 196–212, from the Arabic in *Mutanawwi'at*, Cairo, 1958, pp. 3–28.
14  See Surah 30.30 for the double sense of *fitrat-Ullah* as both (human) nature and (divine) religion.

15   A significant passage in this sense is Surah 49.14–18, where certain Arabs came to the Prophet saying "we have believed". The Qur'an directs him to correct their verb: "You have not believed: you should rather say: 'We have surrendered' (or 'become Muslims') Faith has not entered your hearts." They are warned not to think they are doing a favour to Muhammad. To Allah alone is their duty, given complete sincerity.

16   A passage characterizing Muslims adds: *wa amruhum shura bainahum* which could be translated: "Their way of doing things is by consultation between them", or: "... whose affairs are a matter of counsel". (The word *al-shura* serves as title to the Surah.) *Amr*, however, as well as being "thing" or "matter", has also a sense of "directive", i.e. how they are meant to act.

17   A notable example of strong scepticism was that of the blind philosopher-poet, Abu-l-'Ala al-Ma'ari, sage of Syria (973–1057 CE who defied the dogmatists with his deep register of "the blight of birth" and "the futility of theism". For all his repute he was, however, a recluse and only "Lutheran" in his capacity to defy authority. Another long-suffering "rebel" was the cordwainer-mystic, Al-Hallaj (858–922) who was martyred for his alleged claim to "unitive" identity with God in mystical *fana'*, and also for his social concern in a will to channel Sufi devotion to practical compassion. His tragic career was a signal tribute to the capacity of Islamic piety for radical "revolt".

18   There might even be a temptation to play on words and read also, "The wait in the word".

19   Cited in F. Rajai, *Islamic Values and World View*, London, 1983, p. 54. The dictum would seem to require "reason" to agree to a suspension of its authority in what must constitute an abeyance of its exercise.

## Chapter VII  *Prophethood in Suffering*

1   See W. B. Yeats, "Vision Robart", in *Poems*, ed. P. Allt and K. Alspach, New York, 1957, p. 382. See also Frank Kermode, *The Romantic Image*, London, 1957, p. 74, where Salome's nonchalance is to be "admired". Her captivating eyes matter more to Herod than her vacant mind. Her beauty is cruelly recruited to the malice of her mother as a "persuasion" for the lust of Herod. Meanwhile, the murder of the prophet mocks all truth.

2   Based on Carlyle's Lectures and published in 1841, it fitted Muhammad into Carlyle's theme of "great personality" as clue to history. Long years later it found much favour with Muslims as a pioneer "recognition" despite the curiously robust terms in which Carlyle's "appreciation" of the Qur'an was expressed. On the broad theme of Carlyle and history see: John D. Rosenberg, *Carlyle and the Burden of History*, Oxford, 1985.

3   Prophetic moralism, Biblical and Quranic, stands on divine demands and leaves no room for notions of "natural law". Even so, Hosea (notably) and Isaiah (freely) invoke the contrasts of "nature's" fidelity to argue the folly of human sin. ("The ox knows his owner" etc.). Are pride and wrongdoing in some way, sinful *because* they violate some "law of things"? The frequent

appeal to external nature as a tutor for human nature enlists a certain "natural law" dimension into the theocratic ground.

4 We miss the point of their travail if we think that the prophets, in their conscience against their heritage, are somehow out of love of it. On the contrary, reproach is only the other side of deep identity with what ought to be. Hence the poetry of yearning in the very thrust of accusation.

5 The omnibus title "the Psalms of David" unhappily obscures the strong interplay of psalm and prophet. Cf. "My Tears in Thy Bottle", *The Muslim World Quarterly*, vol. LXXXVIII, no. 4, Oct. 1998, pp. 238–255 reflecting on Psalm 56: 8 – a psalm immersed in a mind like Jeremiah's.

6 Martin Buber, *The Prophetic Faith*, trans. C. Witton-Davies, New York, 1949.

7 In the way in which he seems to speak by rote, by words put on his lips, devoid of conscious participation of his own in their incidence. Oddly, R. R. Wilson, commenting on this, uses precisely the term "conduit" employed about Muhammad by Jalal al-Din Rumi. "The prophet is simply the conduit through which the unaltered divine word comes." Hence, in turn, it cannot be false. In J. L. Mays and P. J. Achtemeier, eds, *Interpreting the Prophets*, Philadelphia, 1987, p. 165. See also chap. 3, note 25 and chap. 4 note 36.

8 There are few more splendidly pictorial passages than chapter 27 of Ezekiel with its exuberant description of the shipping, the commerce, the wealth, wares and clientèle of the great Mediterranean seaport "whose builders perfected her beauty".

9 In its different idiom Psalm 45 actually salutes the divine agency with divine title: "Thy throne, O God, is for ever . . . God, thy God, has anointed thee with the oil of gladness . . ." (vv. 6–7). The significance is not lost on the writer in the Letter to the Hebrews (1: 8).

10 There being no volitional element in sheer victimization, whereas the sense of a bitter "cup" to be taken is the essence of what Jeremiah describes. This is even more the case with Jesus and the antecedents to the Cross. It is grievous for faith and theology that "the lamb of God" analogy has been so sadly traduced to construe the Cross as some arbitrary scheme of divine retributary justice or artificial substitution.

11 The thought is very close to the meaning of *awliya'* (s. *wali*) in the Qur'an – the "trusted ones" of God. In 3.37, 4.89 and 139 the word has the reprobated sense of "patrons" or "allies" of pagans or Satan. "Believers" can fill this role "one to the other" (9.71) for the *awliya'* of Allah, see 10.62, 41.31 (the angels) and the frequent warning to believers of "taking as reliances other than Allah" or those Allah provides. The sense of "prophecy" in Wisdom 7: 27 making "prophets, friends of God" is borrowed, for example, by Ibn 'Arabi who reads Muhammad's "Night Journey" as the divine showing to him of what He has "prepared for His friends", i.e. Paradise. (See *Studia Islamica*, no. 10 and 11, 1959, pp. 158f.). As for Psalm 116, the "grievousness" to God of "the death of His recruited ones" is the theme of CHAPTER VIII.

12  Which is exactly what prophets effectuate, being the insistent "conscience" of society – and such – always liable to rejection, to threats bent on enforcing silence. "Let us hear no more of the word of the Lord" (Isaiah 30: 11) tells their unwantedness.
13  "Appreciation", here, in the original sense of knowing the value of, or "esteeming" rightly. There is much about true and false esteeming in the prophetic saga.
14  W. B. Yeats, *Autobiographies*, London, 1955, p. 186.
15  Nathaniel Hawthorne, *The House of Seven Gables*, New York, 1851, chap. 21, 1965 edn, p. 259.
16  This being the double sense of the one Greek word *airon* in John 1.29 concerning "the lamb of God and the sin of the world".
17  "Vocal" in being a spokesman, not "vocal" in a selfishly querulous way.
18  See note 6, pp. 155–235.
19  For Buber himself concedes that the suffering prophet feels that his travail has import beyond himself and, though intensely private, comes in a public ministry and enters into urgent "dialogue" with Yahweh. *Loc. cit.* p. 165.
20  *Ibid.* p. 218.
21  André Neher, *The Exile of the Word*, New York, 1972, p. 189.
22  Buber, *op. cit.*, readily recognizes that "over against such confusion the true word is almost powerless" (p. 177) and that "the absolute power is for human personality's sake become personality" (p. 195) in the proxy who speaks and, hence, no longer all-compelling.

## Chapter VIII  *Prophethood and God*

1  Is the comma-shaped *wa* of Arabic the progenitor of that sign in English punctuation? Its use characterizes Arabic writing and speech which some critics have charged with the habit of *wa-iyyah*. To be sure, the *wa* that is known as *wa al-hal* (the "and" of purposive copulation) indicating what may locate, or explain or situate the previous verbal action.
2  The "association" word is deliberate. For it underscores a vital distinction we must always make. *Shirk* in Islam, often translated as "association", means "associating" with One God the pseudo-deities of pagan (or contemporary) delusion. Islam, with Christianity, emphatically rejects such distortion or misdirection of worship, power, reliance or belief. But that inclusive repudiation of *Shirk* in no way "dissociates" God from the world. Indeed, the need to correct and disown it, via the sending of "messengers" to educate against it, spells a profound association of God with humankind in history. Of such association prophethood is entire evidence.
3  He meant "man who is not suitably treated as who and what he is". (The business of housing and victuals is derivative.) There is deep theology in the definition of "accommodate", i.e. "To ascribe fittingly a thing to a person, to show a correspondence, to make consistent."
4  The first is an emphatic negative with the *la* of absolute negation. The second

is a nominal sentence which – in form – can be read as singling out Muhammad as *the* apostle of God, though the Qur'an emphasizes that there had been a whole long sequence of prophets whom his finality embraces. It is noteworthy that the two clauses appear in the Qur'an only separately and not in the *Shahadah*'s combination.

5  The "calling down of blessing" upon Muhammad which Surah 33.56 attributes to "God and His angels", and enjoins on all Muslims. Hence the formula, said, written and printed, in Muslim piety, at every mention of Muhammad's name. It enshrines divine acclaim of the Prophet and aligns the believers' salutation of him with that divine register of a divine purpose congenially fulfilled (may we say?) in the human agency. The Islamic term and usage repudiates what Christians have in Christology yet something divinely and humanly reciprocal is unmistakable. It is this "something" we are here at pains to understand.

6  Fazlur Rahman, *Major Themes of the Qur'an*, Minneapolis, 1980. pp. xi and 1–3.

7  *Ibid.*, p. 3.

8  "Human" in the sense that words it finds for its revelatory role it finds in human speech. That necessary fact need not call in question the Islamic conviction that what the reader has is "the words of God". The concept of *wahy* (inspiration) proceeds through Arabic, a language in human currency.

9  The theme here is more fully developed in how human repudiation of Iblis (by conforming to divine *Islam* whereby his strategy of beguilement is frustrated) is powerfully symbolized during Muslim Pilgrimage and the casting of stones against token pillars during the ritual. Hence the descriptive: *Al-Shaitan al-rajim* "the stoned (accursed) Satan". Though active in form the adjective *rajim* is passive in sense. He has to be "made" what he is, namely "accursed".

10  See Surah 16.36. There is also emphasis on "messengers" in the tongues of those to whom they are sent.

11  "Narrowed" in the sense that Israel alone is present at Sinai and takes the ethnic covenant unilaterally theirs, making all the rest of humankind "Gentiles". Long pre-dating Sinai is the Noahid covenant of "seedtime and harvest" in Genesis 8 in which all humanity is involved. To this the Qur'an refers in the cosmic oath of Surah 7.172, responding to Allah's question: "Am I not your Lord?"

12  The command conjoins God and the Prophet in echo of the *Shahadah*. See Surahs 3.32 and 132, 8.1, 20 and 46, 47.33, and 58.13.

13  The congruent word, however, would not be "obey" as to a ruler or legislator, but rather "heed", "hearken", "ponder" or "make heart-place for".

14  For an exploration of the antecedents and meanings of Muhammad's *Tahannuth*, or "soul-seeking" in the environs of Mecca, see, perhaps my: *Returning to Mount Hira'*, London, 1994.

15  From the Greek *en-theos*, "divinely moved". Prophethood might well be

16 If the hearers are in doubt concerning what God has "sent down upon Our servant", they are challenged to "bring a surah like it". Muhammad's "servanthood" consists in textual "recipience". The experience (*wahy*) is traditionally understood, however, as not engaging or recruiting anything from him. He is only a "conduit" where the words are made to flow. The "Our servant" designation of Muhammad occurs also in 8.41. Cf. "His servant" in 17.1, 18.1, 25.1, 39.36, 53.10 and 57.9. In the New Testament, servanthood is the very essence of the "Sonship" of Jesus (cf. Philippians 2: 5–11 and Hebrews 2: 6–13). See below, note 36.

understand, with due safeguards, as a sacred enthusiasm.

17 Notably in respect of Jesus and his Mother, Mary (Surah 23.50).

18 Though the doctrine was challenged and countered by the Mu'tazilites who reasoned the "createdness" of the Qur'an, inasmuch as it was "in time" in the creaturely setting of Muhammad's mission, incorporating domestic details of his household and having incidence only in its *asbab* or "occasions". This seemed to militate against the belief that it could be uncomplicatedly "eternal". The problem is a very familiar one and can only be resolved by "paradox" to which Islam, by and large, is hostile.

19 *The Wisdom of Solomon*, 7: 27. Hebrew "Wisdom" literature was responsive to the Greek influence in the late pre-Christian centuries. The later prophets in the Bible had "discipleships" and "laid-up" deliverances. The entire phenomenon for its Semitic fervour and concern with history could lend itself to Greek categories, epitomized in the very title: "The Wisdom – of Solomon."

20 Using "extravagant" in the strict sense of parting from the true path of rectitude concerning the Prophet's entire human-ness, as the Qur'an – and "orthodox" piety – insisted. Rigorous unitarian thinking in the mood of the Wahhabis and their mentor Ibn Taimiyya reprimanded all deviant celebration of Muhammad's "mysteries", apart from the enjoined *Tasliyah*.

21 Ibn al-'Arabi (1172–1240), of Andalusian origin but widely travelled in the East, developed the most erudite and elusive forms of Islamic esotericism, notably in his *Fusus al-Hikam*, which generated sharp hostility from opponents who saw his "illuminism" and his mystic version of *Tawhid* as treachery to Islam.

22 The traditional use of the concept of Muhammad's complete "illiteracy" was to heighten the total "externality" to his mind of the Quranic deliverances. It demonstrated, on that view, their entire divine origin, verbally and essentially. However, the term *ummi* is more properly read as denoting a prophet to a people as yet "unscriptured". But even if, that way, the Qur'an's "sending on his heart" recruits his mental participation, there would still be place – perhaps sounder place – for supernatural "wisdom" enabling and perfecting such participation.

23 Understanding the phrase only as meaning "one not party in any way to the content of the Qur'an" – in no way impugning authentic vocation.

24 See the pioneer discussion in Fazlur Rahman, *Prophecy in Islam, Philosophy & Orthodoxy*, London, 1957.
25 *Hasrah* means "sharp grief" or "bitter regret". It deplores what has happened, laments what is. The translations of 36.30 vary, but many go for "Woe be to!" (Arberry), or "Alas for . . ." (Bell, Abul-l-Fazl) or "O misery of . . . (Sale) but Muhammad al-Nuwaihy reads "the servants" as prophets and Allah's pity with them in "a suffering identity with creation and humanity". He takes the following clause about any apostle meeting only with derision as evoking this divine "sigh" or "grief" over what His servants undergo. See A. H. Green, ed., *In Quest of an Islamic Humanism, Arabic & Islamic Studies in Memory of Mohammed al-Nuwaihi*, Cairo, 1984, pp. 191-2.
26 Echoing: "We are not of those who are overtaken (or superseded)", Surahs 56.60 and 70.41. The last Judgement is the proof of that but the phrase can have a wider connotation in Allah's perpetual and vigilant sovereignty over all times, places and occasions.
27 All the elements of the Psalm link it with the likeness of Jeremiah (the umbrella title "Psalms of David" should not confuse us). If a "wineskin" is the meaning of "flask" or "bottle" the strange hyperbole is even more arresting. In any event the writer feels that what he is undergoing for God's sake cannot be of no account to God. The sending must somehow mean a sharing. See also chap. 7, note 5.
28 The tiny Hebrew kingdom taunts the great powers that threaten. Zion can "have them in derision". "Be wise, now, therefore, O ye kings", come trembling to make allegiance. The satire is as powerful as the stance is ludicrous – by seeming criteria.
29 Cf. – for *hasb* – Surahs 3.173, 9.59 and 129, 39.38. In 5.104 the polytheists find their *hasb* in their ancestral heritage.
30 The "providence" in the factors leading to the Hijrah and in the safe passage through its hazards, and in its subsequent effects could be read – in Islamic norms – as a sort of making "inviolate" the destiny of Muslims.
31 Flavius Josephus, *The Jewish War*, cited in Yigael Yadin, *Masada*, London, 1966, p. 232.
32 Among its finest exponents is Abraham Heschel, See his *The Prophets*, New York, 1962, and ed. Samuel H. Dresner, *Abraham Heschel: The Circle of the Baal Shem Tov*, Chicago, 1985, and my *Troubled by Truth*, Edinburgh, 1992, pp. 108-26.
33 "Diminished" to "kindly" or "benign" whereas the Latin origin means "suffering with".
34 In the light of the ill-repute in which Nazarenes were held by the élite of Jerusalem. (Cf. John 1: 46.)
35 It is surprising, in the light of the accounts, in Surahs 3 and 19 of the "virgin birth" of 'Isa, that the Islamic Scripture has so little place for what Jesus actually taught. The words "Forgive us our sins" are the only ones, verbatim, that

the Qur'an cites. Nor are the accounts of healing and "the table from heaven" amplified in any significant detail. (See chap. 4, note 23) The Qur'an, in effect, has Jesus only speaking from the cradle (Surah 19. 30–33).

36  Absentee landlords could well be cheated out of their ownership if tenants could "engineer" a fiction that the property had been abandoned or forfeited. This was the point of their defiance of claims on the annual output. In such circumstances, only the son and heir could assert ownership rights (as no servant could do). Hence also the impulse to murder. This explains what, in the parable, would otherwise be inexplicable, namely risking the heir, given the brutality to servants.

37  If these were not reversible, neither could be true. "God in Christ" was Paul's term-making: the whole New Testament speaks the latter. It is well to remember that we owe to the faith in Christology ("the person and the work of Jesus") all record of his words and teaching. For it was only the ultimate faith *about* Him that gave written form to the faith *by* which He lived.

## Chapter IX  Ongoing Finality

1  "Tout le monde existe pour aboutir à un livre." See: Jacques Scherer, *Le Livre de Mallarmé*, Paris, 1957.

2  Matthew 11: 13. The theme of John the Baptist being "the last" turns on the New Testament conviction as to Jesus' Messiahship and, in turn, on that Messiahship as culminating fulfilment of what all prophethood awaited. Thus prophethoods gave way to what was more than they. They were all "fulfilled" in being transcended. The sense in which Islam takes Muhammad as "the seal of the prophets" keeps the culmination within prophethood by disavowing Messiahship except as a title of honour for Jesus *qua* "prophet" in penultimate terms.

3  Which was exactly how, according to the chroniclers, some tribesmen saw the situation. Since their fealty was "submission" to the man, Muhammad, not allegiance to a faith, the man's death freed them from its ties. The distinction, reprehensible when it happens, between being *muslimun* ("submitters") and *mu'minun* ("believers") is explicit in the Qur'an itself. See Surah 49.14.

4  Sikhism, Baha'ism and Mormonism are immediate examples.

5  "Pseudo-prophets" like Musailama in the Prophet's time were roundly denounced, though – in an indirect way – the Qur'an had teased, if not invited, their pretensions by the challenge to equal its eloquence, a challenge oft repeated but scorned when taken up. When, in ambiguous terms, Mirza Ghulam Ahmad, in India, in the third quarter of the 19th century, claimed, or seemed to claim, to be a further (Muslim) prophet, he was denounced. Later his Ahmadiyyah Movement divided over the interpretation of what he claimed. Even so, its "Lahore" segment in Pakistan was declared "un-Islamic" in 1974 and put under duress.

6  Revelation 3: 7 and Matthew 16: 19 with its imagery of "the keys". That "hearts" have their "locks" is an analogy used in Surah 47.24.

7  Some Muslims have been prone to read "into" nuances of the Qur'an anticipations of modern scientific discoveries, in the mistaken conviction that these could be proper confirmation of its "hidden knowledge" – a point of view which ignores how it was always a "religious" Book and never a scientific treatise miraculously ahead of its time. In a different concern, Biblical prophecy has often been suborned to underwrite political, or dogmatic, purposes far removed from intelligent reading.

8  It is basic, in both Bible and Qur'an, that "prophets" belong with "peoples". Kinship was vital given Jewish "covenant". Only a local, Meccan, Arab prophet could fit the self-understanding of the Qur'an. See note 10.

9  See Jesus' foretelling of Muhammad's coming (on the lines of Moses in Deut. 18: 15) in Surah 61.6. There is a large and wearying literature on this issue and its entanglement with the "Gospel" of Barnabas. On the Muslim aligning of John 14: 16 with Surah 61.6 and of *Ahmad* with *parakletos* see my: *Jesus and the Muslim*, London, 1985, pp. 262–8.

10 Despite the intense individualism implicit in prophetic vocation its Hebraic incidence could only be within the nation. How could an alien address "God's people"? (Remember all the trouble Balaam had.) John Skinner makes the point: "In this limitation of religion to the national consciousness of Israel we can see a reason for . . . a special order of men through whom God makes known His will to the nation." *Prophecy & Religion: Studies in the Life of Jeremiah*, Cambridge, 1961, p. 7.

11 Hud, Salih and Shu'aib. The last has been linked with Jethro, whose daughter Moses married. Hud was sent to the 'Ad tribe and Salih to the Thamud.

12 It is tempting to speculate on this significant omission, made the more surprising from these great figures being so much more accessible historically than the likes of Enoch and Shu'aib. Could it be that Amos and they all had a more self-possessed and mind-engaged quality of eloquence than the Qur'an was allowed? Or was it that the ultimate implications of prophetic suffering were at odds with the post-Hijrah patterns in the Qur'an?

13 Ed. Ted Hughes, *A Choice of Coleridge's Verse*, London, 1996, p. 22.

14 Note 7 above and, for example, the idea that the Qur'an "anticipated" the cutting of the Suez Canal by the reference in 55.19: "He let forth the two seas that meet together", when (cf. 25.53) salt and fresh seas are meant.

15 "Heirloom" suits in that it has to do with what is valued and passed down, though "loom" suggests something small and insignificant apart from its associations.

16 In *Sartor Resartus*, first published in 1832, Carlyle made ingenious use of "clothing" in reflecting on human philosophy. W. H. Hudson wrote of it: "Creatures of time and space . . . apprehend the Absolute only when He weaves about Him the visible garments of time and space" (1908 edn, p. xi). Prophets, then, provide the looms.

17 This applies to public reading. Hence the rubric in the Book of Common Prayer requiring the reader to say: "Here begins . . . here ends . . . the Lesson",

lest he introduces his own private words.

18 Ibn Hisham, the 8th century gatherer of traditions of Muhammad. Tabari (839–923), compiler of Quranic exegesis in his great *Tafsir*. Al-Ghazali's "Refutation of the Refutation" sought the vindication of Islamic theology *vis-à-vis* philosophic scepticism. His "Reviving of Religious Knowledge" was a monumental compendium of ethical and religious discipline and faith.

19 These issues troubled the Murjites (how did one explain unbelief, given overall divine will; how identify a faith that only "said" and did not perform; how "check" the Islam of a ruler to whom obedience might be forfeit if his Islam did not pass muster and who was to adjudicate?) The Mu'tazilites wrestled with the question whether the Qur'an was "uncreated" or "created". The theologian Al-Ash'ari "reconciled" the use in worship and faith of the Names of God with the insistence that His "incomparability" excluded any use of human adjectives. None of these issues had been the concern of Mecca and Medina during Muhammad's career.

20 See Fazlur Rahman, *Major Themes of the Qur'an*, Minneapolis, 1980. In *A Faith for all Seasons*, London, 1990, Shabbir Akhtar writes of "problematic parts of revealed Scriptures" (which he says for their part Christians "simply sacrifice") as a duty Muslims must undertake, "learning to face fully the sceptical gaze of modernity" (p. 207). For genuine "fundamentalists" there are no "problematic parts". Sadiq al-'Azm, for example, has boldly undertaken them in his *Naqd al-Fikr al-Dini fi-l-Islam*, Beirut, 1969, "The Criticism of Religious Thought in Islam". Shaikh Muhammad Hasan al-Yasin published a sharp rejoinder, *Hawamish 'ala Kitab Naqd al-Fikr al-Dini*, Beirut, 1971, "Margins on the Book: The Criticism of Religious Thought".

21 See a classic work: Gershom Scholem, *The Messianic Idea in Israel and Other Essays*, New York, 1971.

22 Much conjecture has gathered around how a man could survive swallowing by a whale and be disgorged by it on dry land. But suppose all this allegory about a nation with a mission, running away from it and being re-charged with it after a preserved sojourn in a heathen empire? Or are Daniel and his famous three symbols of Judaic fortitude and preservation through sharp adversity?

23 Ezekiel's meaning is neither served, nor intelligently understood, by wondering how, *in situ*, it is physically conceivable.

24 Cited from *Bal-i-Jabril* (1935) by K. G. Saijidain, *Iqbal's Educational Philosophy*, 3rd edn, Lahore, 1945. The literature on Iqbal is voluminous. See, e.g. Iqbal Singh, *The Ardent Pilgrim*, London, 1951. His major work was *The Reconstruction of Religious Thought in Islam*, Lahore, 1930, London, 1934.

25 *Reconstruction*, pp. 22–3.

26 A. N. Whitehead, the Harvard philosopher, is quoted extensively, *ibid.*, pp. 1, 2, 34, 39, 46, 70 and 133. It is interesting, in our present context, that he leaves "corollaries" (of his views) to the future theologians of Islam,. pp. 72f.

27 The writer is contrasting the "free run" of the Gospel with the imprisonment of its herald. However, the Greek *ou dedetai* says the "the Word" is "unfettered".
28 On this reading, the Qur'an enjoins monogamy, though the verse has long been taken quite otherwise. It is evident that, since Scriptures depend on exegetes, they are liable to how these register the needs and attitudes of changing times. Surah 4.129 says that impartiality between wives is impossible
29 "Non-repugnancy" to the Qur'an was a salient feature of the "Basic Principles" Pakistan sought to enthrone over its constitution-writing and its democracy. It is a more pliant criterion than "actual repugnancy" could be.
30 S. T. Coleridge, *Complete Poetical Works*, ed. E. H. Coleridge, vol. 1, Oxford, 1912, "Dejection – An Ode", p. 365.
31 Caird, London, 1980, Fazlur Rahman, Minneapolis, 1980.
32 *Op. cit.* p. 65. He links the "signs" the Qur'an finds in nature with its concept of *burhan*, "evidently", as the ground of human technology.
33 *Ibid.*, p. 23. Significantly, the *amr* is also that, of God, from which proceeds *wahy*, the coming upon Muhammad of revelatory words. Iqbal, citing Surah 17.85, finds its meaning also in the emerging of ego-entities, human selves, in the spatio-temporal order. *Reconstruction*, p. 193.
34 *Major Themes*, pp. 106–7.
35 *Ibid.*, pp. 128f.
36 A frequent term with a changing connotation. Meaning whatever "tests" and "tempts" (like love of children "tempting" fathers to evade the dangers of combat) it spells "persecution" when the first Muslims were a minority endangered; *fitnah* comes to mean "sedition" against them when they are dominant and empowered.
37 *Op. cit.*, pp. 106 f. and "the end-values of life" in their perpetual "Judgement" of human acts.
38 The point takes us back to the theme of CHAPTER VI. *Major Themes*, with its lively perspective of Muslim intellectual tasks, gives strong prominence to the role of conscience in the obedience the Shari'ah demands. On its relation to *taqwa* and its being at risk with religious custodians, see pp. 29f and 61f. It is what is confronted by "the Hour of Truth", p. 107.
39 It cannot be that history has reached a perfectly attentive and receptive generation. It never does: but had it done so that generation would have passed. Thus, if prophets with "guidance" are necessary at all can they ever credibly be no longer required?
40 See, for example, Gerhard von Rad, *Holy War in Ancient Israel*, trans. M. J. Dawn, Grand Rapids, 1991.
41 Quoting the nonchalant phrasing of the Balfour Declaration, which, in 1917, dealt with "Palestine" (for which it had no other name) but forebore to refer to any "Palestinians" who "existed" only as "non-Jewish".
42 On the nuances and ambiguities of "the territorial dimensions of Judaism"

see the careful study under that title by W. D. Davies, Berkeley, 1982.
43 Citing Psalm 39: 3. Aspects of this "question" are reviewed in my *Palestine: The Prize and Price of Zion*, London, 1997, chap. 11.
44 It is often alleged that Christianity was/is a "Gentile" development, a sorry "de-Judaising" of all that Jesus was. While, by a Jewish opting-out later in the 1st century, it did become a majority "Gentile" thing, this in no way diminishes the founding role of Jewish apostles. All the New Testament writers – save Luke – were Jews. "Jesus the Jew" is a deeply right emphasis, keeping in mind "what sort of Jew?" On that the original Jewish apostles had their verdict.
45 Dudley Young, *Out of Ireland: The Poetry of W. B. Yeats*, Cheadle, 1975, pp. 24–5.
46 Does the familiarity of these words conceal from us how startling, enigmatic, they would have sounded prior to the actual Cross of Jesus?
47 At Caesarea Philippi in Matthew 16 but also, dramatically, in Mark 10: 32.
48 Traditionally Qur'an copies, located in different centres and probably differing textually in places, were "collected" during the Caliphate of 'Umar (634–644) and "finalized" in the time of the third Cailph, 'Uthman (644–656). But see John Burton, *The Collection of the Qur'an*, Cambridge, 1977.
49 However, this formal "programmatic" for the precept that "How they should be is by counsel among themselves" (Surah 42.38) was hedged about by the pundits, interested in the writ of their own "expertise" and minded to argue that "the gate of Ijtihad" was "closed" or that would-be participants in it lacked what it required. Organs of change are always called into question by diehards.
50 *Op. cit.*, p. 83.
51 This "occultation" – as the term was – resulted in two Schools of the Shi'ah, happening in the one case after the seventh Imam, and in the other after the twelfth. Hence the "Seveners" and the "Twelvers...". The "hidden-ness" of the Imam aroused mystical speculation and also kindled the doctrines of "re-appearance" which underlie Mahdism in its several forms.
52 The central role of an Ayatollah was demonstrated in an extra-ordinary way in the 1979 Iranian Revolution, where "the masses" had their vital supporting part in crowding into the streets. In that sense the phrase *Ilah al-nas*, "the God of the people" in Surah 114.3, could be seen to have its point, but only as released by and recruited for the "clerical" authority. This is a far cry from the Sunni concept of *Ijma'*.
53 The infamous day in 680 when the forces of the new Ummayyad Caliph Yazid slaughtered the hapless retinue of Husain who had marched from Medina to lower Iraq anticipating local support in a campaign to recover the Caliphate for the house of 'Ali.
54 A phrase (akin to "great victory") much used in the post-Hijrah Qur'an both in celebration and to emphasize how successful issue there has to be and to

be unmistakably evident.
55 Hence the "Passion Play" on the 10th of Muharram recalling and pleading the virtue of the martyrs. See Mahmud Ayyub, *Redemptive Suffering in Islam: A Study of the Devotional Aspects of 'Ashura' in Twelver Shi'ism*, The Hague, 1978.
56 Ibn Khaldun, *Al-Muqaddimah*, trans. Franz Rosenthal (sub-titled: *An Introduction to History*), New York, 1958, vol. 1, p. 415. He quotes the tradition on p. 253.
57 See T. F. Fretheim, *The Suffering of God*, Philadelphia, 1984.
58 Gerhard von Rad, *Old Testament Theology*, Vol. 2: *The Theology of Israel's Prophetic Traditions*, trans. D. M. G. Stalker, New York, 1965, p. 274.
59 Samuel L. Terrien, *The Elusive Presence*, New York, 1978, p. 246. "Ongoing Finality" might pause over the plea of Ecclesiasticus 49: 10: "As for the twelve prophets, may their bones flower again from the tomb, since they have comforted Jacob and redeemed him in faith and hope." The "tomb" is surely, rather, the womb of their communal possession.

# Index of Themes

absolute, the, 91, 174, 188
accusation
    exterior,8, 31, 111, 154, 168
    interior,8, 18
    self,77
adversity, prophets',20, 32, 65, 72, 78, 79, 81, 93, 106, 131
*afflatus*,9, 41
agency, divine,7, 8, 19, 48, 76, 93, 117f., 122, 123, 134, 142, 146
    in Islam,125, 127, 166, 169
anguish, prophetic,12, 154, 166 (*see also* grief)
anointing, 7, 60
antecedents, to call, 45
anthropomorphism, 54
antipathy, 19, 20
apocalyptic, 1, 83, 156
apostacy, 8, 73, 96
artistry, 41, 48, 63, 172
authoring, 44, 50, 152, 173, 176
authority, 46, 89, 99, 100, 106, 110, 141, 143, 151, 160, 164, 181
    of conscience, 90f.
awe, 70

biography, prophetic, 2, 13, 16, 23, 26, 32
    in Hosea, 28, 58
blasphemy, 90
burden, the prophetic, 1f., 14f., 18, 26, 30, 32, 59, 73, 74, 82, 92, 102f., 110, 124, 134, 166
    divine, 134, 135
    in Jeremiah, 65

calligraphy, 43, 126
call narratives, 29, 313, 48, 92, 123
Canon, role of, 1, 63, 88, 138, 145, 146, 170

the Biblical, 9, 33
paradox of, 141
"casting", 4, 13, 14f.
celebration, of nature, 12 (*see also* Nature)
Christ-event, the, 45, 116, 127, 136, 137, 166
Christhood in Jesus, 2, 3, 20, 115, 152, 160
    a suffering, 10, 11, 20 (*see also* the Cross)
Christology, 3, 12, 118, 128, 136, 137, 167, 184, 187
Church, the Christian, 10, 11, 118, 129, 136, 164
    making of, 159, 160
communion, with God, 2
community, 27, 60, 61, 97, 139f., 155, 160, 166
compassion, 29, 59, 90, 95, 135, 181
complacence, 77, 154
conscience, 6, 8, 25, 40, 56, 88f., 107, 132, 134, 154, 158, 159, 183, 190
    and divine law, 89f., 96
conscientization, 93
consciousness, 2, 22, 90, 99
continuity, 1, 10, 87, 138, 163, 166 (*see also* finality)
controversy, 55, 74, 91, 167
    "the Lord's", 73, 74
courage, 104
covenant, Hebraic, 4, 6, 7, 25, 27, 29, 37, 38, 56, 63, 72, 73, 76, 77, 83, 91, 105, 131, 155, 156, 188
    the new, 32 (*see also* New Testament)
creation, 12, 34, 50, 51, 118, 121, 152, 175, 180, 186
    creation myths, 60
creaturehood, human, 12, 13, 51, 72, 115, 118, 120, 122, 144, 188

## Index of Themes

creaturehood, human *(continued)*
  and prophethood, 120f.
credentials, 10, 11, 24, 45, 46, 139, 142, 149
Cross, the, 20, 45, 66, 103, 113, 134, 135, 136, 159, 160, 166, 182, 191

death, of prophets, 103, 104, 110, 159, 182
despair, ultimate, 112, 159
determinism, and free-will, 100
development, of meaning, 144, 145, 191
  (*see also* exegesis)
dialogue
  with hearer, 67, 83
  with Yahweh, 32, 33, 62, 65, 82
differences between Biblical & Quranic
  prophethoods, 6, 7, 8, 10, 23, 26, 30, 40, 41, 55, 56, 72, 73, 79, 92, 94, 122, 123, 128, 133, 134, 147, 172

ecstacy, 41
election, Hebraic, 4, 8, 27, 48, 59, 79, 84, 105, 122, 131, 155, 156
eloquence, Biblical, 44, 46, 52, 62, 76
  Quranci, 49, 50, 126
endurance, 8, 15, 131
engagement, 42
eschatology, 158
ethics, 90, 92, 95, 106, 133
  and God, 119f.
  Islamic, 98, 120
  social, 51
ethnicism, Arab, 85
  Jewish, 146 (*see also* peoplehood)
event(s), 40, 48, 113, 118, 161
  stress of, 107
evil, human, 8, 33, 68, 74, 110, 129, 159
exceptionality, Jewish, 12, 56, 63, 67, 76, 78, 84, 105
exclusivism, 82, 84
  and theology, 84f.
exegesis, 148f., 158, 162, 169, 179, 189
exile, 6, 7, 37, 63, 67, 76, 78, 79, 85, 93, 106, 108, 147, 156, 179
expectation, 7, 20 (*see also* hope)
experience, prophetic, 2, 12, 14, 23, 26, 30, 32, 43, 58, 74, 86, 105, 107, 109, 115, 128, 129, 135, 157, 158, 159, 166

falsehood, 104, 105
fate, 104, 129
Fatherhood, divine, 2, 137, 151

"fear of the Lord", 37, 89, 153
fertility cults, in Hosea, 59
fidelity, divine/human, 81, 110, 113, 161, 172
finality, 40, 71, 138f., 160, 167, 184
  in Eucharist, 161
folk religion, 39
"forwarding", Quranic, 53, 95, 153
futility, 108, 155, 158, 181
futurism, 7, 20, 80, 82, 108, 141, 142, 158

genius, theme of, 41, 42
Godwardness, in humans, 118
good, overcoming evil, 110, 113, 159 (*see also* redemption)
grace, 13, 113, 115, 118, 137, 152
gratitude, 50, 51, 70
grief, prophetic, 32, 75, 82, 107, 110, 111, 113, 114, 115, 128, 132, 160, 164, 166, 168, 186
guidance, 37, 116, 121, 139, 160, 161, 190
guilt, 6, 8, 19, 29, 38, 59, 89, 94, 102, 170

heart-break, 102f., 108, 109
heart-sickness, 75, 107, 177
heredity, factor of, 39, 163, 164
heroic, the, 104
history, place of, 37, 47, 54, 58, 77, 85, 91, 106, 107, 111, 121, 138, 144, 146, 152, 178
  criticism, 42, 145
  as retrospect, 83, 104
holiness, divine, 29, 30, 105, 106, 156
honesty, 110, 129, 130
hope, 7, 20, 57, 67, 80, 87, 110, 111, 112, 116, 137, 142, 146, 147, 156, 158
humility, 104
hymnology, 82

iconoclasm, 55
idiosyncrasies, in prophets, 19, 23, 48, 66, 67
idolatry, 30, 50, 54, 72, 76, 85, 86, 91, 174, 179
ignorance, 73, 74, 122
"illiteracy" of Muhammad, 125, 126, 185
  (*see also* ummi)
illumination, 38, 39, 118, 185
imagery, 15, 21, 33, 50, 52, 56, 57, 60, 61, 62, 64, 103, 109, 110, 144, 149, 151, 152, 169
  in Ezekiel, 16, 17, 149, 182
  in Qur'an, 25 (*see also* signs)

194

# Index of Themes

imitation, of Christ, 161
immaculate status, of Muhammad, 39
"implacable" Qur'an, 50, 51
incarnation, 2, 66
Incarnation, the, 127 (*see also* Christ-event)
incidence, 40, 70
  of Qur'an, 24, 100
individualism, 170, 188
  and conscience, 90, 94, 104
infallibility, 43, 74
infanticide, 25, 95
inspiration, 16, 19, 35, 36, 40, 43, 56, 67, 69, 100, 122, 167, 169, 173, 176, 184, 189
instrumentality, 43, 122, 127
intelligibility, 41
intention, moral, 99 (*see also* niyyah)
interpretation, 150f., 164, 174 (*see also* exegesis)
intimidation, 18, 36, 105
irony, 33, 50, 53, 65, 83, 91, 103, 106, 128, 132
judgement, the last, 95, 142, 153, 154, 171, 190
  oracles of, 77 (*see also* Al-Akhirah)
justification, 111, 113, 172

karmic law, 112
"kingdom of priests", 3 (*see also* nature, trust of)

"Lamb" imagery, 81, 109, 110, 118, 129, 182
land, the, 60, 72, 73, 76, 78, 79, 85, 93, 106, 132, 147, 155, 156, 157, 168, 177, 178
  forfeiture, 80
language, 2, 16, 21, 22, 40f., 49, 54, 63, 64, 68, 117f., 148f., 164, 174, 184
  and meaning, 153
  in Qur'an, 9, 45
  as "sacred", 44, 45, 162
last day, the, 98
law, natural, 106, 181
  and prophethood, 80f., 92, 149, 154
liability, human, 50, 97, 98, 99, 108
loneliness, 104, 105, 108
long-suffering, divine, 82

manwardness, in God, 118f.
memory, 57
Messiah (ship), 7, 66, 79, 82, 103, 115, 116, 125, 134, 136, 147, 159, 160, 164, 167, 168, 172, 187, 191
  and God, 107, 117f. (*see also* theology)
  "servant" antecedents 117f., 128, 136
Messianic hope, 11, 28, 37, 158
"Messianic secret", the, 81
metaphor, 16, 53, 56f., 62, 66, 104, 109, 113, 152, 153, 170, 175
metaphysics, 52, 125
ministry, of Jesus, as Messianic prelude, 135f., 158
monasticism, 180
monolatry, 84, 85, 155, 176
monotheism, 4, 54, 56, 84, 85, 155, 175
  (*see also* unity, divine)
mythology, 173

"name in vain" the, 106, 141
narrative art, of Qur'an, 54, 55
nationalism, Islamic, 146
nations, heathen, 77, 78, 79, 80, 83
nature, invocations of, 50, 51, 59, 60, 62, 63, 106, 180, 181, 182, 190
  in human trust, 45, 120, 121, 180
non-repugnancy, to Qur'an, 152, 190

oath, the cosmic, 50
obduracy, human, 53, 73, 74, 83, 104, 103, 108, 116, 131
obedience, community of, 128, 146, 160, 189, 190
oblation, vain, 91
occasionalism, in Qur'an, 26, 70, 76, 101, 152, 161, 171 (*see also* asbab al-nuzul*)
"offering, a pure", 84, 111, 114
omnipotence, 76
ongoingness, in "the word", 139f.
ostracism, 105

paganism, 4, 25, 50, 56, 73, 75, 76, 79, 87, 92, 131, 163, 172
parable method, 50, 136, 170
paradox, 8, 30, 36, 39, 41, 53, 57, 60, 62, 64, 76, 93, 106, 108, 109, 139, 145, 154, 155
parataxis, 117, 119, 184
partiality, in exhortation, 112
partnership, divine/human, 47, 48 (*see also* agency, divine)
passion, 37, 56, 62, 156
passivity, in prophets, 100
patience, 3, 8, 24, 26, 103, 124, 131
penitence, 33, 57, 59, 78, 83, 110, 145

# Index of Themes

peoplehood, 28, 59, 62, 74, 84, 93, 106, 118
perpetuity, 138f. (*see also* finality)
perplexity, 32, 33, 34, 64, 65, 76, 108, 134, 155, 156
persecution, in Mecca, 7 (*see also fitnah*)
personality, 2, 5, 15, 19, 21f., 25, 27, 28, 33, 41, 78, 88, 121, 167
   in Hosea, 26
   in Jeremiah, 31, 32, 78
   truth through, 12, 66
perspectives, in history, 10, 112, 149, 150
perversity, human, 7, 13, 19, 30, 33, 53, 75, 129, 158
piety, imaginative, 39
pluralism, 76, 99, 119
poetry, 9, 41, 42, 61, 80, 81, 138, 169
   in Qur'an, 42, 49, 51, 53, 176, 180
politics, 19, 82, 93, 128, 133, 162, 163, 165
   and conscience, 93, 95
post-modernity, 145
power-community, 5, 96, 97, 162, 163
power-dimension, in faith, 6, 33, 94, 97, 105, 106, 108, 132, 133, 157, 183
preaching, 5, 18, 19, 78, 104, 105, 109, 112
presence, divine, 67, 79, 123, 157, 166, 170
priest/prophet tension, 91, 106
principalities, 105
privilege, 105
procreation, 51
prolepsis, 30, 58, 114, 171
prophethood, 1f., 14f., 20, 57, 58, 71, 76
   and psalmody, 34, 107, 123, 130, 137
   and situation, 69f., 102f., 118f., 138f., 146
   and suffering, 102f.
prophetism, early, 9, 107
prophetology, 36, 118f., 123, 129
   in Islam, 38, 39, 119f., 126f.
prophets, extra-Biblical, 94
"prosperity of His servant", 109, 110, 140
proxy-hood, for God, 21, 40f., 108, 109, 111
   in Jeremiah, 32f.
purity, 156
   ritual, 90
puzzle in closure of prophethood, 138f., 143
psyche, the, 40, 98, 118, 150, 156
   Jewish, 84, 85

rationality, 36, 37, 51, 52, 101, 118, 147, 181
realism, 53, 94, 111
   in Messianic task, 110, 136
   political
redemption, 7, 20, 110, 128, 131, 160, 167
   in Shi'ah Islam, 192
refuge, 65
remnant, 28, 33
responsibility, human, 50, 51, 52, 94, 98
resurrection, the, 136, 150
retribution, 6, 30, 52, 60, 70, 77, 80, 103, 154
revelation, 2, 12, 16, 38, 40, 43, 47, 58, 117f., 145, 152
   and conscience, 89, 90
   Qur'an on, 53, 54, 120, 125
reverence, 96
rhetoric, 15, 49, 50, 51, 53, 57, 65
   in Isaiah, 63
righteousness, 105, 106, 133, 142, 158

sacrifice, 59, 90, 106, 109, 113, 156
"saying", 16
scapegoat, the, 109
scepticism, 181, 189
schools of Prophets, 105
science, 52
"seal of prophets", 138, 139, 140, 155
secularity, 52, 86, 90
self-awareness, 24, 58, 59, 97
self-deceit, human, 75, 99
self-exoneration, 103, 104
self-reproach, moral, 79 (*see also* guilt)
self-wronging, 97, 100 (*see also zulm*)
servanthood, 3, 123, 124, 167, 185
   and "Son", 125
   and suffering, 64, 79, 102f., 113, 158
"servant songs", the, 64f., 81
shame, 29, 30, 33
signs, 67, 68, 105, 124, 125, 152, 190
   and "Emmanuel", 150, 151
   Quranic, 125
"sin of the world", 115 (*see also* wrong)
sincerity, 99, 181
situations, 48, 66, 69f., 76, 79, 84, 100, 102, 104, 148, 155
Sonship, divine, 2, 20, 125, 139, 167
sovereignty, divine, 50, 84, 135, 163
   and suffering, 109
speech, divine, 16, 43, 46, 169
"spoils of war", 96
"success, manifest", 5

## Index of Themes

suffering, 20, 37, 81, 102f., 105, 133, 135, 158, 160, 183, 188
   and God, 129, 130, 133, 158, 192
superstition, 39
suspicion, 52
symbolism, 56, 65, 82, 83, 107, 143, 149, 175
   in Ezekiel, 66, 67

Temple, the role of, 8, 34, 54, 62, 65, 79, 82, 85, 105, 147, 156
   in Isaiah, 29, 30, 123
testament, of prophets, 144, 147, 154f.
text, 46, 70, 122, 144, 148f., 157, 161, 173
theocracy, 13, 154
theology, 39, 49, 52, 67, 82, 86, 91, 108, 109, 113, 114, 115, 117f., 127, 132, 134, 146, 182
   in "god and ...", 118, 129, 130
   "process", 150
   of society, 96
   in the Qur'an, 53, 119, 121, 122, 124, 130, 134, 146, 169, 173
   among Shi'ah, 164
theophany, 33, 78, 166
thought-schools, 155
tradition, 21, 55, 70, 104, 106, 125, 138, 142, 147, 160, 165, 167, 171
Tradition, 15, 25, 38, 89, 95, 161, 162, 168, 173
transcendence, 119
translation, 45, 46
travail, prophetic, 20, 103, 108, 110, 111, 121, 128, 158, 159, 182
   divine, 134
tribalism, 3, 25, 72, 79, 84, 85, 86, 96, 177
tribal raiding, 96, 97
tribulation, 103, 108, 116
Trisagion, the, 29
truth, 32, 47, 74, 107, 115, 153, 165
   cost of, 109, 110
   maligned, 30, 52
   through personality, 12, 66, 81, 117f., 123

uncreatedness, of the Qur'an, 9, 46, 47, 185
unity, divine, 12, 54, 72, 73, 86, 99, 125, 151, 176
   and prophethood, 93, 117f., 125 (*see also* prophetology)
universality, 80, 82, 84, 114
utterance, 9, 22, 56, 68

veil, behind a, 25
veneration, 36
vested interests, 104, 130, 131, 143
vicariousness, 2, 19, 107, 109, 115, 129, 131, 164, 166, 179
   excluded in Islam, 94
   in the Cross, 183
victory, manifest, 8, 164, 191
vindication, 8, 104, 110, 113, 130, 131, 163, 166
vindictiveness, 104
vineyard parable, 61, 62, 178, 187
violence, 34
vision, 78, 93, 149
   of Isaiah, 28, 29, 123
   of Muhammad, 24
vocabulary, 23, 49, 52, 55, 70, 120, 124, 144, 148, 153
vocation, 15, 19, 21, 22, 23, 29, 34, 42, 56, 73, 75, 82, 91, 93, 101, 104, 108, 116, 122, 132, 148, 155, 178, 188
voice, crying, 22, 40, 55, 105
vulnerability, 19, 82, 103, 107, 129, 170
   divine, 70, 129

warfare, in Qur'an, 97
wealth, as duty, 96 (*see also zakat*)
"weighting", 1, 13, 17, 18, 47, 48, 110, 114, 124, 128, 134, 159, 158
wilderness, the, 62, 68, 93, 105, 106, 155
wilfulness, human, 75, 76 (*see also zulm*)
wisdom, 16, 36, 41, 50, 63, 121, 125, 127, 147, 156, 160, 172, 185
"Woes", 33, 61, 63, 68
wonder, 49, 52, 95
word(s), 1, 16, 22, 26, 40, 49, 58, 65, 93, 104, 122, 123, 147, 150, 151, 152, 153, 159, 160, 174, 176, 183, 184
word, and person, 36, 56, 65 (*see also* personality)
word-play, 56, 65, 109, 181
"Word made flesh, the", 2, 127, 159, 160, 166
worship, 70, 86, 87, 95, 119, 172, 176
   cultic, 29, 73
   nature, 59, 119
   plural, 5, 54, 76, 86, 125
wrong, human, 7, 19, 30, 33, 52, 53, 76, 77, 94, 95, 97, 109, 110, 112, 133, 151, 159, 165

Yahwism, 38, 56, 84, 178
Yahweh's counsel, 108, 110
"Yeas", 68

# Index of Names and Terms

Aaron, 88
Abel, 36
'abd, 123
Abraha, 70
Abraham, 5, 12, 21, 54, 72, 74
  as iconoclast, 55
  as "monotheist", 25
Abu Lahab, 131
Abu Talib, 86
Adam, 74
Ahab, 18, 110
Ahaz, 150
Ahl al-Bait, 38, 39, 164
Ahl al-Jahiliyyah, 73, 122, 131, 172, 177
Ahmad, 143, 169, 188
Al-Akhirah, 153, 154
Akhtar, Shabbir, 189
Alexander, 54
Alexandria, 147
'Ali, 164, 191
Allah, 8, 19, 23, 25, 39, 54, 70, 73, 76, 86, 99, 117, 119, 120, 122, 128, 130, 134, 139, 152
  names of, 36, 135
  and *Tasliyah*, 38, 39
  exclusion of, 51, 74
*Allahu akbar*, 120
Allat, 85
*amr*, 100, 155, 181
Amos, 5, 6, 8, 10, 11, 12, 14, 21, 23, 31, 33, 36, 37, 40, 42, 55, 56, 59, 70, 77, 88, 92, 94, 101, 105, 107, 123, 129, 138, 143, 175, 180, 188
Anathoth, 15, 32, 65
*Ansar*, 135
Apocrypha, the, 38
Arabia, 85, 127
Arabic, 46f., 125, 141, 173, 183, 184
Arabs, 44, 47, 85, 179

Aramaic, 45
Arberry, A.J., 174, 186
Aristotle, 126
Arjuna, 96
*Asbab al-nuzul*, 70, 152, 161, 185
Assyria, 33, 58, 70, 77, 78, 85, 180
Ayyub, 8
Ayyub, Mahmud, 192
Al-'Azm, Sadiq, 189

Babylon, 67, 79, 81, 82, 85, 93, 107, 157
Bacon, Francis, 86, 179
Badr, battle of, 132, 177
*balagh*, 19, 125, 170
Barnabas, Gospel of, 188
Bathsheba, 89
Beersheba, 57
Begin, Menahem, 147
Ben Gurion, 147
Bergson, Henri, 150
Bethlehem, 151
Bhagavad Gita, the, 96
Bible, the, 41, 47, 56, 88, 89, 105, 138
  as Hebrew, 45, 117, 153
Bradford, William, 18, 170
Brecht, Bertolt, 151
Buber, Martin, 107, 114, 115, 182, 183
Al-Busiri, 75, 177
Byzantium, 4, 85, 178

Caesarea Philippi, 136, 191
Caird, George, 9, 153, 190
Caliphs, 29, 133, 139, 146, 164
Canaan, 60
Carlyle, Thomas, 35, 104, 145, 181, 188
Chebar, the river, 16, 34, 66
Christianity, 20, 25, 76, 134, 144, 147, 155, 166, 179, 191
*chronos*, 138

## Index of Names and Terms

Coleridge S. T., 151, 153, 188, 190
Cyrus, 6, 60, 80, 81, 108

Damascus, 77, 92
*Al-damir*, 90
Daniel, 45, 95, 148, 189
*Dar al-Islam*, 165
David, 4, 5, 6, 21, 54, 57, 74, 77, 89, 90, 106, 169
  Psalms of, 34, 54, 89, 182, 186
Davidson, A. B., 2
*Dawlah*, 132, 163
"Day of the Lord", 33, 37, 78
Deuteronomy, Book of, 4, 142, 172
Dhammapada, the, 45
*Dhu al-Kifi*, 54
*Dhu al-Qarnain*, 54, 178
*Dies Irae*, 33
*Din*, 163
Donne, John, 1, 151
Dostoevsky, 27

Easter, 166
Ecclesiastes, Book of, 37, 83
Edom, 83, 92
Egypt, 36, 60, 147
Eliazar, 132
Elijah, 18, 83, 129, 144
Elisha, 12, 71, 144
Emmanuel, 150
Enoch, 12, 71
Ethiopia, 33, 85
Euphrates, the, 65, 85
Exodus, the, 57, 60, 78, 85, 105, 142, 155
Ezekiel, 6, 17, 19, 21, 23, 34, 38, 41, 65f., 79, 83, 94, 105, 107, 145, 147, 149, 152, 189
  against Tyre, 8, 35
  eating the roll, 35
  resemblance to Muhammad, 35, 66, 67, 168
  speechlessness, 67
  strangeness in, 34, 60, 149

*fana'*, 24
Al-Farabi, 126
Al-Faruqi, Ismail, 174, 179
*fasad*, 52
Fazlur-Rahman, 119, 123, 153, 154, 162, 164, 169, 171, 174, 184, 186, 189, 190
*fiqh*, 162
*fitnah*, 92, 154, 163, 168, 190
*fitrah*, 98, 180

Five Pillars, the, 99
Flaubert, Gustave, 102
Frost, Robert, 27

Galilee, 135, 161
Gath, 57
Gethsemane, 104, 135, 167
Al-Ghazali, 146, 189
Gogol, Nicolai, 27
Gomer, 27, 175
Good Friday, 159, 166, 176
Gospels, the, 136, 137, 158, 160
Greece, 127

Habakkuk, 33, 34, 40, 61, 78, 166, 172
*Hadith*, 38, 88
Haggai, 17, 36, 61, 82, 108
*Hajj*, 180
Al-Hallaj, 181
Hanameel, 66
Handel, G. F., 64, 111, 176
*hanif* (pl. *hunafa'*), 25, 171
*Hasbuna Allah*, 131, 186
Hastings, James, 167
Hawthorne, N., 112, 180
Haykal, M. H., 180
Herodias, 102
Herzl, Theodor, 147
Heschel, Abraham, 172, 186
Hijaz, 4, 21, 23, 75, 78, 85
*Al-Hikmah*, 36, 125, 126, 172
Hijrah, the, 20, 71, 72, 96, 128, 130, 131, 132, 133, 162, 177
Hira', Mount, 5, 25, 26, 30, 123, 167, 171, 184
Homer, 58
Horeb, 148
Hosea, 1, 2, 5, 9, 12, 21, 23, 26, 27, 30, 38, 58f., 63, 71, 73, 74, 77, 105, 122, 123, 134, 142, 147, 149, 157, 166, 177, 181
Hud, 5, 54, 71, 72, 94, 188
*huda*, 119, 139, 161
*hudud*, 98
Hughes, Ted, 143, 188
Husain, Imam, 164, 192
Husain, M. K., 97, 98, 178, 180

Iblis, 121
Ibn al-'Arabi, 126, 182, 185
Ibn Hisham, 146, 189
Ibn Khaldun, 165, 192
Ibn Sina, 126, 173
Ibn Taimiyya, 126, 185

199

## Index of Names and Terms

*Ijtihad*, 88, 100, 162, 163
*Ijma'*, 162, 191
*'Ijaz*, 173
*ikhlas*, 99, 100
*Ilaf*, 69, 70, 176
Iqbal, Muhammad, 149, 150, 189, 190
*Iqra'*, 124
Isa ibn Maryam, 7, 163
    birth narratives, 24
Isaiah, 21, 30, 37, 40, 60, 62, 73, 78, 80, 82, 92, 94, 105, 113, 116, 123, 127, 132, 145, 152, 155, 157, 178, 179
    call, 29, 60
Islam, 38, 75, 83, 89, 90, 99, 119, 120, 146, 148
*isnad*, 41
Israel, 8, 27, 33, 58, 73, 80, 85, 106, 129

Jabotinsky, Vladimir, 147
Jacob, 84
Jehoiakim, 107
Jeremiah, 1, 2, 4, 6, 12, 13, 18, 20, 23, 26, 27, 31, 32, 36, 40, 65, 74, 78, 81, 89, 94, 105, 106, 109, 116, 122, 123, 142, 166
    Confessions of, 5, 9, 32, 33, 65, 81, 107, 114, 168
    Letter to exiles, 147
    Temple sermon, 5, 105, 132
Jerusalem, 4, 25, 33, 34, 38, 63, 74, 76, 78, 82, 85, 93, 108, 114, 136, 142, 149, 157, 162, 174, 186
Jesus, 9, 55, 66, 103, 113, 115, 124, 128, 135, 136, 143, 147, 151, 158, 160, 166, 168, 173, 179
    as the Christ, 2, 11, 20
    as 'Isa, 7, 163
Jewry, 1, 25, 43, 48, 63, 84, 111, 112, 143, 156
Jezebel, 110
Jezreel, 60
Job, 8, 33, 37, 61, 85
Joel, 26, 36, 61, 63, 142, 143, 145
John Baptist, 102, 138, 187
Jonah, 71, 143, 148, 177
Jordan, the river, 65, 93
Joseph, 55, 72, 104, 169
Josephus, 132, 186
Joshua, 61, 77, 93
Joshua, the High Priest, 83
Josiah, 4
Judah, 29, 73, 77, 85, 114, 115, 150, 180
Judaism, 89, 118, 144, 147, 148, 155, 157
Judea, 21, 75, 80

Justin Martyr, 151

*Ka'bah*, the, 70, 72, 74, 149, 177, 180
Karbala', 164, 192
*khilafah*, human, 146, 174, 175, 180
Khomeini, Ayotallah, 47, 101, 174, 191
*Al-Kitab*, 172
*kufr*, 20, 53, 100

*la'ala*, 50
*al-Lawh al-Mahfuz*, 127
Lebanon, 61
Lewis, C. S., 175
Logos, the divine, 125
Luther, Martin, 100

Al-Ma'ari, 181
Maccabees, 1, 37, 140, 146
Machiavelli, 94
Mada'in Salih, 5
Malachi, 1, 3, 5, 6, 14, 23, 55, 71, 82, 83, 91, 108, 138, 170
Mallarmé, Stephane, 138, 187
*Manat*, 85
*marad*, 177
Marduk, 106
*Markabah*, 123
Mary, 173, 185
Masada, 132
*mawlid*, 125, 173
Mecca, 1, 5, 6, 7, 18, 20, 23, 24, 25, 30, 55, 66, 69, 72, 74, 76, 83, 91, 127, 131, 149, 162, 177, 178
Medes, 85
Medina, 1, 5, 6, 7, 20, 66, 131, 162
Mediterranean, the, 147, 182
Mernissi, Fatimah, 179
Micah, 12, 26, 40, 61, 63, 134, 142, 157
*al-Mi'raj*, 126
Moabites, 33
Moses, 5, 12, 14, 21, 25, 37, 54, 59, 72, 77, 88, 138, 142, 143, 148, 177, 188
"Mother of the Book", 47
Muhammad, 1, 3, 4, 5, 10, 15, 18, 22, 30, 32, 35, 46, 48, 55, 56, 65, 69, 70, 76, 85, 86, 92, 94, 95, 115, 117, 123, 128, 130, 162
    call, 24f., 38, 45, 144
    in devotion, 2, 35f., 119, 125 (isee *tasliyah*)
    finality of, 139f., 164
    as "genius", 38, 39, 125
    "literacy" of, 48, 125
    as orphan, 26, 175

## Index of Names and Terms

and the "paraclete", 142f.
  as "seal", 71, 139f., 170
  as *unmi*, 9, 23, 43, 126, 143
*muhkamat*, 53, 54
*mujtahidun*, 163
Mu'minun, 140
*munafiqun*, 133, 163, 168
*muru'ah*, 85, 145
*mutashabihat*, 53, 54

Nahum, 26, 78, 92
*Na'im al-wakil*, 131
Najran, 4, 25, 85
*nass*, 161
Nathan, 87
Nazareth, 20, 66, 135
Nehemiah, 82, 83, 140
Neher, André, 113, 172, 183
New Testament, 19, 33, 37, 40, 45, 55, 60, 63, 81, 103, 113, 115, 135, 138, 144, 148, 158, 163, 172, 179, 185, 187
  Letters in, 160
Nietzsche, F., 88
*nifaq*, 96, 100, 163, 168
Night Journey, the, 24, 38, 126, 149, 182
Nile, the, 4, 57, 85
Nineveh, 33
*niyyah*, 99
Noah, 5, 72, 95

Obadiah, 83
Orlinksy, H. M., 179

Pakistan, 150, 187, 190
Pali, 45
*Paracletos*, 143, 169, 188
Paradise, 85, 92
Paul, 34, 40, 105, 113, 115, 148, 160, 167, 172, 187
Peace Movement (Israel), 157f.
"people of the Book", 43
Persia, 4, 36, 63, 81, 85, 178
Peter, 115, 136, 160
Philo, 147, 173
Plato, 40, 126, 169, 173
  Dialogues, 40
Potiphar, 55
Proverbs, Book of, 37

*qadar*, 153
*Qiblah*, 168
Qoheleth, 27, 83, 158

Quraish, 4, 8, 43, 46, 69, 70, 76, 85, 97, 129, 131, 177

*Rahbaniyyah*, 180
*ra'i*, 100
Al-Rasul, 23, 123, 170
Red Sea, 23
Revelation of St. John, 84, 118, 129
*Riddah*, the, 133, 140
Robinson, H. W., 169, 176
Rumi, Jalal al-Din, 35, 66, 176, 182

Sabbath, 160
*Sabr*, 8
*Salat*, 99
Salih, 5, 54, 71, 72, 94, 188
Salome, 102
Samaria, 5, 10, 93
Sanskrit, 45
Satan, 14, 47, 121, 154, 178
Saul, 90
Scholem, Gershom, 189
Seleucids, the, 71
Sennacherib, 80
Septuagint, the, 22, 45, 147, 150, 153
*Shahadah*, the, 86, 93, 117, 119, 121, 122, 123, 128, 129, 130, 134, 168, 184
Al-Shahrastani, 126
*Al-Shaitan al-Rajim*, 154, 184
Shakespeare, Wm., 18, 65, 170, 177
*Sharh al-Sadr*, 38, 126, 173
Shari'ah, 4, 5, 89f., 161, 162
Sheba, 85
*Shechinah*, 34, 67, 93, 107, 157
Shi'ah, the, 54, 71, 72, 94, 188
*Shirk*, 76, 183
Shoah, the, 112
Shu'aib, 54, 71, 72, 94, 188
*Shura*, 100, 181
Siddiqui, Ataullah, 171
Sadrah tree, 145
Sinai, 4, 12, 25, 27, 59, 73, 88, 89, 90, 93, 116, 189
Sirach, Ben, 36, 37
*Sirah*, 20, 71, 88, 167
Sirius, 85
Skinner, John, 2, 26, 167, 171, 188
Smith, Margaret, 170
Solomon, 37, 74
  pseudo, the, 37
Sunni Islam, 42, 100, 163, 165, 179
Al-Suyuti, Ialal al-Din, 177
Syrians, 105

## Index of Names and Terms

Al-Tabari, 86, 146, 179, 189
Tabuk, 5, 167
*tadabbur*, 145, 146
*taghut*, 154
*tahannuf*, 171
*tahannuth*, 25, 26, 184
*tajwid*, 125
*takdhib*, 32, 52
*tanzil*, 18, 26, 38, 42, 47, 48, 54, 88, 125, 140, 185
Tarsus, 34
*tasliyah*, 38, 119, 122, 184, 185
*Tawhid*, 54, 151, 185
Tekoa, 15, 57, 70, 170, 175
Thamud, Banu, 5
Tiglath Pileser, 86
Tigris, River, 4, 85
Torah, 4, 5, 90, 143, 147, 156
Tyre, 8, 108, 182

*ulama*, 88
*Ummah*, 88, 96, 126, 165
*Umm al-Kitab*, 148, 161
Ummayyads, 133, 191
*ummi*, 9, 43, 168, 171
'Uthman, 139, 191
Al-'Uzza, 85

Verdi, G., 75
Von Rad, 169, 179, 190, 192

*wahy*, 18, 25, 42, 43, 48, 101, 123, 126, 139, 150, 185
Wahhabis, 39, 185

Whitehead, A. N., 19, 150, 170, 189
Wisdom Literature, 83, 103, 140, 158
Wisdom of Solomon, 36, 83, 103, 110, 113, 182, 185
Wordsworth, Wm., 169

Yahweh, 6, 10, 12, 22, 25, 27, 29, 31, 32, 34, 37, 59, 61, 63, 73, 76, 80, 83, 93, 108, 118, 130, 134, 147, 156, 160, 161, 168
  's controversy, 73, 82
  and covenant, 4, 29, 83, 84
*Yawm al-Furqan*, 177
Yeats, W. B., 102, 111, 112, 181, 183, 191
Yemen, 70
Yunis, 71
Yusuf, 55

*Zabur*, 54
Zadok, 108
*Zakat*, 96
*zann*, 52
Zealots, 132, 140, 146, 156
Zechariah, 8, 71, 82, 108, 143, 147, 158
Zephaniah, 8, 26, 33, 63, 78
Zerubbabel, 82, 83
Zia al-Haq, 150
Zion, 57, 61, 157, 179, 186
Zionism, 142, 147, 156, 157
Zulaika, 55
*zulm*, 53, 97, 178, 180
*zulm al-nafs*, 75, 97, 98, 100

# Scriptural Citations

**Qur'an Cited**

Surah 2
  v.13   79
  v.23   123
  v.30   120
  v.87   104
  v.97   126
Surah 3
  v.7   53, 148, 149
Surah 4
  v.52   50
  v.105   122
Surah 5
  v.3   139
  v.97   149
Surah 6
  v.54   122
Surah 7
  v.57   17
  v.153   17
  v.172   50, 178, 184
Surah 12
  v.2   45, 55
Surah 17
  v.1   126, 149
  v.95   52, 53
  v.116   101
Surah 18
  v.6   32, 75
Surah 20
  v.113   45, 100
Surah 26
  vv.193–4   47, 126
Surah 27
  v.24   85
Surah 30
  v.30   180
Surah 33
  v.33   38
  v.56   38
Surah 36
  v.30   128, 130, 186
  v.75   128
Surah 37
  v.96   51
Surah 40
  v.41   74
Surah 41
  v.3   45
  v.37   85
  v.44   140
Surah 42
  v.7   45
  v.24   50
  v.38   100
  v.51   25, 100
Surah 43
  v.3   45
  v.4   47
Surah 46
  v.9   17
Surah 49
  vv.14–18   133, 181
Surah 51
  vv.50–52   72
Surah 52
  v.40   17
Surah 53
  vv.4–11   24, 126
  vv.13–18   24
  vv.19–23   85
Surah 55
  vv.10–32   52
  v.29   150
Surah 56
  vv.57–74   52
Surah 68
  v.46   17
Surah 73
  v.1   24, 144
  vv.5–6   4, 14, 24, 40
Surah 74
  v.1   24, 144
Surah 75
  v.17   100
Surah 77
  vv.1–11   49
Surah 81
  vv.8–9   95
Surah 85
  v.22   46
Surah 90
  v.2   178
Surah 91
  vv.1–6   49
Surah 93
  vv.1–4   95
Surah 94
  vv.1–2   26, 38
  v.3   18, 168
Surah 96
  v.1   22, 23, 24, 53
Surah 100   97, 180
Surah 106   69, 70
Surah 112   99, 135, 151

**Hebrew Bible Cited**

Genesis 37.19–20   104
Exodus 23.3   90
Numbers
  11.29   138, 177
Deuteronomy
  7.6–8   155
  18.15–18   142, 143
1 Kings 18.17   18
2 Kings 10.11   60
Psalm 19.13–14   89

## Scriptural Citations

27.8   123
34.27   109
35.27   177
56.8   130, 169, 182, 186
87   175, 178
105.15   131, 169
116.15   110
130.1   137
Proverbs 20.27.   36
Ecclesiastes 3.1   28
Isaiah
  1.3–23   73, 106
  1.4–19   61, 62, 132
  3.13   63
  5.8   142
  5.26–30   61
  6.1f.   15, 28, 29, 30, 60
  7.10–17   150
  8.16–20   61
  10.5   78
  11.1   62
  13.19–22   61
  14.4–23   61
  27.1   60
  30.11   108
  30.28–32   61
  35.2   62
  40.3   22
  40.25   62
  41.1–11   61
  42.10–16   61
  43.24   134
  45.1   60, 80
  45.10   62
  48.19   62
  49.1   80
  50.4–6   81, 106
  51.9   60
  52.13–53.12   64, 79, 104, 109, 111, 114, 135, 140
  63.1–3   62
  65.11–12   62
Jeremiah
  1.5f.   31
  1.1–15   65
  8.7.   74
  11.19   109
  12.5   65
  13.1–7   66
  14.7   65
  15.5   142
  15.10   108
  15.18   65, 104
  16.1   66
  17.9   75
  17.14–18   107
  18.1–6   66
  18.20   65, 66
  18.20–23   107
  20.7   65, 172, 176
  20.14f.   31
  29   66, 79
  31.31   32
  32.6   79
  38   60
Ezekiel
  2.3–7   66
  3.4   34, 35, 104
  3.22–27   67
  4.1–7   34, 67
  5.1   34
  10.18   79
  21.6   34
  24.23–27   67
  32   66
  33.21f.   67
  33.32–33   41
  37.16–20   67
Hosea
  2.21–23   60
  3.1f.   27
  6.6   59
  10.11–12   60
  11.4   59
  12.2   63
  12.13   59, 142
  13.9   73
Joel 3.9–25   83
Amos
  3.3–6   58, 70, 177
  5.1   17
  5.18–20   172
  6.3–6   57
  7.14   10
  8.11–13   57
  9.13–15   57
Micah 6.2   63
Nahum
  1.15   78
  2.1–19   78
  3.19   78
Habakkuk
  1.2–4   33
  2.4–20   33, 113
  3.1–16   34
Haggai
  1.1   17
  2.1   17
  2.19–23   61, 83
Zechariah
  2.1–15   82
  3.10   61
  5.1–4   83
  6.9–15   83
  8.23   82, 104
  14.1–19   63, 84
Malachi
  1.11   83, 84
  4.4–6   83, 84

**New Testament Cited**

Matthew
  11.9.   20
  11.13   102
  16.13–23   136, 160
  21.33–42   136
Mark
  8.27–29   136
  12.1–12   136
Luke
  9.18–20   136
  20.9–19   136
  24.13–32   136, 148
John
  1.11–12   159
  14.16   142, 163
Romans 1.17   113
1 Corinthians 10.4   148
Galatians 6.17   160
Philippians 2.7   167, 185
Hebrews
  1.1–2   139
  11.4   36
  12.3   102, 167
2 Timothy 3.16   175
1 Peter 4.1   160